Frommer's®

Rome day BY day

1st Edition

by Sylvie Hogg

Wiley Publishing, Inc.

Contents

Published by:
Wiley Publishing, Inc.

111 River St.
Hoboken, NJ 07030-5774

ISBN-13: 978-0-7645-7614-0
ISBN-10: 0-7645-7614-3

Editor: Alexis Lipsitz
Special Thanks to Amy Lyons
Production Editor: Heather Wilcox
Photo Editor: Richard Fox
Cartographer: Roberta Stockwell
Production by Wiley Indianapolis Composition Services
Savvy Traveler illustrations by Rashell Smith and Karl Brandt

For information on our other products and services or to obtain technical support, please contact our Customer Care Department within the U.S. at 800/762-2974, outside the U.S. at 317/572-3993 or fax 317/572-4002.

Wiley also publishes its books in a variety of electronic formats. Some content that appears in print may not be available in electronic formats.

Manufactured in China

5 4

A Note from the Publisher

Organizing your time. That's what this guide is all about.

Other guides give you long lists of things to see and do and then expect you to fit the pieces together. The Day by Day guides are different. These guides tell you the best of everything, and then they show you how to see it *in the smartest, most time-efficient way*. Our authors have designed detailed itineraries organized by time, neighborhood or special interest. And each tour comes with a bulleted map that takes you from stop to stop.

Hoping to relive the glory days of Ancient Rome, or to tour the highlights of Vatican City? Planning a walk through Piazza Navona, or a whirlwind tour of the very best that Rome has to offer? Whatever your interest or schedule, the Day by Days give you the smartest route to follow. Not only do we take you to the top sights and attractions, but we introduce you to those special moments that only locals know about—those "finds" that turn tourists into travelers.

The Day by Days are also your top choice if you're looking for one complete guide for all your travel needs. The best hotels and restaurants for every budget, the greatest shopping values, the wildest nightlife—it's all here.

Why should you trust our judgment? Because our authors personally visit each place they write about. They're an independent lot who say what they think and would never include places they wouldn't recommend to their best friends. They're also open to suggestions from readers. If you'd like to contact them, please send your comments my way at mspring@wiley.com, and I'll pass them on.

Enjoy your Day by Day guide—the most helpful travel companion you can buy. And have the trip of a lifetime.

Warm regards,

Michael Spring

Michael Spring, Publisher
Frommer's Travel Guides

About the Author

California-raised and Ivy League–educated **Sylvie Hogg** first visited the Eternal City as a 1-year-old. Twenty-eight years and many world travels later, she is still convinced that Rome is the most amazing place on earth . . . by far. As well-versed in classical archaeology as she is in designer shoes, she can be spotted drinking *prosecco* at the Vineria, taunting visiting teams at the Stadio Olimpico, or—most often—gazing spellbound at the ruins of ancient Rome. She is the author of *Frommer's Irreverent Guide to Rome* and has also written for numerous other American and British guides to Rome.

Acknowledgements

To Mom, Dad, and Katie, for being so rad; Fabrizio Cuneo, for being my Roman brother and hilarious observer of his fellow natives; Jennifer C., Anne L., Emily C., and Claire H., for living the fab (and not-so-fab) expat life with me; Pierluigi and Fulvia, for loving Rome with their heart and soul; Frank Bruni; the Dartmouth Classics department; and Alexis at *Frommer's*.

An Additional Note

Please be advised that travel information is subject to change at any time—and this is especially true of prices. We therefore suggest that you write or call ahead for confirmation when making your travel plans. The authors, editors, and publisher cannot be held responsible for the experiences of readers while traveling. Your safety is important to us, however, so we encourage you to stay alert and be aware of your surroundings.

Star Ratings, Icons & Abbreviations

Every hotel, restaurant, and attraction listing in this guide has been ranked for quality, value, service, amenities, and special features using a **star-rating system.** Hotels, restaurants, attractions, shopping, and nightlife are rated on a scale of zero stars (recommended) to three stars (exceptional). Within each tour, we recommend cafes, bars, or restaurants where you can take a break. Each of these stops appears in a shaded box marked with a coffee cup–shaped bullet.

The following **abbreviations** are used for credit cards:

AE	American Express	DISC	Discover	V	Visa
DC	Diners Club	MC	MasterCard		

Frommers.com

Now that you have the guidebook to a great trip, visit our website at **www.frommers.com** for travel information on more than 3,000 destinations. With features updated regularly, we give you instant access to the most current trip-planning information available. At Frommers.com, you'll also find the best prices on airfares, accommodations, and car rentals—and you can even book travel online through our travel booking partners.

A Note on Prices

Frommer's provides exact prices in each destination's local currency. As this book went to press, the rate of exchange was 1€ = US$1.30. Rates of exchange are constantly in flux; for up-to-the-minute information, consult a currency-conversion website such as www.oanda.com/convert/classic.

In the Take a Break and Best Bets section of this book, we have used a system of dollar signs to show a range of costs for one night in a hotel (the price of a double-occupancy room) or the cost of an entrée at a restaurant. Use the following table to decipher the dollar signs:

Cost	Hotels	Restaurants
$	under $100	under $10
$$	$100–$200	$10–$20
$$$	$200–$300	$20–$30
$$$$	$300–$400	$30–$40
$$$$$	over $400	over $40

An Invitation to the Reader

In researching this book, we discovered many wonderful places—hotels, restaurants, shops, and more. We're sure you'll find others. Please tell us about them, so we can share the information with your fellow travelers in upcoming editions. If you were disappointed with a recommendation, we'd love to know that, too. Please write to:

Frommer's Rome Day by Day, 1st Edition
Wiley Publishing, Inc. • 111 River St. • Hoboken, NJ 07030

M AGRIPPA L F

15 Favorite **Moments**

15 Favorite **Moments**

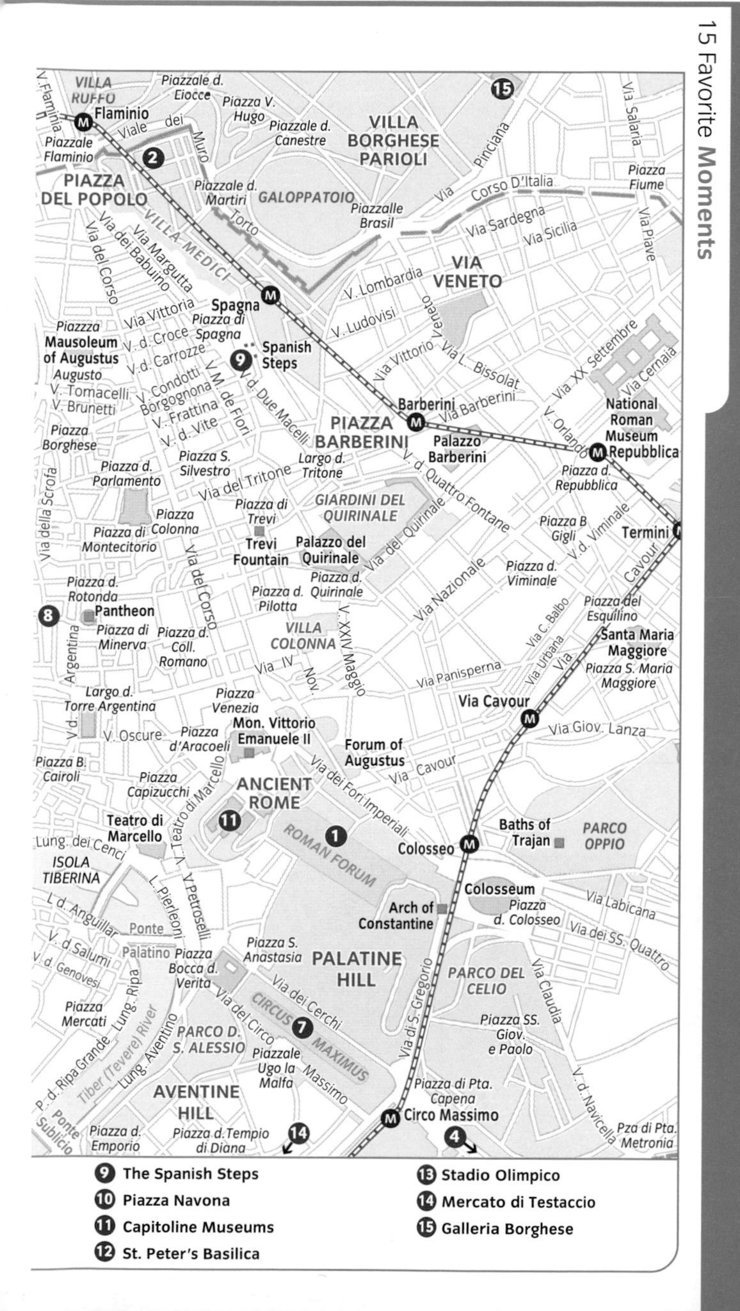

9 The Spanish Steps
10 Piazza Navona
11 Capitoline Museums
12 St. Peter's Basilica
13 Stadio Olimpico
14 Mercato di Testaccio
15 Galleria Borghese

When it comes to experiencing the best of Rome, sun-drenched days at the Colosseum are only the beginning—the Eternal City virtually bombards you with ways to enjoy yourself, from the visual to the gastronomical. Get off the tourist track, and accept the fact that there's traffic and pollution. With its unrivalled concentration of art and history, romantic scenery, and vibrant people, Rome embraces all with a monumental, irresistible charm. Here are the most sublime moments in our ongoing love affair.

1 Gazing over the ruins of the Roman Forum and Palatine from the Capitoline Hill terraces in the evening and, from there, strolling down Via dei Fori Imperiali, where strategically placed floodlights cast dramatic glows over solitary columns and the arches of the Colosseum. The ruins of Rome at night are truly, disarmingly spectacular. *See p 24.*

2 Taking your lover to the Pincio terraces, whose theatrical ivy-covered stone balustrades and view are virtually unchanged since the Renaissance, when maidens, courtiers, and the occasional knave no doubt met here for trysts and double-crossings. *See p 45.*

3 After a long day of sightseeing, joining the rest of Rome for an *aperitivo* at one of the outdoor bars on Campo de' Fiori. Have a seat, praise Bacchus for having created inexpensive, drinkable wine, and watch the world go by. *See p 56.*

4 Treading the ancient paving stones along the leafy Via Appia Antica, and leaving the hustle and bustle of the *centro* far behind. From the catacombs to the ruined villas of Roman patricians, there's a quiet but heavy sense of history here. Umbrella pines and farmland that seem to be steeped in antiquity perfume the air, transporting you back to the time when this was Rome's *Regina Viarum* (Queen of Roads). *See p 97.*

5 Riding a scooter, half-fearing for your life, on a sunny day, over the

The Pincio terraces make for a romantic rendezvous.

Romans enjoying an alfresco lunch at a sunny trattoria.

broad cobblestone avenues of Rome's archaeological areas, past umbrella pines and 2,000-year-old ruins. A thrill ride and history lesson all in one.

❻ **Wandering the untouristed, narrow back streets of Trastevere** and discovering shops, eateries, and slices of local life not listed in any guidebook. Separated from the rest of the old city by the river, this picturesque neighborhood has been able to maintain its own identity since ancient times, when it was called simply *Trans Tiberim* ("across the Tiber"). *See p 58.*

❼ **Standing along the high, western rim of the Circus Maximus** and absorbing the view from the umbrella pines across to the ruins of Palatine Hill. As you do, imagine being one of the 300,000 fans cheering on the raucous ancient Roman chariot races. *See p 66.*

❽ **Mastering the art of taking a caffè at a real Roman bar.** Walk in to the bar, greeting all with a smile and *"Buon giorno."* Pay for your drink at the *cassa*, and take your receipt to the bar counter. Slip a 10- or 20-cent tip on top of the receipt, and place your order with the *barista*. Drink your coffee as the Romans do—standing up at the bar.

❾ **Doing some serious retail damage around the Spanish Steps,** and then enjoying a cocktail at the Hotel de Russie's glamorous garden bar (where you might want to change into those new Gucci slingbacks). *See p 76.*

❿ **Spending hours over lunch or dinner** at a typical Roman trattoria or pizzeria, with a steady, wonderfully affordable flow of wine, water, and delicious food. Look for such Roman classics as *spaghetti alla carbonara* (pasta with bacon, black pepper, and eggs) or *saltimbocca alla romana* (thin slices of veal with cheese, ham, and sage). *See p 101.*

⓫ **Going to the Capitoline Museum's Palazzo Nuovo** in late afternoon on a crisp winter day, when no one else is there. Your only companions are half-drunk, smirking fauns and busts of Hadrian and Homer. *See p 31.*

⓬ **Taking your first step over the threshold of St. Peter's Basilica.** When the ethereal light of the low afternoon sun is broken into celestial beams by the basilica's well-placed windows, Bernini's stained-glass dove of the Holy Spirit against the church's terminal apse flickers with searing tones of amber. *See p 48.*

Soccer fans wave colorful team scarves at a match in Stadio Olimpico.

⓭ Going to a Roma or Lazio soccer (football) game on a sunny Sunday afternoon and joining in the infectious, unbridled exhilaration that floods the stadium when the home team scores. You're likely to be hugged and spun around by complete strangers. *See p 132.*

⓮ Mixing with locals at the lively Mercato di Testaccio. No other market in the city has such a strong sense of community: Yuppies and jovial retirees shuffle from stall to stall, passionately debating the latest political scandal—or soccer (football) league standings—while they expertly pick out the freshest culinary delights. Perhaps more so than any other Roman neighborhood, Testaccio has a salt-of-the-earth flavor drawn from its working-class slaughterhouse past. *See p 74.*

⓯ Encountering Bernini's sculptures at Galleria Borghese. Grimace in determination as *David* does against daunting adversary Goliath, or gape at the amazing detail of *Apollo and Daphne.* The paintings and ceiling frescoes throughout the gallery make for colorful counterpoints. *See p 30.* ●

Bernini statue amid the ceiling frescoes at Villa Borghese.

1 The Best **Full-Day Tours**

The Best of Rome **in One Day**

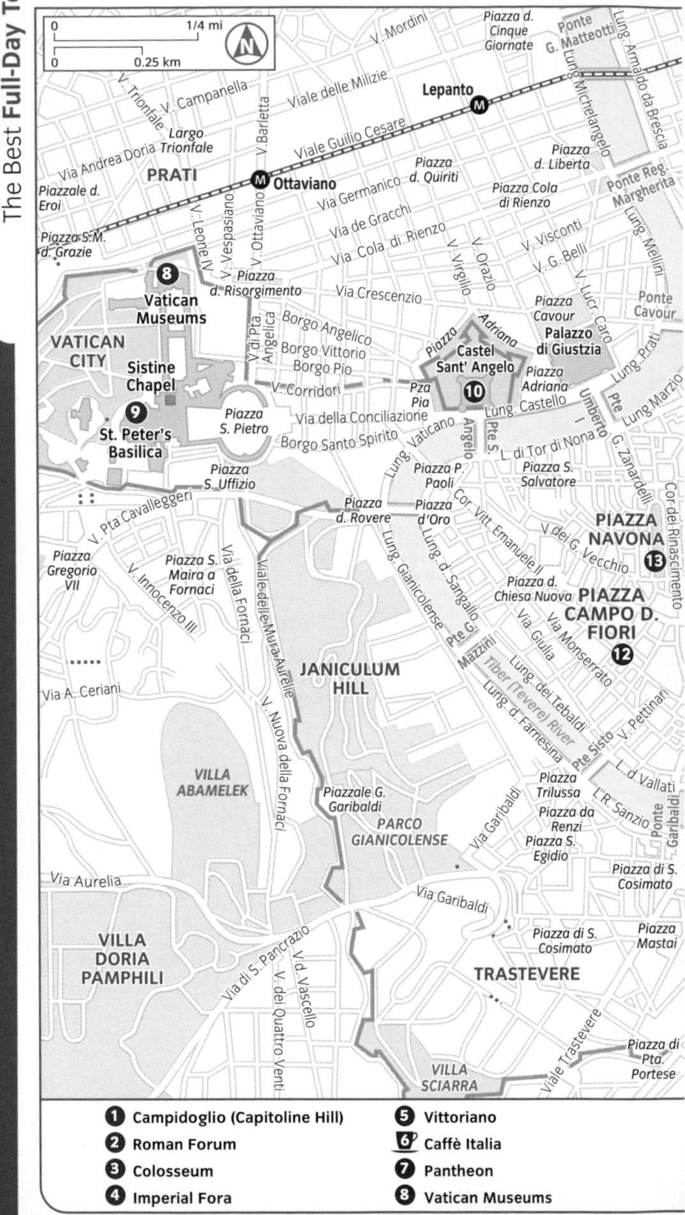

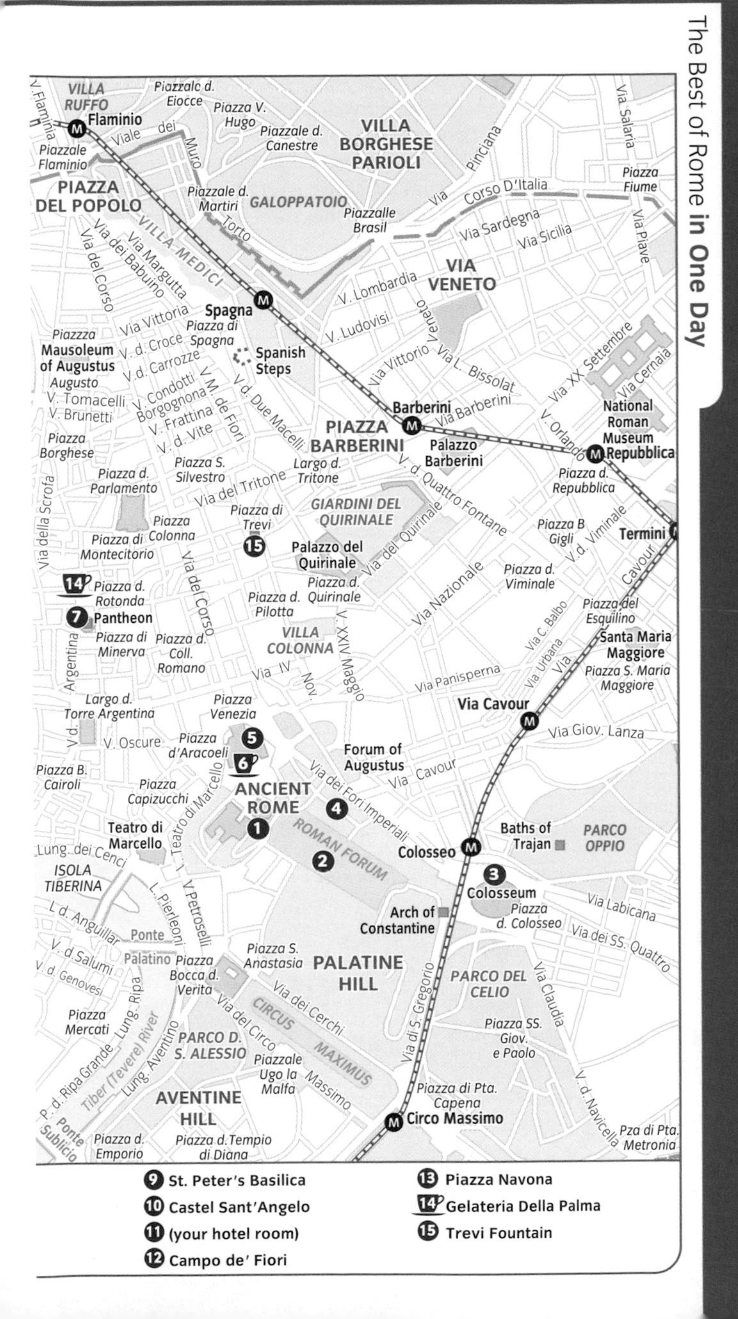
VILLA RUFFO
Piazzale d. Eiocce
Piazza V. Hugo
Flaminio
V. Flaminia
Viale dei Muro
Piazzale Flaminio
Piazzale d. Canestre
VILLA BORGHESE PARIOLI
Via Pinciana
Via Salaria
Piazza Fiume
PIAZZA DEL POPOLO
Piazzale d. Martiri
Torto
GALOPPATOIO
Piazzalle Brasil
Via Corso D'Italia
Via Sardegna
Via Sicilia
Via Piave
VILLA MEDICI
Via del Corso
Via dei Babuino
Via Margutta
VIA VENETO
V. Lombardia
Spagna
Piazza di Spagna
Via Vittoria
Piazzza Mausoleum of Augustus
Augusto
V. Tomacelli
V. Brunetti
V. d. Croce
V.d. Carrozze
Spanish Steps
V. Ludovisi
Via Veneto
Via Vittorio
Via L. Bissolat
Via XX Settembre
Via Cernaia
V. Condotti
Borgognona
V. Frattina
V. d. Vite
V. M. de Fiori
V. d. Due Macelli
Barberini
Via Barberini
National Roman Museum
V. Orlando
Piazza Borghese
PIAZZA BARBERINI
Palazzo Barberini
Repubblica
Piazza d. Parlamento
Piazza S. Silvestro
Largo d. Tritone
Via del Tritone
V. d. Quattro Fontane
Piazza d. Repubblica
Via della Scrofa
Piazza Colonna
Piazza di Montecitorio
Piazza di Trevi
GIARDINI DEL QUIRINALE
Piazza B Gigli
V.d. Viminale
Termini
15
Palazzo del Quirinale
Via del Quirinale
Cavour
14
Piazza d. Rotonda
Via del Corso
Piazza d. Quirinale
Piazza d. Pilotta
Via Nazionale
Piazza d. Viminale
7 Pantheon
Piazza di Minerva
Piazza d. Coll. Romano
VILLA COLONNA
V. XXIV Maggio
Via C. Balbo
Via Urbana
Piazza del Esquilino
Santa Maria Maggiore
Piazza S. Maria Maggiore
Argentina
Via IV Nov.
Via Panisperna
Via
Largo d. Torre Argentina
Piazza Venezia
Via Cavour
V. d.
V. Oscure
Piazza d'Aracoeli
5
6
Via Giov. Lanza
Forum of Augustus
Piazza B. Cairoli
Piazza Capizucchi
Via dei Fori Imperiali
Via Cavour
ANCIENT ROME
4
Teatro di Marcello
Via Teatro di Marcello
1
ROMAN FORUM
2
Baths of Trajan
PARCO OPPIO
Colosseo
Lung. dei Cenci
ISOLA TIBERINA
3
Colosseum
L. Pierleoni
V. Petroselli
Piazza d. Colosseo
Via Labicana
L. d. Anguillar
Ponte Palatino
Arch of Constantine
Via dei SS. Quattro
V. d. Salumi
V. d. Genovesi
Piazza Bocca d. Verita
Piazza S. Anastasia
PALATINE HILL
Via di S. Gregorio
PARCO DEL CELIO
Via Claudia
Via dei Cerchi
CIRCUS MAXIMUS
Piazza Mercati
Lung. Ripa
Tiber (Tevere) River
Lung. Aventino
PARCO D. S. ALESSIO
Via del Circo Massimo
Piazza SS. Giov. e Paolo
Piazzale Ugo la Malfa
P. d. Ripa Grande
AVENTINE HILL
Piazza di Pta. Capena
V. d. Navicella
Circo Massimo
Ponte Sublicio
Piazza d. Emporio
Piazza d. Tempio di Diana
Pza di Pta. Metronia
9 St. Peter's Basilica
10 Castel Sant'Angelo
11 (your hotel room)
12 Campo de' Fiori
13 Piazza Navona
14 Gelateria Della Palma
15 Trevi Fountain

Seeing the top sights of Rome in one day requires an early start, discipline, and a bit of stamina, but it's actually quite doable. This "greatest hits" itinerary begins with an overview of the highlights of ancient Rome; after lunch, cross town and spend a few hours at the Vatican. Conclude your day with a leisurely evening walking tour of the gorgeously floodlit fountains and piazzas of the *centro storico.* **START: Take bus 30, 40, 62, 64, 70, 87, 95, 170, 492 or 628 to Piazza dell'Ara Coeli and climb the stairs to Piazza del Campidoglio.**

Travel Tip

Seasonal opening hours of some attractions may require modification of the itinerary below: For example, because of the Vatican Museums' shorter winter hours, from November to February, you'll need to do the Vatican in the morning and ancient Rome in the afternoon.

1 ★★★ Campidoglio (Capitoline Hill). The most sacred of Rome's hills was given its present look in the 1500s, when Michelangelo designed the star-patterned square and surrounding buildings of the Capitoline Museum (see p 31, bullet 5). The bronze statue of Marcus Aurelius in the center of the piazza is a copy; the 2nd-century-A.D. original is inside the museum. The western slopes of the hill, with their steep red tufa walls and tangled vegetation, still look much the same as they would have in the primordial days before the rise of Rome. Don't miss the majestic view of the Roman Forum from the south-facing terraces on either side of the bell-towered Palazzo Senatorio (city hall). 🕘 *15–30 min. Also gorgeous—and deserted—at night. Bus: 30, 40, 62, 64, 70, 87, 170, or 492.*

2 ★★★ Roman Forum. While the Forum is not one of the better-preserved archaeological sites of ancient Rome, it is the most historically significant. The Forum was the nerve center of the most powerful Western civilization in history for the better part of a thousand years, where political decisions were made, public speeches were heard,

The ruins of the Roman forum were excavated in the 19th century.

The Colosseum takes on a spectral glow at dusk.

and market activities took place. The remains here—of 2,000-year-old temples, law courts, and victory monuments—are impressive but skeletal, and can be difficult to decipher. *30–45 min. See p 24, bullet 7 for full details.*

3 ★★★ Colosseum. The Flavian amphitheater (A.D. 72–80) never fails to impress—for its elegant, enduring bulk, and its disturbing former function as a theater of slaughter. In the empire's heyday, games were held almost every other day; in times of special celebration, games could last for weeks or months on end. Free *tesserae* (tickets) were distributed to about 65,000 Romans, who could be seated in the arena in a matter of minutes, thanks to an efficient system of 80 numbered *vomitoria* (entrance/exit passageways). Against slashing swords and gnashing lions' teeth, gladiators and *bestiarii* (animal fighters) fought to the death, hoping to someday win their freedom. (In the Colosseum's 400-year history, fewer than 100 men ever did.) A visit inside the massive structure is certainly rewarding, but if you're pressed for time or cash, a walk around the exterior is fine. If there's a long queue, buy your tickets at the Palatine (p 26, bullet 8) and go straight to the turnstiles. *30–45 min. See p 26, bullet 10 for full details.*

4 ★★ Imperial Fora. Mussolini blazed the broad thoroughfare of Via dell'Impero—now Via dei Fori Imperiali—to trumpet the glories of his ancient forebears and propagate his own ambitions of empire. Along the east side of the boulevard, the ruins of the forums built by emperors Nerva, Augustus, and Trajan can be seen protruding from the ancient street level, 7.6m (25 ft.) below. On the west side, near the Colosseum, don't miss the fascinating marble maps (also from the Fascist period) charting the spread of the Roman Empire, which ultimately reached as far east as Iran (Parthia). *30 min. Via dei Fori Imperiali.*

5 ★ Vittoriano. Locals revile the 100-year-old monument to Victor Emanuel II, the first king of united Italy, as a tasteless and over-the-top neoclassical "typewriter," but tourists can't seem to take their eyes off the plus-size marble confection on the south side of Piazza Venezia. Either way, the views from the uppermost terraces are spectacular. *30–45 min. Free admission. Daily 10am–4:30pm. Bus: 30, 40, 60, 62, 64, 70, 85, 87, or 492.*

6 ★ Caffè Italia. Take a breather at this alfresco cafe halfway up the summit of the Vittoriano, to the left of the gigantic bronze statue of the king on horseback. ***Il Vittoriano.*** *06-6780905.*

7 ★★★ Pantheon. As the best-preserved and most elegant ancient building in the city—if not the world—the Pantheon ("temple to all gods") merits multiple visits. It was designed and possibly built by Hadrian from A.D. 118 to 125, in a form governed by circles and squares—shapes which, as Vitruvius wrote (and Leonardo later immortalized in his drawing, the *Vitruvian Man*), the human body most naturally occupies. The Pantheon's perfectly hemispherical, poured concrete dome is 43m (141 ft.) tall and wide, 1m (3 ft.) wider than the dome of St. Peter's. ***15–30 min.*** ***See p 54, bullet 11.*** *Take a taxi from the Pantheon to the Vatican Museums.*

This stained-glass window is one of the treasures of the Vatican Museums.

8 ★★★ Vatican Museums. After lunch, the crowds have left the Vatican, making it much more pleasant to explore. Stay focused, however, and make sure you see the starring ancient sculptures—the gut-wrenching emotion and dynamism of *Laocoon,* the transcendent composure of *Apollo Belvedere*—in the Pio-Clementine section of the museums, and then hightail it for the Vatican's biggest guns, Raphael's *stanze* and Michelangelo's frescoes in the Sistine Chapel. The art here, by two of the greatest painters in history, is a triumph of Renaissance achievement, bold in color, lofty in concept, and monumental in scale. ***1½ hr.*** ***See p 49, bullet 6 for a more comprehensive review.***

9 ★★★ St. Peter's Basilica. The incomprehensibly voluminous Vatican basilica boasts incalculable riches, from the marble and gold that cover its every surface to masterpieces like Michelangelo's *Pietà* and Bernini's baldacchino. ***30 min. Dome visit not absolutely necessary.*** ***See p 48, bullet 2.***

10 ★★ Castel Sant'Angelo. You probably won't have the time or energy to go inside, but the view of this mausoleum-turned-fortress, from Ponte Sant'Angelo—where angels by Bernini wince and moan—is not to be missed. ***15 min.*** ***See p 53, bullet 1 for full details.***

11 Your hotel room. By now, it's 4 or 5pm—a good time to return to your hotel, rest your feet, and freshen up before heading back out for dinner and your evening walking tour. Just don't crash completely. If it's after 5, and you're feeling energetic, skip the hotel and proceed directly to 12, below.

athletic stadium of Domitian, boasts Bernini's fantastic Fountain of the Four Rivers and Borromini's church of Sant'Agnese in Agone, as well as the smaller Fontana del Moro and Fontana di Nettuno. There are also a number of cafes to tempt you with after-dinner treats—it's touristy, but the setting sure is pretty. *20–30 min.* *See p 38, bullet 1, and p 53, bullet 6.* *Bus: 30, 40, 62, 64, 70, 87, 116, or 492.*

14 ★★ **Gelateria Della Palma.** Some call this gelateria a tourist trap; we say, "So what?" The upper half of the store has gaudy candy displays even Willy Wonka wouldn't dream of; on the lower level, a huge, horseshoe-shaped ice-cream bay attracts plenty of locals with its delicious traditional gelato, sorbet, and mousse (and not-so-delicious soy-based imitation gelato). *Via della Maddalena 20–23.* ☎ *06-68806752.*

15 ★★★ **Trevi Fountain.** Rome's most celebrated fountain, designed by Nicola Salvi and built 1732–62, is impressive enough during the day, but at night, the floodlights make it look cleaner and doubly spectacular—so gorgeous that you won't even mind the crowds. *20 min. Piazza di Trevi. Bus: 62, 85, 95, 175, or 492.*

The Trevi Fountain lit up at night.

12 ★★★ **Campo de' Fiori.** By early evening (6–6:30pm), this square in the very heart of the *centro storico* is abuzz with all kinds of people taking an *aperitivo* at the many outdoor bars. (We recommend **Vineria** and **Taverna del Campo,** p 114.) Campo de' Fiori and nearby Piazza Navona, the starting points of your evening tour, are also prime zones for dinner. *1 hr.* *See p 101.* *Bus: 30, 40, 62, 64, 70, 87, 116, or 492.*

13 ★★★ **Piazza Navona.** The most famous baroque square in Rome, built on the site of the ancient

St. Peter's Basilica fronting St. Peter's Square.

The Best of Rome **in Two Days**

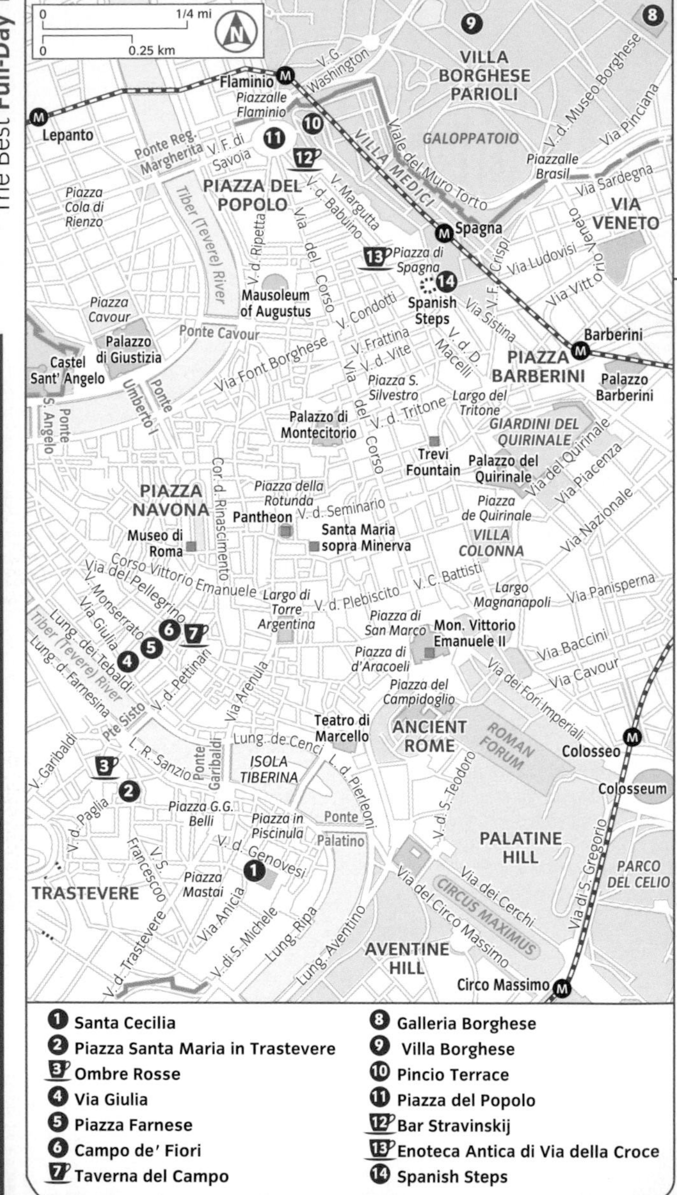

1 Santa Cecilia
2 Piazza Santa Maria in Trastevere
3 Ombre Rosse
4 Via Giulia
5 Piazza Farnese
6 Campo de' Fiori
7 Taverna del Campo
8 Galleria Borghese
9 Villa Borghese
10 Pincio Terrace
11 Piazza del Popolo
12 Bar Stravinskij
13 Enoteca Antica di Via della Croce
14 Spanish Steps

On your second day, spend the morning wandering the picturesque squares and alleys of Trastevere and Campo de' Fiori, Rome's oldest and most authentic quarters. Have lunch, and then cross town to feast your eyes on the crown jewels of baroque art In the Galleria Borghese. Go for a stroll through the Villa Borghese, making your way to the Pincio terraces and their enchanting view over the city and the Vatican. Finish the day by visiting the elegant Tridente district below, where such *dolce vita* activities as shopping, drinking, and eating abound. Allow 2½ hours for the morning tour of Trastevere and Campo de' Fiori. START: **Take bus 23, 271, or 280 to Lungotevere degli Anguillara, and walk to Piazza di Santa Cecilia; or take bus H, 780, or tram 8 to Piazza G.G. Belli, and walk.**

1 ★ Santa Cecilia. This incredibly peaceful basilica—an 18th-century reworking of a medieval church—is dedicated to the patron saint of music, who was martyred here in the 3rd century A.D. Inside, altar mosaics dazzle, and fragments of Pietro Cavallini's wonderful 13th-century fresco of the *Last Judgment* can be seen at limited times. Cecilia was exhumed from her tomb in the crypt here in 1599, long enough for Stefano Maderno to sculpt the lovely (but disturbing—her throat is slashed) statue of the saint's still-uncorrupted body below the altar. The church is one of the most popular in Rome for weddings, as evidenced by omnipresent grains of rice on the ground near the front door. *20 min. Piazza di Santa Cecilia. ☎ 06-5899289. Daily 9:30am–12:30pm, 4–6:30pm. Cavallini frescoes: Tues, Thurs 10am–noon, Sun 11:30am–12:30pm. Bus: 23, 271, 280, 780, or H. Tram: 3 or 8.*

2 ★★ Piazza and Basilica di Santa Maria in Trastevere. The first church in Rome dedicated to the Virgin Mary is spectacular inside and out, with a landmark Romanesque brick bell tower, colorful frescoes, mosaics, and loads of recycled ancient marbles. The eponymous square in front of the church acts as a kind of common living room for the neighborhood—it seems that every resident of Trastevere crosses the wide expanse of cobblestones here

A 9th-century apse mosaic in the Santa Cecelia Basilica.

at some point or another during the day. See also p 39, bullet 8, and p 43, bullet 9. *20 min. Piazza Santa Maria in Trastevere. ☎ 06-5814802. Daily 7:30am–9pm. Bus: 23, 271, 280, 780, or H. Tram: 8.*

3 ★ **Ombre Rosse.** This cafe with a porchlike view over a charming piazza is more stylish than the average neighborhood bar, but still frequented by born-and-bred, local *trasteverini,* and perfect for cappuccino-sipping and people-watching. *Piazza Sant' Egidio 12. ☎ 06-5884155.*

4 ★★ **Via Giulia**. Bearing straight toward the Vatican from Ponte Sisto, this former pilgrim route is home to many art galleries and high-end, original boutiques. Via Giulia's most fetching feature is an arch—with overgrown ivy draped luxuriously toward the pitch-black cobblestones—that spans the road behind Palazzo Farnese. *15 min. Bus: 23, 271, or 280. Tram: 8.*

5 ★★ **Piazza Farnese.** Sophisticated and regal Piazza Farnese is where locals come to read the newspaper or push a stroller in peace, against the stately, yellow-brick backdrop of 16th-century Palazzo Farnese. The sleepy square seems a world away—in reality, it's only a block—from the hubbub of Campo de' Fiori. See also p 39, bullet 10, and p 56, bullet 3. *15 min. Bus: 23, 30, 40, 62, 64, 70, 87, 116, or 492. Tram: 8.*

6 ★★★ **Campo de' Fiori.** Rome's market square par excellence, the *Campo* is the perfect embodiment of the myth of Italy. Every morning from Monday to Saturday, the square hosts a lively fruit, vegetable, and trinket bazaar. By early evening, where grocery shoppers eyed *pachino* tomatoes a few hours before, Rome's bright young things are scoping out each other over sparkling wine and effervescent conversation, indulging in the carefree atmosphere and centuries-old charm of the place they call home. See also p 39, bullet 11, and p 56, bullet 1. *20–30 min. Bus: 23, 30, 40, 62, 64, 70, 87, 116, or 492. Tram: 8.*

7 **Taverna del Campo.** Break for lunch on or around Campo de' Fiori before beginning the second part of the day's tour. For savory pizza-bread sandwiches and piazza views, Taverna del Campo can't be beat (p 114).

8 ★★★ **Galleria Borghese.** Reel in amazement at sculptures by

Tomatoes for sale at the market in the Campo de' Fiori.

The Spanish Steps are the city's favorite gathering place.

Bernini (and other masterpieces) at one of the world's most outstanding small museums. Visits must be booked at least 1 day in advance: Go for the 1pm or 3pm time slots. See also p 30, bullet 3. *1 hr. Piazzale Museo Borghese. ☎ 06-32810. Admission 8.50€. Tues–Sun 9am–7pm (last visit 5pm). Bus: 116 or 910.*

9 ★★ Villa Borghese. Go for a relaxing stroll among the refreshing greenery of Rome's most central public park. Boats can be rented at the picturesque *laghetto*. See also p 92. *30 min. Daily 6am–sunset. Metro: Spagna. Bus: 52, 53, 63, 116, or 910. Tram: 3 or 19.*

10 ★★★ Pincio Terrace. All hearts flutter at the impressive perspective on the Vatican from this panoramic spot above Piazza del Popolo. Gloriously sun-filled by day, ultraromantic by night. See also p 45, bullet 3. *15 min. Metro: Flaminio.*

11 ★★ Piazza del Popolo. Romans and tourists alike bask in the late afternoon sun that floods this vast, traffic-free oval space just below the Pincio. Graced in the center by a massive, hieroglyphed pink granite obelisk, the "square of the people" is wonderfully elegant and uncluttered—perfect for idling and gelato-licking, and a fitting introduction to the good-life Tridente district that spreads out pronglike to the south. See also p 38, bullet 4, and p 61, bullet 1. *15 min. Metro: Flaminio.*

12 ★★ Bar Stravinskij. Make like a movie star being hounded by the paparazzi and duck into this glamorous bar inside the Hotel de Russie. In warm weather, sit outside in the gorgeous interior garden, sloping up toward the Pincio; in winter, get cozy at the piano bar's indoor tables. *Via del Babuino 9. ☎ 06-328881.*

13 ★★ Enoteca Antica di Via della Croce. Grab a barstool or sidewalk seat and enjoy a well-earned snack (or meal) of wine and tantalizing plates of meats, cheeses, and olives. *Via della Croce 76B. ☎ 06-6790896.*

14 ★★★ Spanish Steps. Fortunately, the sweeping beauty of the *Scalinata di Piazza di Spagna* transcends the sometimes-ugly crowds of tourists that populate the square day and night. The climb to the high terrace covers 12 curving flights of steps of varying width—you'll trip if you don't watch where your feet are—but the view from the top is exhilarating. Come between 2 and 6am, and you'll enjoy that rarest of Roman treats—having the fabulous stage of the Spanish Steps to yourself. See also p 63, bullet 11. *30 min. Metro: Spagna.*

The Best of Rome **in Three Days**

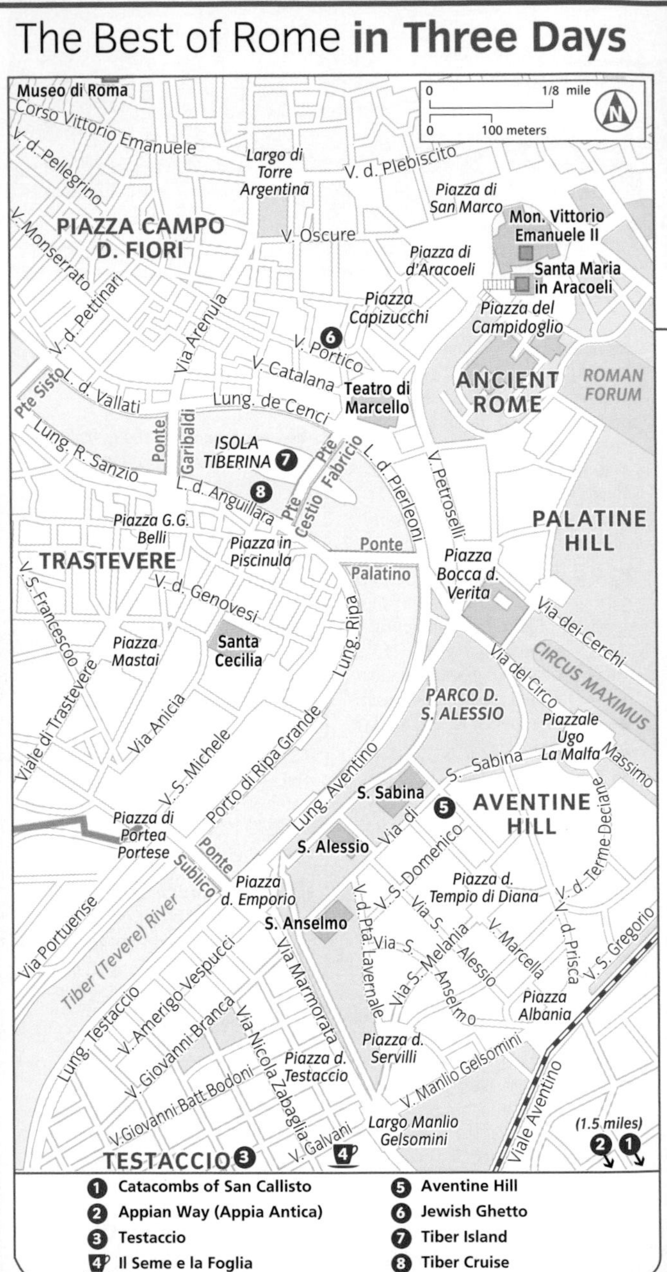

1. Catacombs of San Callisto
2. Appian Way (Appia Antica)
3. Testaccio
4. Il Seme e la Foglia
5. Aventine Hill
6. Jewish Ghetto
7. Tiber Island
8. Tiber Cruise

One of the best and most surprising things about Rome is how quickly you can escape the urban chaos and enjoy the rustic tranquillity of the city's greener areas, just a few miles away from the tourist hordes. On your third day, visit the catacombs and breathe the spicy, rural air along the history-saturated Appian Way. Then, go for a stroll in the contrasting, adjacent neighborhoods of Testaccio and the Aventine. Finish the day back in the *centro storico* with a walk through the Jewish Ghetto and Tiber Island. (Alternatively, get out of town entirely, and go for a day trip to Ostia Antica or Tivoli. See p 150 and 148.) **START: Take bus 118 or a taxi to the Catacombe di San Callisto on the Appian Way (the entrance is 3.2km/2 miles south of Porta San Sebastiano gate).**

1 ★★★ Catacombs of San Callisto. Twelve miles and four levels of hand-dug tunnels make up the underground network of Rome's largest catacombs, home to the tombs of half a million Christians, buried here from the 1st to the 4th centuries A.D. Deep within the complex, a labyrinth of 9m-high (30-ft.) tunnels, whose walls are perforated up to the ceiling with *loculi* (tomb niches), is especially impressive (and uncannily reminiscent of college library stacks). See also p 46. *45 min. Via Appia Antica 110. ☎ 06-5130151. Admission 5€. Open Thurs–Tues 8:30am–noon, 2:30–5pm. Bus: 118.*

2 ★★★ Appian Way. Few places in Rome transport you to ancient times as well as the Via Appia Antica, whose black basalt cobblestones, still bearing the wheel ruts of ancient cart traffic, stretch south of the city from Porta San Sebastiano. A few miles from the city walls, a rustic, agrarian landscape opens up on either side of the 4th-century-B.C. highway; the scenery is scattered with imposing or modest remains of ancient tombs and villas, and shepherds drive flocks of sheep from pasture to pasture, right across the "Queen of Roads." Even the scent of the Appian Way is ripe with antiquity: Once you smell it, the combination of bright notes of umbrella pine needles, musty sunbaked brick and marble, and the acrid pungency of leaves burning in farmyards becomes indelible in your memory. See also p 94. *1 hr. Bus: 118.*

A sarcophagus in the Catacombs of San Callisto.

3 ★★ Testaccio. Anchored by an artificial hill made of ancient pottery cast-offs and populated by salt-of-the-earth *romani de' Roma* (and the odd sheep or goat), the authentic neighborhood of Testaccio oozes character. See also p 72. *1 hr. Metro: Piramide. Bus: 30, 60, 75, 95, 118, or 170. Tram: 3.*

4 ★ Il Seme e la Foglia. With views of the old slaughterhouse and the potsherds of Monte Testaccio, this hip corner joint is a great place for a casual, quick lunch of enormous and tasty salads and sandwiches. *Via Galvani 18. ☎ 06-5743008.*

❺ ★★★ **Aventine.** Oblivious to the noise of the *centro* below, Aventine Hill is mostly residential, and home to several churches, whose dignified and simple red-brick exteriors and grassy grounds are a welcome contrast from the fussy facades and cramped quarters of many Roman churches. The 5th-century-A.D. church of Santa Sabina is cavernous and calming—a sublime example of the basilican form. See also p 64. ⌚ ***1 hr. Metro: Circo Massimo. Bus: 30, 60, 75, 81, 95, 118, 175, or 628. Tram: 3.***

A wall-fountain at Santa Sabina.

❻ ★★ **Jewish Ghetto.** As the area where Roman Jews were confined from the 16th to the 19th centuries, the medieval quarter between the Capitoline and the Tiber has seen its share of dark days. Today, however, the Ghetto is an upbeat, characteristic part of the *centro storico* that many tourists miss. From towering ancient ruins like the Theater of Marcellus, to sculptural gems like the Fountain of the Tortoises in Piazza Mattei, to the triumphant synagogue, this small area has a lot to see. See also p 68. ⌚ ***45 min. Bus: 30, 40, 62, 64, 70, 81, 87, 170, 492, or 628. Tram: 8.***

❼ ★★ **Tiber Island.** This boat-shaped protuberance in the middle of the river, between the Ghetto and Trastevere, is an oasis of calm; ever since the Greek god of medicine, Aesculapius, washed up here disguised as a snake, the island has been the city's sanctuary of medicine. Check out the lower promenade (water level permitting), with its great views of the ancient bridges nearby. See also p 68. ⌚ ***30 min. Bus: 23, 30, 40, 62, 64, 70, 81, 87, 170, 280, 492, or 628. Tram: 8.***

❽ ★★ **Tiber Cruise.** If you have time, going for a ride on the new *Battelli* riverboat service is a great way to relax while seeing Rome from the interesting perspective of this historic waterway, now largely overlooked by the modern city. Hop on at the dock opposite Tiber Island, and cruise all the way up to the Foro Italico (p 131) for a sunset stroll among the Fascist-inspired athletic cult mosaics and statues. ⌚ ***1 hr. Lungotevere Anguillara. ☎ 06-69380264. Admission 1€. Bus: 23, 280, 780, or H. Tram: 8.*** ●

Tiber Island is an oasis of calm.

2 The Best Special-Interest Tours

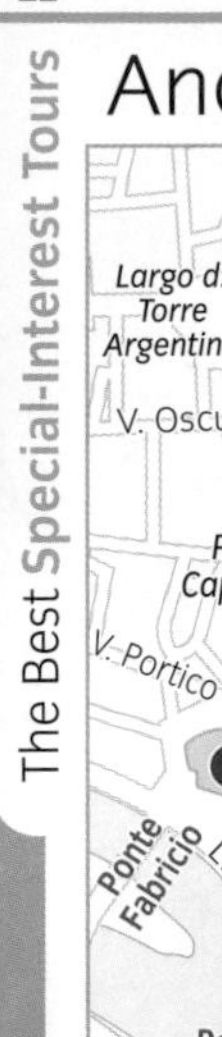

Ancient Rome

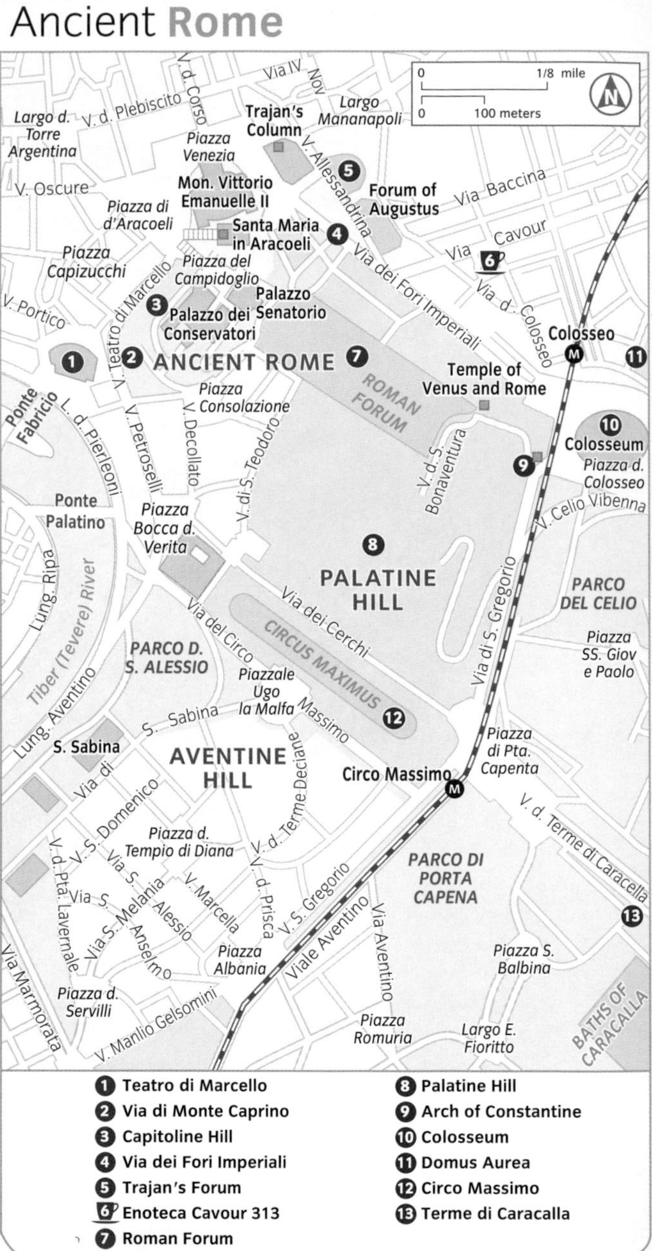

In towering brick or crumbling marble, the awe-inspiring ruins of ancient Rome are concentrated in the archaeological park south of the *centro storico*. Here, in an undulating topography drenched in history and dotted with umbrella pines, lie such famed sights as the Forum and the Colosseum, as well as the most sacred hills of Rome, the Capitoline and the Palatine. Bring a bottle of water and a picnic, and wear comfortable shoes for this half- or full-day tour. In summer, avoid these sites during the intense heat of midday. **START: Take bus 30, 95, 170, or 628 to Via del Teatro Marcello, or take bus 40, 62, 64, 70, 87, or 492 to Via d'Aracoeli or Piazza Venezia, and walk.**

The ruins of the Theater of Marcellus.

1 ★ Teatro di Marcello. The familiar arches of this 1st-century-B.C. theater, used for plays and concerts, inspired the design of the Colosseum, built 100 years later. Via del Teatro di Marcello.

2 ★ Via di Monte Caprino. Past shade trees and weathered fountains, this charming path winds its way up the Capitoline Hill's western slope. In 390 B.C., the Gauls attempted to storm the Capitol under cover of darkness and the dense vegetation here, but the sacred geese of Rome, kept in a pen nearby, detected their movement and sounded the alarm, thwarting the raiders. (The Capitoline guard-dogs, who slept through it, were later crucified.)

3 ★★ Capitoline Hill. Analogous to the Acropolis in Athens, this was the citadel and religious nerve center of ancient Rome. Atop this spur of red tufa, augurs monitored the flight of birds for omens, and traitors were hurled from the infamous Tarpeian Rock. The temple of Jupiter here, now lost, dominated the Roman skyline for centuries. Though it was redubbed Campidoglio in the Middle Ages and architecturally restyled during the Renaissance, the Capitoline's air of antiquity remains palpable. Be sure to visit the hill's southern terraces for staggeringly gorgeous views over the Roman Forum. See p 45, bullet 7 for Piazza del Campidoglio, and p 31, bullet 5 for the Capitoline Museum.

4 ★★ Via dei Fori Imperiali. Mussolini created this tree-lined boulevard, running dead-straight from his balcony at Palazzo Venezia to the Colosseum, to showcase the reminders of Rome's glory days and military might. On the east side of the street, from north to south, are the Forums of Trajan, Augustus, and Nerva; on the west side are the Forum of Julius Caesar and the original Roman Forum.

5 ★★ **Trajan's Forum.** Majestic and overtly phallic, the 40m-high (130-ft.) marble Column of Trajan was dedicated in A.D. 113 to commemorate the Romans' victory over Dacia (modern Romania). The ascending spiral band of sculptured reliefs depicts all stages of the military campaign, down to the finest detail. The most dominant feature in Trajan's Forum is the massive, concave-fronted, brick structure known as Trajan's Markets. Built on three levels, the markets were the world's first mall, housing 150 shops and commercial offices. While we recommend an up-close-and-personal walk through the site, the view of these monuments from the street is fine if you're pressed for time. *45 min. Via IV Novembre 94. ☎ 06-6790048. 6€. Daily 9am–7pm. Bus: 30, 40, 62, 64, 70, 85, 87, 95, 170, 175, or 492.*

6 **Enoteca Cavour 313.** Rest your feet at this wine bar just up the hill from the Forum. Light meals and non-alcoholic beverages are available, as well as plenty of wines by the glass. *Via Cavour 313 (at Via Annibaldi). ☎ 06-6785496.*

7 ★★★ **Roman Forum.** The Forum was the beating heart of republican and imperial Rome and the most important civic space in all of Western civilization for much of antiquity. It was here, in temples, basilicas, and markets that range in date from the 6th century B.C. to the 5th century A.D., that the Roman people carried out their daily religious, political, and commercial activities. Today, the Forum is a picturesque and evocative ruin that bears the deep scars of Roman "recycling"—when power over Rome passed from the emperors to the popes, church fathers dismantled the pagan buildings for their precious marble and bronze. From the late Middle Ages, dirt, debris, and cow manure accumulated in the Forum, reaching a height of 9m (30 ft.) by the 1890s, when excavations began.

The Roman Forum, with the Arch of Titus in the background.

Roman Forum

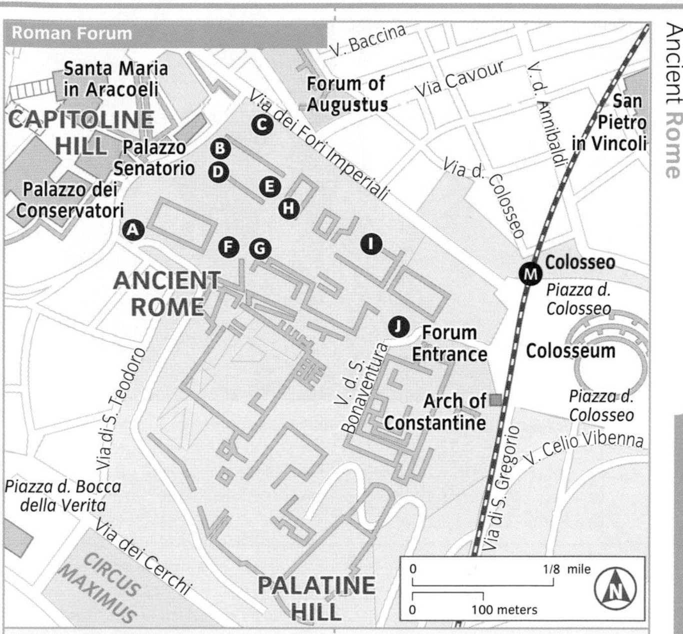

The eight columns of the 7A ★ **Temple of Saturn** tower over the north end of the Forum, indicating the former height of all the structures here. Nearby, the 7B ★★ **Arch of Septimius Severus** was erected in the 3rd century A.D. to celebrate that emperor's triumph in Parthia (modern Iran). The tall brick 7C ★★ **Curia Julia** (29 B.C.) is where the Roman senate met. The low, brown 7D ★ **Rostra,** or orator's stage, is where Mark Antony addressed friends, Romans, and countrymen. All that's left of the 7E ★ **Temple of Julius Caesar** (29 B.C.), which once had a hexastyle (six-columned) front, is its podium. Under its green metal roof is the rocky mound where Caesar's funeral pyre burned for 7 days in 44 B.C., culminating in the appearance of a comet. Near here, the picturesque *tria columna* of the 7F ★★ **Temple of Castor and Pollux** have helped centuries of poets imagine the splendor of Rome in its heyday. A curved grouping of smaller columns in this area are the ruins of the 7G ★ **Temple of Vesta,** where the six Vestal Virgins tended the eternal flame of Rome. Opposite, the hexastyle 7H ★★ **Temple of Antoninus and Faustina** (A.D. 141) survives because it was reconsecrated as a church in the medieval period. The three soaring vaults of the spectacular, 4th-century-A.D. 7I ★★★ **Basilica of Maxentius** represent only one-third of the law court's original size. Sculptural reliefs on the 7J ★★ **Arch of Titus** (A.D. 81) glorify the sack of Jerusalem.

1 hr. Apr–Oct, go after 2pm to avoid crowds. Largo Romolo e Remo. ☎ 06-6990110. Free admission. Daily 9am–1 hr. before sunset. Metro: Colosseo. Bus: 60, 75, 85, 87, 95, or 175.

The Palatine Hill archaeological park contains the ruins of imperial palaces.

❽ ★★ **Palatine Hill.** Back in 753 B.C., Romulus killed Remus and founded Roma on the Palatine. Later, emperors and other ancient bigwigs built their palaces and private entertainment facilities here. Nowadays, it's a sprawling, crowd-free archaeological garden, with plenty of shady spots good for picnicking and cooling off in summer. The Palatine's extensive ruins are time-consuming to explore and not very well marked, which is fascinating for some but frustrating for those in a hurry. ⌚ *45 min. Entrances near Arch of Titus and at Via di San Gregorio 30.* ☎ *06-6990110. 10€ (includes Colosseum). Daily 9am–1 hr. before sunset. Metro: Colosseo. Bus: 60, 75, 85, 87, 95, or 175. Tram: 3.*

A relief sculpture on the Arch of Titus depicts the triumphant return of the emperor and the spoils of the great temple of Jerusalem.

❾ ★ **Arch of Constantine.** Decorated largely with sculpture looted from earlier emperors' monuments, this arch was dedicated in A.D. 315 to commemorate the Battle of the Milvian Bridge (A.D. 312), in which Constantine defeated his co-emperor, Maxentius, after having a vision of the Christian cross. The superstitious Constantine legalized Christianity in A.D. 313 with the Edict of Milan, ending centuries of persecution.

❿ ★★★ **Colosseum.** Occupying the masses' free time with escapist, high-testosterone spectacles, the games at the Flavian amphitheater were the NASCAR of antiquity. Inaugurated in A.D. 80 over the site of

Nero's lake, the Colosseum hosted 65,000 fans every other day with its gory contests between men and animals. The enormous scale and masterful architecture of the amphitheater, supported entirely on radial and lateral arches, can be appreciated well enough from the outside, but inside, a modern catwalk allows visitors to stand at the same level where gladiators and hippos once fought to the death. Below, an ingenious system of 32 elevator shafts and trapdoors kept the action constant, replenishing the arena with new combatants and props when one fight ended. In A.D. 523, well after the rise of Christianity, the fights ended for good. Over the years, earthquakes, popes, barbarians, and the environment have all played a role in the Colosseum's decay. The pockmarks that riddle the travertine walls indicate where metal-hungry Lombards gouged into the stone in the 9th century to extract the lead fasteners between the blocks. ⌚ ***45 min.; crowded until late afternoon—buy tickets at Palatine Hill to skip the queue. Piazza del Colosseo. ☎ 06-7005469. 10€ (includes Palatine). Daily 9am–1 hr. before sunset. Metro: Colosseo. Bus: 60, 75, 85, 87, 95, or 175. Tram: 3.***

⓫ ★★ **Domus Aurea.** The maniacal emperor Nero snatched up most of the city land that burned in the catastrophic fire of A.D. 64 and built himself a palace that extended from the Palatine to the Oppian Hill, where the underground ruins of the "Golden House" can now be visited. ***See p 46, bullet*** ❷.

⓬ ★ **Circo Massimo.** Before there was Russell Crowe in *Gladiator,* there was Charlton Heston in *Ben-Hur.* In the world of ancient Roman sports, it was the chariot races at the Circus Maximus that held fans—300,000 of them—most in thrall. ***See p 66, bullet*** ❶.

⓭ ★★ **Terme di Caracalla.** Luxurious bathing complexes, like those built by Caracalla in A.D. 212 below the Aventine Hill, were a sort of country club in ancient times, but open to rich and poor, and as integral to the Romans' daily life as shuffling through the Forum on business or watching gladiators slug it out in the Colosseum. ***See p 67, bullet*** ❾.

The Baths of Caracalla are the best-preserved baths from Ancient Rome.

The Best Museums

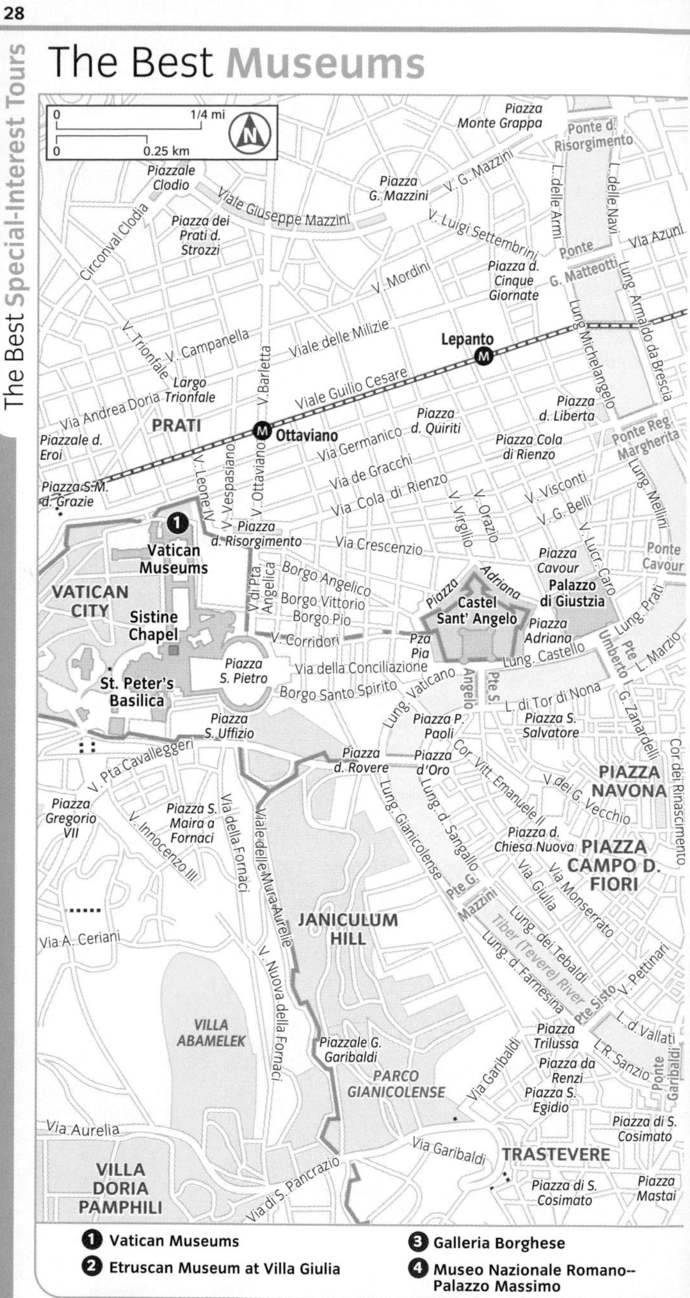

1 Vatican Museums
2 Etruscan Museum at Villa Giulia
3 Galleria Borghese
4 Museo Nazionale Romano--Palazzo Massimo

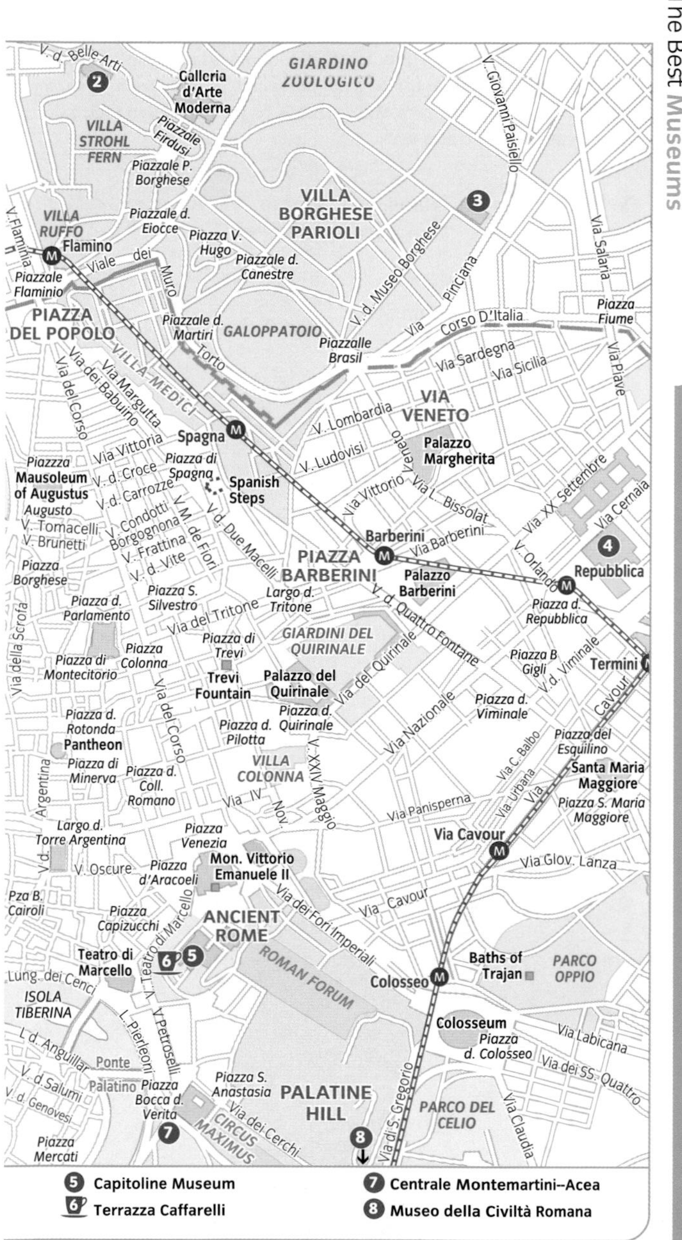
V. d. Belle Arti
2
Galleria d'Arte Moderna
GIARDINO ZOOLOGICO
V. Giovanni Paisiello
VILLA STROHL FERN
Piazzale Firdusi
Piazzale P. Borghese
VILLA BORGHESE PARIOLI
3
VILLA RUFFO
Piazzale d. Eiocce
Piazza V. Hugo
V. Flaminia
Flamino
Viale dei Muro Torto
Piazzale d. Canestre
V. d. Museo Borghese
Via Pinciana
Via Salaria
Piazzale Flaminio
PIAZZA DEL POPOLO
Piazzale d. Martiri
GALOPPATOIO
Piazzalle Brasil
Corso D'Italia
Piazza Fiume
VILLA MEDICI
Via Sardegna
Via Sicilia
Via Piave
Via del Corso
Via dei Babuino
Via Margutta
VIA VENETO
V. Lombardia
Spagna
Via Vittoria
Palazzo Margherita
Piazzza
Mausoleum of Augustus
Augusto
V. d. Croce
Piazza di Spagna
Spanish Steps
V. Ludovisi
Via Vittorio Veneto
V. d. Carrozze
Via L. Bissolat
Via XX Settembre
Via Cernaia
V. Tomacelli
V. Brunetti
V. Condotti
Borgognona
V. M. de Fiori
V. d. Due Macelli
Barberini
Via Barberini
4
V. Frattina
V. d. Vite
V. Orlando
Piazza Borghese
PIAZZA BARBERINI
Palazzo Barberini
Repubblica
Piazza d. Parlamento
Piazza S. Silvestro
Largo d. Tritone
V. d. Quattro Fontane
Piazza d. Repubblica
Via del Tritone
Via della Scrofa
Piazza di Trevi
GIARDINI DEL QUIRINALE
Piazza Colonna
Piazza B Gigli
Termini
V. d. Viminale
Piazza di Montecitorio
Trevi Fountain
Palazzo del Quirinale
Via del Quirinale
Cavour
Piazza d. Quirinale
Piazza d. Viminale
Piazza d. Rotonda
Pantheon
Piazza d. Pilotta
Via Nazionale
Piazza del Esquilino
Via C. Balbo
Piazza di Minerva
Piazza d. Coll. Romano
VILLA COLONNA
V. XXIV Maggio
Via Urbana
Santa Maria Maggiore
Argentina
Via IV Nov.
Via Panisperna
Piazza S. Maria Maggiore
Largo d. Torre Argentina
Piazza Venezia
Via Cavour
V. d.
V. Oscure
Piazza d'Aracoeli
Mon. Vittorio Emanuele II
Via Glov. Lanza
Pza B. Cairoli
Via dei Fori Imperiali
Via Cavour
Piazza Capizucchi
ANCIENT ROME
V. Teatro di Marcello
Teatro di Marcello
6
5
ROMAN FORUM
Baths of Trajan
PARCO OPPIO
Lung. dei Cenci
Colosseo
ISOLA TIBERINA
L. Pierleoni
V. Petroselli
Colosseum
Piazza d. Colosseo
Via Labicana
L. d. Anguillar
Ponte Palatino
Via dei SS. Quattro
V. d. Salumi
Piazza Bocca d. Verita
Piazza S. Anastasia
PALATINE HILL
Via di S. Gregorio
V. d. Genovesi
Via dei Cerchi
CIRCUS MAXIMUS
PARCO DEL CELIO
Via Claudia
7
8
Piazza Mercati
5 Capitoline Museum
6 Terrazza Caffarelli
7 Centrale Montemartini–Acea
8 Museo della Civiltà Romana

Out of the more than 100 museums in Rome, those listed here are our favorites for all-around interest, from intimate family collections to Fascist-era didactic museums. **START: Take bus 23, 49, or 492 to the entrance of the Vatican Museums, or take tram 19 to Piazza Risorgimento, or take Metro Line A to Ottaviano-San Pietro or Cipro-Musei Vaticani, and walk.**

1 ★★★ Vatican Museums. From mummies to moon rocks, the papal collections have the best of everything. *See p 49, bullet 6.*

2 ★★ Etruscan Museum at Villa Giulia. Pope Julius III's gorgeous Mannerist villa houses priceless artifacts, including intricate gold jewelry and a charming his-and-hers sarcophagus, from the civilization that ruled Italy before the Romans. *45 min. Piazza Villa Giulia (at Viale delle Belle Arti). ☎ 06-3226571. 4€. Tues–Sun 9am–7pm. Tram: 2, 3, or 19.*

3 ★★★ Galleria Borghese. Immensely entertaining and mercifully manageable in size, the collection at this 17th-century garden estate is museum perfection. Ancient Roman mosaics in the entrance salon depict gory scenes between gladiators and wild animals. In Room 1, Canova's *Pauline Bonaparte* (1805–08) lies, topless, on a marble divan. Bernini's staggeringly skillful sculptures of *David, Apollo and Daphne,* and *Rape of Persephone* (1621–24), in Rooms 2 to 4, are so realistically rendered that their subjects seem to be breathing. The paintings by Caravaggio in Room 8 range in tone from luscious (*Boy with a Basket of Fruit,* 1594) to strident and grisly (*David and Goliath,* 1610). Renaissance masterpieces like Raphael's *Deposition* (1507) and Titian's *Sacred and Profane Love* (1514) hang casually upstairs in the *pinacoteca*. *1 hr. Piazzale Scipione Borghese. ☎ 06-32810. www.galleriaborghese.it. Reservations required. 8.50€. Tues–Sun 9am–7pm. Bus: 116 or 910.*

4 ★★ Museo Nazionale Romano—Palazzo Massimo. An embarrassment of ancient

A close-up of Michelangelo's Sistine Chapel ceiling fresco depicts God reaching out to Adam.

The Capitoline Museum lies on the perfectly proportioned Piazza del Campidoglio.

riches—paintings, mosaics, statues, and inscriptions—are displayed at this recently restored, bright, and airy palazzo near the train station. Frescoes teeming with delightful animal and vegetable motifs, rescued from the bedrooms and dining rooms of Roman villas, are the highlight here, and totally unique among Rome's museums. ⌚ ***1 hr. Largo di Villa Peretti 1 (at Via Giolitti).*** ☎ ***06-48903501. 6€. Tues–Sun 9am–7pm. Metro: Termini. Bus: 40, 64, 70, 170, 175, or 492.***

❺ ★★★ **Capitoline Museum (Musei Capitolini).** In the Michelangelo-designed buildings of Piazza del Campidoglio are some of the most important Roman sculptures in the world. The Palazzo dei Conservatori houses the 5th-century-B.C. bronze *Capitoline she-wolf,* mascot of Rome, in Room 4, and the photogenic fragments of the colossal statue of *Constantine* in the courtyard. The *pinacoteca* has a number of fine works by Caravaggio, Titian, Tintoretto, and Guido Reni. Across the square in the Palazzo Nuovo are the majestic 2nd-century-A.D. bronze of *Marcus Aurelius,* haunting busts of emperors and philosophers in Rooms 4 to 5, and myriad marble fauns and satyrs throughout. Not to be missed, the ponderous tufa blocks of the *tabularium* (Roman archive hall, 78 B.C.) connect the two wings of the museums and offer dramatic views over the Forum. ⌚ ***1½ hr. Best in late afternoon. Piazza del Campidoglio.*** ☎ ***06-67102071. 7.80€. Tues–Sun 9:30am–7pm. Bus: 30, 40, 62, 64, 70, 87, 95, 170, or 492.***

❻ ★ **Terrazza Caffarelli.** The Capitoline Museum's cafe has fresh sandwiches and drinks—and a commanding view of the *centro storico.* Non-museumgoers can access the cafe from the northern wall of Palazzo dei Conservatori.

❼ ★★ **Centrale Montemartini—Acea.** Luminous ancient sculpture is exhibited against the heavy iron machinery of an old power station—think "Venus in the Boiler Room." ⌚ ***30 min. Via Ostiense 106.*** ☎ ***06-5748030. 4.20€. Tues–Sun 9am–7pm. Metro: Piramide. Bus: 23 or 271.***

❽ ★★ **Museo della Civiltà Romana.** It's worth the subway ride to Mussolini's fantasyland—EUR—to see the enormous, 1:250 scale plastic model of ancient Rome. ***Piazza Agnelli 10.*** ☎ ***06-5926135. Tues–Sat 9am–7pm; Sun 9am–2pm. Metro: Fermi.***

Baroque Rome

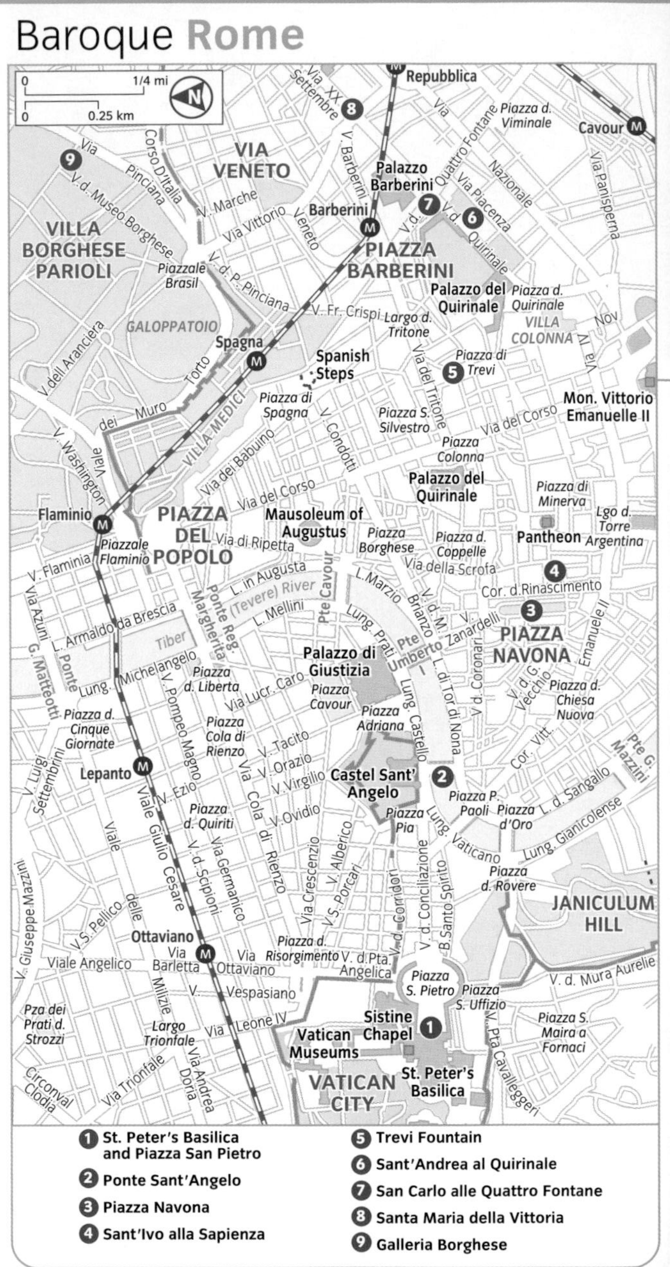

Straight lines and right angles? Ugh—so 1500s! The 17th century in Rome saw a boom in artistic patronage—the biggest in the city since the days of the Caesars—that heralded the arrival of a new style, called *barocco* ("irregular pearl"), in which sculptors and architects traded the balance and symmetry of the Renaissance for dynamism and theatrical flourish. The two greatest exponents of Roman baroque were Francesco Borromini and Gian Lorenzo Bernini, who left their respective curricula vitae virtually strewn about the city. Occasionally over-the-top, but always fun, the baroque style is what gave Rome its signature sinuous building facades and its myriad playful fountains. It's what makes an aimless stroll through the *centro storico* so rewarding. START: **Take bus 23, 40, 62, or 64 to Piazza Pia/Via della Conciliazione.**

1 ★★★ St. Peter's Basilica and Piazza San Pietro. Reaching out from either side of the church, the curving, colonnaded arms of Piazza San Pietro were designed by Bernini in the 1640s to mimic a gigantic human embrace, clutching visitors, caliper-like, inexorably toward the bosom of St. Peter's Basilica. Under the dome, Bernini's corkscrew-legged bronze baldacchino is flecked with tiny bumblebees, the symbol of his—and the baroque's—greatest patron, Pope Urban VIII Barberini. *See p 48, bullets 1 and 2.*

This angel is a copy of one of Bernini's original sculptures atop the Ponte Sant'Angelo.

2 ★★ Ponte Sant'Angelo. The angels studding this bridge to Castel Sant'Angelo are copies of original sculptures by Bernini. Each figure holds an instrument of the passion of Christ; their masterfully rendered emotions run the gamut

The Ponte Sant'Angelo at dusk.

from introverted sorrow to wrenching pain to that Bernini warhorse, the parted-lips swoon. ◷ *15 min. Best at night. Between Castel Sant' Angelo and Lungotevere Sant'Angelo. Bus: 40, 62, or 64.*

3 ★★★ **Piazza Navona.** Rome's grandest baroque square is the stage for an architectural smackdown between Borromini and Bernini. Weighing in on the western side of the oblong piazza is Borromini's **Sant'Agnese in Agone** (1653–57), a small church whose proud bearing is enhanced by its telescoping bell towers, oversized dome, and concave facade—a popular baroque feature, designed to draw in passers-by. A bare basin for centuries, the **Fountain of Neptune** was only given its namesake figure and fanciful decoration in the 1800s. In the center, Neptune engages an octopus in fierce battle as unfazed duos of seahorses, nymphs, and aquatic cherubs cavort around the fountain's edge. In the center of the square, Bernini's action-packed, obelisk-crowned **Fountain of the Four Rivers** (1651; see chapter opening photo) is a feisty competitor, with four reclining figures representing the Danube, Plata, Ganges, and Nile. The fountain's base is a mass of travertine, hewn in the pre-weathered, organic style so favored in the 17th and 18th centuries. And any baroque sculptor worth his salt would sooner be caught dead than design a fountain that didn't include cavorting animals—today, overheated tourists and mentally unstable locals splash (illegally) alongside Bernini's "hippopotamus" (which is just a horse, wading) and river serpents. Between Borromini and Bernini, who wins? After 350 years, the jury is still out—but if you look up at the left bell tower of the church, a devastatingly *superb* statue of St. Agnes, placed there after the fountain's completion, seems to have the last laugh. *See also p 53, bullet* **6**.

4 ★ **Sant'Ivo alla Sapienza.** Borromini always created drama in his architecture by employing elements of curvaceous tension; here, an upside-down marble tornado of a dome crowns a dizzying, star-shaped church. ◷ *15 min. Corso Rinascimento 40. Bus: 30, 40, 62, 64, 70, 87, 116, or 492.*

5 ★★★ **Trevi Fountain.** The tourist swarms are annoying, but Nicola Salvi's fountain (1732–62) is a

The Fontana del Nettuno (Fountain of Neptune) in the Piazza Navona.

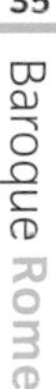

Sleeping Hermaphrodite *sculpture in the Galleria Borghese.*

monumental feast for the eyes that never fails to delight—and to surprise, given its hidden location. An ingeniously sculpted base of faux boulders and "fallen" building cornices gives rise to a dynamic pageant of mythological figures, over which thousands of gallons of water per minute thunder to the inviting blue pool below. ◷ ***30 min. Piazza di Trevi. Crowded from 10am–midnight. Bus: 62, 95, 116, 175, or 492.***

❻ ★ **Sant'Andrea al Quirinale.** The smallest church Bernini designed, known as the "pearl of the baroque," is understated only in size. Amid a rich dessert of pink marble and gilded stucco, a plaster St. Andrew steals the show, rising to the heavens past the broken pediment above the altar. ◷ ***15 min. Via del Quirinale 29. Metro: Barberini. Bus: 40, 64, 70, 170, or H.***

❼ ★★ **San Carlo alle Quattro Fontane.** It feels almost like being trapped inside an elaborate crystal in Borromini's tiny church (his favorite). This is an oppressive, colorless frenzy of concave chapels, jutting cornices, intricate coffers, and tricks of light. ◷ ***15 min. Via del Quirinale 23. Metro: Barberini. Bus: 40, 62, 64, 70, 95, 116, 170, 175, or 492.***

❽ ★★ **Santa Maria della Vittoria.** Still risqué after all these years, Bernini's *Ecstasy of St. Teresa* (in the Cornaro Chapel, to the left of the altar) captures the mystical saint in a moment of spiritual rapture that looks for all the world like another kind of climax. From their "box seat" to the side, the animated Cornaro family members react to the ambiguously scandalous spectacle. ◷ ***15 min. Via XX Settembre 17. Metro: Repubblica. Bus: 60, 62, or 910.***

❾ ★★★ **Galleria Borghese.** The word "incredible" is often used lightly, but Bernini's chisel wizardry here truly confounds belief. In his sculptures of *Apollo and Daphne, Rape of Persephone,* and *David,* he defies the physical properties of marble, involving us emotionally with his subjects and reverentially with his skill. The museum's strict reservations policy keeps crowds to a blessed minimum; be sure to book at least a few days in advance. ***See p 30, bullet ❸.***

Bernini's Ecstasy of St. Teresa *in the Santa Maria della Vittoria.*

Rome's Best Piazzas

0 1/4 mi
0 0.25 km
N
V. Mordini
Piazza d. Cinque Giornate
Ponte G. Matteotti
Lung. Armaldo da Brescia
Lung. Michelangelo
V. Trionfale
V. Campanella
Viale delle Milizie
Lepanto
V. Barletta
Largo Trionfale
Viale Guilio Cesare
Via Andrea Doria
PRATI
Piazza d. Liberta
Piazza d. Quiriti
Piazzale d. Eroi
Ottaviano
Via Germanico
Piazza Cola di Rienzo
Ponte Reg. Margherita
V. Leone IV
V. Vespasiano
V. Ottaviano
Via de Gracchi
Piazza S.M. d. Grazie
Via Cola di Rienzo
V. Visconti
Lung. Mellini
V. Virgilio
V. Orazio
V. G. Belli
Piazza d. Risorgimento
Via Crescenzio
V. Lucr. Caro
Vatican Museums
Piazza Cavour
Ponte Cavour
V. di Pta. Angelica
Borgo Angelico
Adriana
Palazzo di Giustzia
VATICAN CITY
Borgo Vittorio
Piazza
Castel Sant' Angelo
Borgo Pio
Piazza Adriana
Lung. Prati
Sistine Chapel
V. Corridori
Pza Pia
Umberto I
Pte
Lung. Marzio
Piazza S. Pietro
Via della Conciliazione
Lung. Castello
St. Peter's Basilica
Borgo Santo Spirito
Lung. Vaticano
Angelo
Pte S.
L. di Tor di Nona
G. Zanardelli
Piazza S. Uffizio
Piazza P. Paoli
Piazza S. Salvatore
Cor. dei Rinascimento
V. Pta Cavalleggeri
Piazza d. Rovere
Piazza d'Oro
Cor. Vitt. Emanuele II
V. dei G. Vecchio
PIAZZA NAVONA
Piazza Gregorio VII
Piazza S. Maira a Fornaci
Via della Fornaci
Viale delle Mura Aurelie
Lung. Gianicolense
Lung. d. Sangallo
Piazza d. Chiesa Nuova
PIAZZA CAMPO D. FIORI
V. Innocenzo III
Pte G. Mazzini
Via Giulia
Via Monserrato
Via A. Ceriani
JANICULUM HILL
Tiber (Tevere) River
Lung. dei Tebaldi
V. Nuova della Fornaci
Lung. d. Farnesina
V. Pettinari
Pte Sisto
L. d. Vallati
VILLA ABAMELEK
Piazzale G. Garibaldi
Piazza Trilussa
L. R. Sanzio
Ponte Garibaldi
PARCO GIANICOLENSE
Via Garibaldi
Piazza da Renzi
Piazza S. Egidio
Via Aurelia
Via Garibaldi
VILLA DORIA PAMPHILI
Via di S. Pancrazio
V. d. Vascello
V. dei Quattro Venti
Piazza di S. Cosimato
Piazza Mastai
TRASTEVERE
Viale Trastevere
Piazza di Pta. Portese
VILLA SCIARRA

1. Piazza Navona
2. Piazza della Rotonda
3. Piazza San Lorenzo in Lucina
4. Piazza del Popolo
5. Caffè Rosati
6. Bar Canova

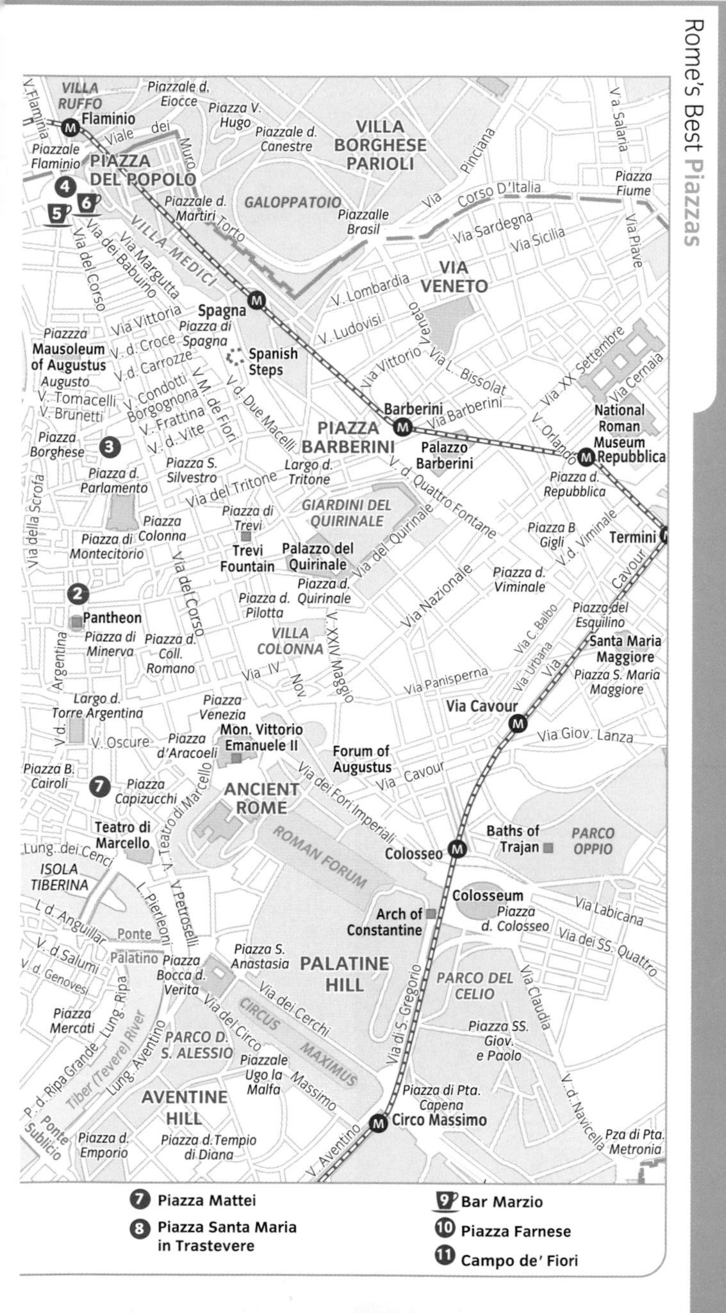
VILLA RUFFO
Piazzale d. Eiocce
Piazza V. Hugo
Piazzale d. Canestre
VILLA BORGHESE PARIOLI
Flaminio
V. Flaminia
Viale dei Muro Torto
Piazzale Flaminio
PIAZZA DEL POPOLO
Piazzale d. Martiri
GALOPPATOIO
Piazzalle Brasil
Via Pinciana
Corso D'Italia
Via Sardegna
Via Sicilia
V.a Salaria
Piazza Fiume
Via Piave
Via del Corso
Via dei Babuino
Via Margutta
VILLA MEDICI
VIA VENETO
V. Lombardia
Spagna
V. Ludovisi
Via Vittoria
Piazza di Spagna
Spanish Steps
Piazzza Mausoleum of Augustus Augusto
V. d. Croce
V. d. Carrozze
V. Condotti
V. Borgognona
V. Frattina
V. d. Vite
V. M. de Fiori
V. d. Due Macelli
Via Vittorio Veneto
Via L. Bissolat
Via XX Settembre
Via Cernaia
V. Tomacelli
V. Brunetti
Barberini
Via Barberini
National Roman Museum
Piazza Borghese
PIAZZA BARBERINI
Palazzo Barberini
V. Orlando
Repubblica
Piazza d. Parlamento
Piazza S. Silvestro
Largo d. Tritone
V. d. Quattro Fontane
Piazza d. Repubblica
Via della Scrofa
Via del Tritone
Piazza di Trevi
GIARDINI DEL QUIRINALE
Piazza Colonna
Piazza di Montecitorio
Trevi Fountain
Palazzo del Quirinale
Via del Quirinale
Piazza B Gigli
V. d. Viminale
Termini
Cavour
Piazza d. Quirinale
Via Nazionale
Piazza d. Viminale
Pantheon
Piazza d. Pilotta
Piazza del Esquilino
Santa Maria Maggiore
Piazza di Minerva
Piazza d. Coll. Romano
VILLA COLONNA
V. XXIV Maggio
Via C. Balbo
Via Urbana
Via IV Nov.
Via Panisperna
Piazza S. Maria Maggiore
Argentina
Largo d. Torre Argentina
Piazza Venezia
Via Cavour
V. d.
V. Oscure
Piazza d'Aracoeli
Mon. Vittorio Emanuele II
Forum of Augustus
Via Giov. Lanza
Piazza B. Cairoli
Piazza Capizucchi
Via Cavour
ANCIENT ROME
Via dei Fori Imperiali
V. Teatro di Marcello
Teatro di Marcello
ROMAN FORUM
Baths of Trajan
PARCO OPPIO
Lung. dei Cenci
Colosseo
ISOLA TIBERINA
Colosseum
Piazza d. Colosseo
Via Labicana
L. Pierleoni
V. Petroselli
L. d. Anguillar
Ponte Palatino
Arch of Constantine
Via dei SS. Quattro
V. d. Salumi
V. d. Genovesi
Piazza Bocca d. Verita
Piazza S. Anastasia
PALATINE HILL
PARCO DEL CELIO
Via Claudia
Lung. Ripa
Via dei Cerchi
Via di S. Gregorio
Piazza Mercati
Via del Circo Massimo
CIRCUS MAXIMUS
Piazza SS. Giov. e Paolo
PARCO D. S. ALESSIO
Piazzale Ugo la Malfa
Lung. Aventino
Tiber (Tevere) River
P. d. Ripa Grande
V. d. Navicella
AVENTINE HILL
Piazza di Pta. Capena
Circo Massimo
Ponte Sublicio
Piazza d. Emporio
Piazza d. Tempio di Diana
V. Aventino
Pza di Pta. Metronia
7 Piazza Mattei
8 Piazza Santa Maria in Trastevere
9 Bar Marzio
10 Piazza Farnese
11 Campo de' Fiori

Giving every city neighborhood its own alfresco salon, with newsstands, cafes, and room to breathe, the piazza is one of the great Italian urban inventions. In Rome, some are grandiose gifts to the city from politically minded popes; others are the incidental result of streets meeting at odd angles; but the best piazzas are those where Romans act out their daily pageants, fully aware of their dramatic backdrops. **START: Take bus 30, 40, 62, 64, 70, 87, 116, or 492 to Corso Vittorio Emanuele or Corso Rinascimento.**

❶ ★★★ **Piazza Navona.** This theatrical baroque platter retains the shape of the ancient stadium over which it was built. Vying for your attention at the center of the oval are Bernini's dynamic Fountain of the Four Rivers and Borromini's haughty Church of Sant'Agnese in Agone. Cafes and restaurants abound on the square, but you'll never find locals dining here. Piazza Navona is at its best before 10am, when the tourist hordes and trinket sellers start to descend, so come for a morning cappuccino to enjoy an unspoiled view. *See p 53, bullet ❻. Bus: 30, 40, 62, 64, 70, 87, 116, or 492.*

The pink granite obelisk in the Piazza del Popolo.

❷ ★★★ **Piazza della Rotonda.** Despite a 9m (30-ft.) rise from the surrounding ground level, the 2nd-century-A.D. Pantheon still stands, awesomely imposing, at the southern end of this square; the fountain is 18th century. Stop by in the late evening for a drink, when the atmosphere is more intimate and tourist-free. *Bus: 30, 40, 62, 64, 70, 85, 87, 95, 116, or 175. Tram: 8.*

❸ ★ **Piazza San Lorenzo in Lucina.** Tourists have taken over Piazza di Spagna, but well-heeled locals in the Tridente shopping district still have this wedge-shaped square when they want to sit down for Campari and sandwiches. The two cafes here—Ciampini and Teichner—are almost identical, and great for watching big-spending Romans on parade. *Metro: Spagna. Bus: 62, 85, 95, 175, or 492.*

❹ ★★★ **Piazza del Popolo.** A 4,000-year-old pink granite obelisk with wonderful hieroglyphics presides over this grand, newly pedestrianized expanse at the top of the Tridente. On the north side of the piazza, Santa Maria del Popolo (p 61, bullet ❷) is a trove of art treasures. *Metro: Flaminio.*

5 ★ **Caffè Rosati.** A bit touristy, but what the hell—it still feels fabulous to soak up the Art Nouveau decor and view at this haunt of Roman glitterati. *Piazza del Popolo 4. ☎ 06-3225859.*

6 Bar Canova. The *other* Piazza del Popolo cafe, preferred by Fellini for its morning shade. ***Piazza del Popolo 16. ☎ 06-3612231.***

Trastevere is full of colorful sights, like these green shutters set against a rust-red facade.

7 ★ Piazza Mattei. A scrappy little square in the old Jewish ghetto charms all with its endearing *Fontana delle Tartarughe* (Fountain of the Tortoises), begun in 1588 by Giacomo della Porta and Taddeo Landini and given its namesake amphibians by Bernini in 1638. ***Bus: 23, 30, 40, 62, 63, 64, 70, 87, 170, 280, or 492.***

8 ★★ Piazza Santa Maria in Trastevere. The crossroads of daily life in village-y Trastevere meets all criteria: a sprinkling of cafes and restaurants, children with *nonna* in tow, a graceful fountain, and a big church. ***Bus: H, 23, 280, or 780. Tram: 8.***

9 ★ Bar Marzio. The outdoor tables here offer a prime view across the square to the splendid facade of Santa Maria in Trastevere. ***Piazza Santa Maria in Trastevere 15. ☎ 06-5816095.***

10 ★★ Piazza Farnese. Just steps away from the buzz of the Campo, Piazza Farnese is elegant, sedate, and open, graced on its west side by the stately Palazzo Farnese, designed in part by Michelangelo and now the French embassy. The fountains here are granite bathtubs filched from the Baths of Caracalla in the 1500s and topped by the Farnese family emblem, the iris. ***Bus: 23, 30, 40, 62, 64, 70, 87, 116, 280, or 492. Tram: 8.***

11 ★★★ Campo de' Fiori. With a produce market in the morning and a booming social scene at its many bars in the evening, this former "field of flowers" is the liveliest square in the *centro storico*. The Campo may lack the architectural refinement of other Roman piazzas, but its round-the-clock utility and heavy traffic of locals are tough to beat. ***Bus: 30, 40, 62, 64, 70, 87, 116, or 492. Tram: 8.***

An array of pumpkins in the produce market at the Campo de' Fiori.

Rome's Best Churches

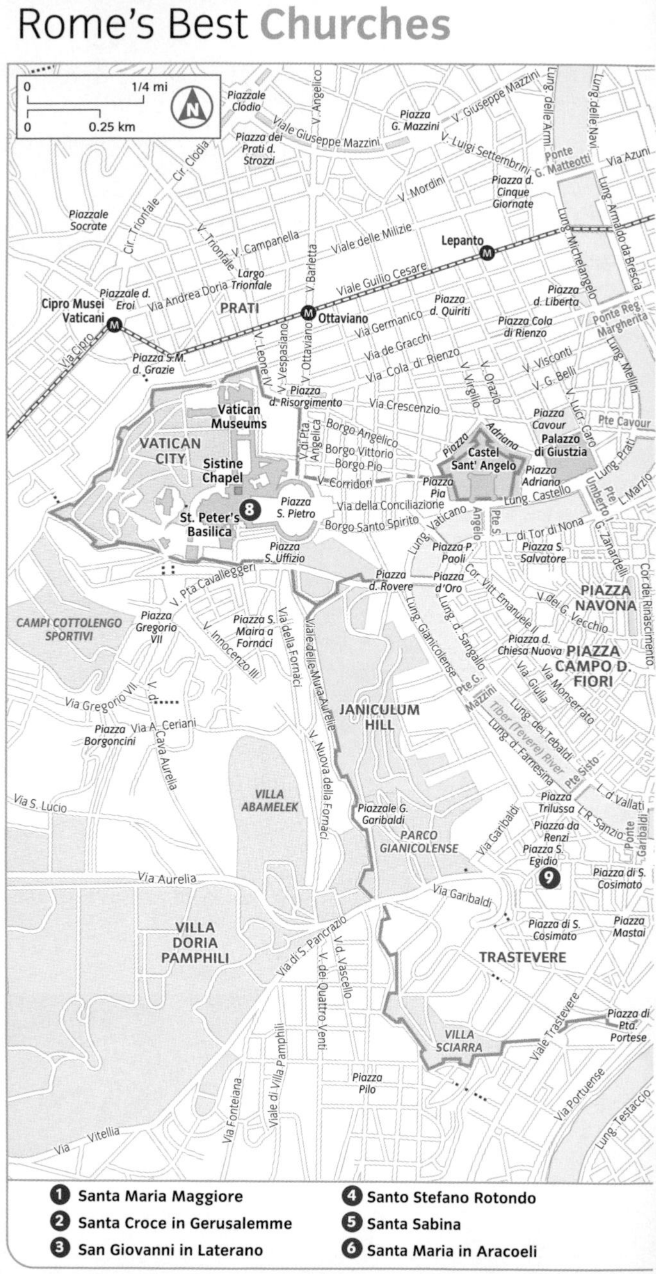

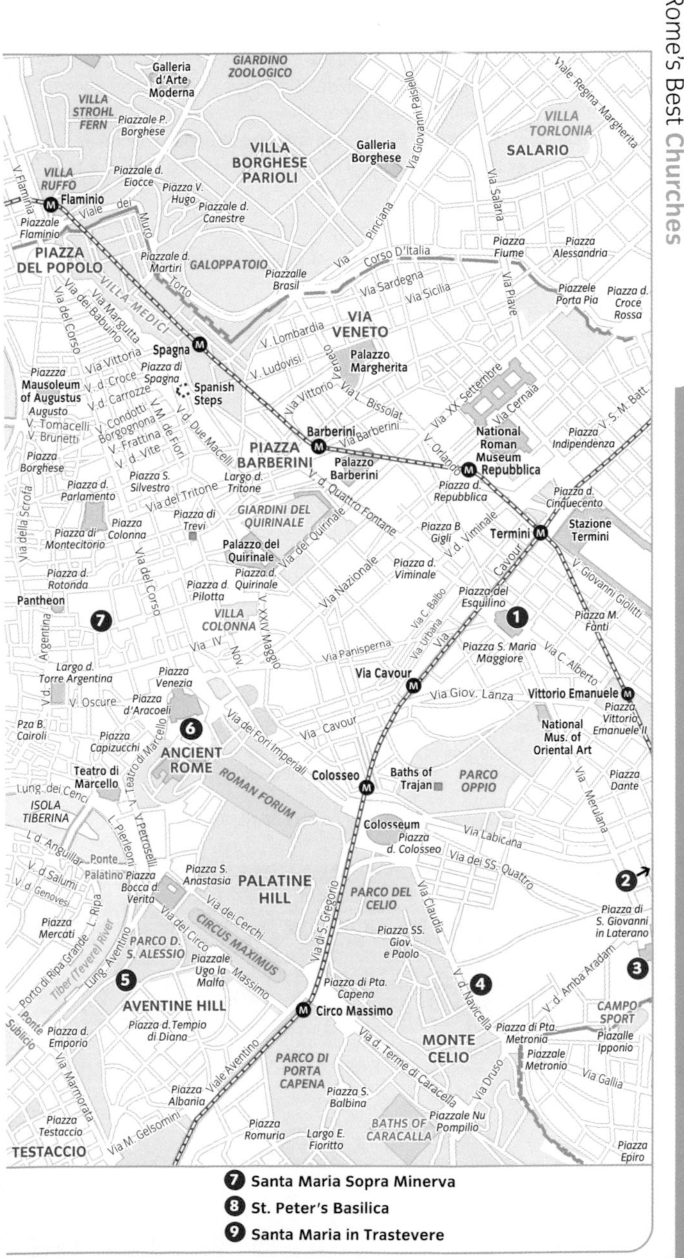

7 Santa Maria Sopra Minerva
8 St. Peter's Basilica
9 Santa Maria in Trastevere

The city's best all-around churches have artistic treasures, relics, and fascinating histories, as well as architecture—humbling or haunting—that reinforces the religious function of the space. All churches in Rome are free of charge and refreshingly cool in summer, but opening hours are notoriously subject to change. **START: Take bus 70 or 75 to Piazza Santa Maria Maggiore, or take Metro Line A or B, or bus 40, 64, 170, 175, 492, or H to Stazione Termini, and walk.**

1 ★★ Santa Maria Maggiore. In this perfect example of the prototypical basilica, the main nave, flanked by two lower and narrower side aisles, terminates in a curved apse, which is decorated with dazzling polychrome and gold mosaics. Near the right side of the main altar, a modest marble slab marks the tomb of baroque superstar Gian Lorenzo Bernini; the epitaph, inlaid in bronze, is a pithy summary of his life: "He decorated the city." *Piazza di Santa Maria Maggiore. ☎ 06-483195. Free admission. Daily 7am–7pm. Metro: Termini. Bus: 70, 75, 649, or 714.*

2 ★ Santa Croce in Gerusalemme. The mother lode of relics here includes a piece of the True Cross, remnants of the Crown of Thorns, and the finger of doubting St. Thomas. (Photos aren't allowed, but postcards of all can be purchased at the church gift shop.) *Piazza di Santa Croce in Gerusalemme 12. ☎ 06-7014769. Metro: Manzoni. Bus: 81 or 649. Tram: 3.*

3 ★★ San Giovanni in Laterano. The cathedral of Rome and mother church of the world is not St. Peter's in the Vatican, but this church dedicated to St. John. The spare, slightly grave interior is by Borromini (1646); the facade, with its chorus line of saints, dates from 1735. In a separate building across the piazza are the *Scala Santa* (holy stairs) and the *Sancta Sanctorum* ("holy of holies"), boasting rare 13th-century frescoes by Cimabue and relics of furniture from the Last Supper. *Piazza San Giovanni in Laterano. ☎ 06-69886433. Free admission to church and Scala Santa; 3€*

Elegant columns adorned with mosaics by the artist Vassalleti are found in San Giovanni in Laterano.

A nun strolls through St. Peter's Square.

Sancta Sanctorum. Church daily 7am–6:30pm. Scala Santa daily 6:30am–noon, 3–6pm. Sancta Sanctorum Tues, Thurs, Sat 10:30–11:30am, 3:30–4:30pm. Metro: San Giovanni. Bus: 85, 87, or 117. Tram: 3.

4 ★ Santo Stefano Rotondo. Deep in the rustic Celio Hill, this ancient church is reminiscent of a railway roundhouse. The walls of the ambulatory are frescoed with R-rated scenes of gruesome martyrdoms. *Via di Santo Stefano Rotondo 7. ☎ 06-421191. Nov–Mar Mon–Sat 2–4pm, Tues–Sat 9am–1pm; Apr–Oct Mon–Sat 3:30–6pm, Tues–Sat 9am–1pm. Bus: 81.*

5 ★★ Santa Sabina. *See p 66, bullet 3.*

6 ★★ Santa Maria in Aracoeli. Raised 120 steps from street level, the "altar of the sky" is far removed from the chaos of traffic below. The church's biggest claim to fame is the feverishly revered *Bambinello*—though it's a copy of the original that was stolen from here in 1994, this wooden statue of the baby Jesus is purported to have the same miraculous disease-healing powers. *Piazza del Campidoglio 4. ☎ 06-6798155. Free admission. Daily 9am–12:30pm, 2:30–5:30pm (Nov–Mar); 9am–12:30pm, 3:30–6:30pm (Apr–Oct). Bus: 30, 40, 62, 64, 70, 87, 95, 170, or 492.*

7 ★★ Santa Maria Sopra Minerva. The only Gothic church in the city is a soothing contrast to the sometimes-gaudy baroque interiors of many Roman churches. Pointy medieval arches—meant to emphasize heaven—create soaring vaults that are decorated with a cool, blue, starry sky motif. To the right of the main altar is Michelangelo's underwhelming *Christ Carrying the Cross* (1514–20); the ridiculously prudish golden loincloth was added later. *Piazza della Minerva 42. ☎ 06-6793926. Daily 7am–7pm. Bus: 30, 40, 62, 64, 70, 87, 116, or 492.*

8 ★★★ St. Peter's Basilica. The facade is the pompous result of too many architects' tinkerings, but the sublime interior of St. Peter's (built 1506–1626) is astounding, visit after visit. The church is, quite simply, huge. Its vastness plays out in the building's every feature, from the 2m-tall (6-ft.) Latin inscription to the 45-story-high dome, designed by Michelangelo to "crown" the Roman skyline. *See p 48, bullet 2.*

Dress Code

St. Peter's has a hard-and-fast dress code that makes no exceptions to the rule: **Men and women in shorts, above-the-knee skirts, or bare shoulders** will not be admitted to the Vatican City basilica. Period.

9 ★★ Santa Maria in Trastevere. Best visited just after Mass has let out, when the basilica is still fragrant with incense. *See p 58, bullet 6.*

Romantic Rome

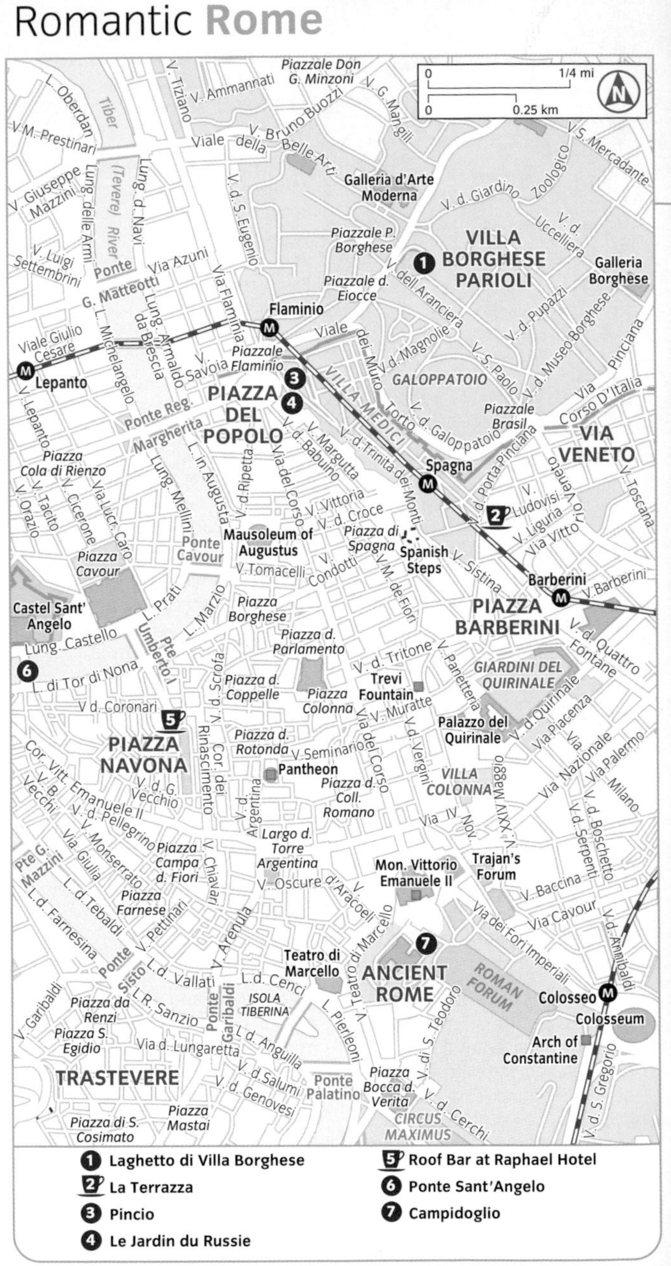

Between gorgeous lookouts, intimate piazzas, panoramic bars, and the general ardor of the natives, Rome is one sprawling romantic setting. Against your best defenses, the itinerary below will have you waxing sappy and gushing *"Ti amo"* from dusk till dawn. **START: Take bus 490 or 495 to Villa Borghese/Viale Fiorello La Guardia, or tram 3 or 19 to Villa Borghese/Viale delle Belle Arti, or bus 52, 53, or 116 to Via Veneto/Piazza San Paolo del Brasile, and walk.**

1 ★ Laghetto di Villa Borghese. Take your lover for a gentle row around Villa Borghese's idyllic lake, surrounded by trees and faux temples. Boats can be rented from 9:30am to sunset daily. *Bus: 116, 490, or 495. Tram: 3 or 19.*

2 ★★ La Terrazza. Toast the sweetness of life at this bar on the top floor of the Hotel Eden, where it almost seems possible to reach out and touch the church domes and bell towers, by now aglow in the golden light of sunset. *Via Ludovisi 49. ☎ 06-478121. Metro: Spagna.*

The roof bar at the Raphael Hotel.

3 ★★★ Pincio. The utterly trystworthy Pincio gardens have secluded corners, umbrella pine bowers, and spectacular stone balustrades overlooking the rooftops of the *centro* and across to St. Peter's. Recommended during the lingering glow after sunset, or in the full dark of night. *Metro: Flaminio.*

4 ★★ Le Jardin du Russie. Have dinner—or another drink—at the Hotel de Russie's fabulous interior garden, whose lush, candlelit terraces are the ultimate in Mediterranean luxury. *Via del Babuino 9. ☎ 06-32888870. Reservations required for dinner. Metro: Flaminio.*

5 ★★ Roof Bar at Raphael Hotel. After dinner, stroll over to this Piazza Navona–area hotel, whose romantic rooftop is perfect for a post-meal *digestivo*. *Largo Febo 2. ☎ 06-682831. Bus: 30, 70, 87, 116, or 492.*

6 ★★★ Ponte Sant'Angelo. The Bernini angels lining this bridge are especially bewitching by night. *Bus: 30, 40, 62, 64, or 571.*

7 ★★★ Campidoglio. The sublime, deserted piazza is a fine place to be at night in romantic company, but the view from the Campidoglio terraces over the Roman Forum, where floodlit marble columns and arches recede majestically into the dark valley below toward the ghosts of the ancients, is quite possibly the most rapturous sight in the world. *Bus: 30, 40, 62, 64, 70, 87, 95, 116, 170, or 492.*

Underground Rome

In a city whose street level has risen about 9m (30 ft.) (due to flooding of the Tiber) since the days of the Caesars, it's only natural that a whole other Rome should exist hidden away beneath the modern buildings. The catacombs have been drawing visitors underground for centuries, but there are also plenty of places (some newly opened) within the city center that permit visitors a fascinating descent into the bowels of history. **START: Take bus 118 or a taxi to the Catacombs of San Callisto or San Sebastiano, on the Via Appia Antica.**

1 ★★ Catacombs of San Callisto and San Sebastiano. Rome's most famous underground tourist attractions, the catacombs, are outside the city walls, as ancient Roman law forbade burials within the sacred *pomerium,* or city boundary. Of Rome's 65 known catacombs—networks of hand-dug tunnels that became massive "dormitories" for the dead—only a handful are open to the public. The catacombs of San Callisto are the largest, with 500,000 burial niches *(loculi).* Nearby, the catacombs of San Sebastiano are more intimate. *See p 95.*

2 ★★ Domus Aurea. The cavernous halls of nutty Nero's former pad feature nymphaeums (ornamental grottoes built as shrines to water nymphs) with fake stalactites, rooms frescoed in the *grotesque* (grotto-esque) style, and the famed octagonal dining room. *45 min. Via della Domus Aurea. ☎ 06-39967700. Reservations required. 6€. Wed–Mon*

9am–7:45pm. Metro: Colosseo. Bus: 60, 75, 85, 87, 95, or 175. Tram: 3.

3 ★★ **San Clemente.** This "lasagna of churches" is the best place in Rome to understand the city's archaeological evolution. Descend 18m (60 ft.) through medieval and paleo-Christian layers to the lowest level, where adherents of the ancient cult of Mithras met and performed grisly rituals in the long, rectangular *mithraeum*. *30 min. Via di San Giovanni in Laterano. 06-70451018. 3€. Mon–Sat 9am–12:30pm, 3–6pm; Sun 10am–12:30pm, 3–6pm. Metro: Colosseo. Bus: 60, 75, 85, 87, 95, or 175. Tram: 3.*

4 ★ **Divinare.** Stop in for a glass of wine or water and a plate of cheese and cured meats at this well-stocked neighborhood *enoteca. Via Ostilia 4 (at Via di San Giovanni in Laterano). 06-7096381.*

5 ★ **Case Romane di Santi Giovanni e Paolo.** Recent excavations beneath this Romanesque church on the Celio Hill revealed 1st-century-A.D. Roman houses with splendid wall frescoes. *45 min. Piazza Santi Giovanni e Paolo 13. 06-70454544. www.caseromane.it. 6€. Reservations required for guided tour, 3.50€. Thurs–Mon 10am–1pm, 3–6pm. Metro: Colosseo. Bus: 60, 75, 85, 87, 95, or 175. Tram: 3.*

6 ★ **Mamertine Prison.** Dank and oppressive, these black-rock chambers are said to be where saints Peter and Paul were imprisoned before their martyrdoms. Claustrophobes, steer clear. *15 min. Clivo Argentario 1. 06-6792902. Donation expected. Daily 9am–noon, 2:30–5pm. Bus: 60, 85, 87, 95, or 175.*

7 ★★★ **Crypt of the Capuchin Monks.** Macabre yet oddly pleasing, this must-see church crypt is decorated with thousands of artfully arranged monks' bones. Each chapel is a bizarre diorama where propped-up monks, still in their desiccated skin and cassocks, strike cautionary poses. *20 min. Via Veneto 27. 06-4871185. Donation expected. Daily 9am–noon, 3–6pm. Metro: Barberini. Bus: 62, 95, 116, 175, or 492.*

8 ★★ **Stadium of Domitian.** At the northern end of Piazza Navona, explore the fascinating remains of the 1st-century-A.D. athletic venue that gave the square its oblong shape. *45 min. Piazza di Tor Sanguigna 16. 06-67103819. 6€. Sat–Sun 10am–1pm. Bus: 70, 87, 116, or 492.*

9 ★★ **Necropolis of St. Peter's.** Positively chill-inducing, these humble, narrow tunnels beneath the immense Vatican basilica make for an unforgettable descent into early Christian history. *See p 49, bullet* **4**.

One of the fascinatingly macabre chapels in the Crypt of the Capuchin Monks.

Vatican City

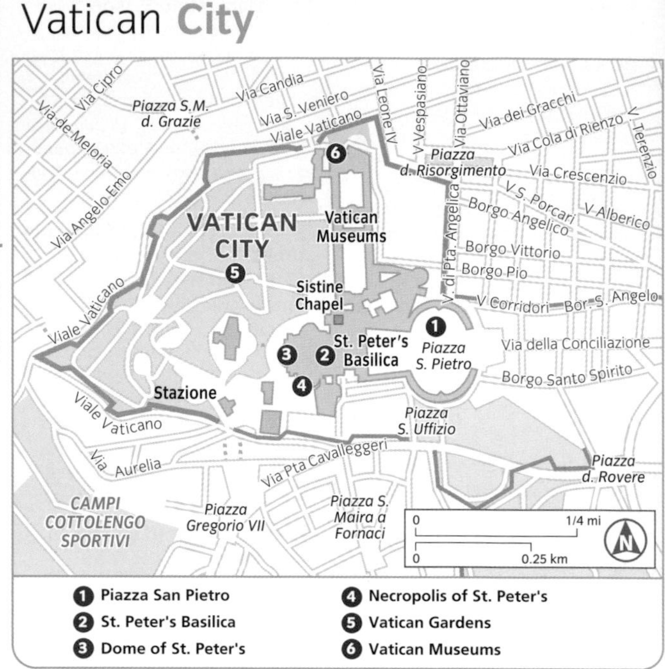

Welcome to Popeland, the sovereign state of visual delights. From the star-studded halls of the Vatican Museums to the gargantuan volume of St. Peter's Basilica, the Holy See is brimming with things for the tourist to see and do. Allow the best part of 4 hours to take it in. **START: Take bus 23, 49, or 492 to Viale Vaticano/Viale dei Bastioni di Michelangelo, or take Metro Line A to Ottaviano-San Pietro or Cipro-Musei Vaticani, and walk.**

1 ★★★ Piazza San Pietro.

Designed in the 1630s by Bernini to mimic a human embrace, this sweeping colonnade is the gateway to the largest church in the world. In the center stands an Egyptian obelisk that once marked the center of Nero's Circus, where St. Peter was martyred in A.D. 64. Along the south wall of the square are official Vatican souvenir and bookshops and a branch of the Vatican post office. ⏲ *30 min. Free admission.*

2 ★★★ St. Peter's Basilica.

Everything in St. Peter's is made of marble, bronze, or gold, and what appear to be altar paintings are actually mosaics with minuscule *tesserae*. The outstanding artworks in the basilica include Michelangelo's intensely moving *Pietà* (1499) and Bernini's spiral-legged bronze baldacchino (1633). ⏲ *45 min. Free admission. Daily 7am–7pm; can vary with papal appearances and religious holidays.*

St. Peter's Square and basilica at night.

3 ★ **Dome of St. Peter's.** Recommended for those who can't visit a European city without climbing a dome—its perspective on the Vatican is impressive, but its general city view is overrated. A coffee bar was opened at the midway point in late 2004. *45 min. Queue is shortest in early am or late afternoon. Piazza San Pietro. 5€ (lift, then stairs); 4€ (all stairs). Daily 9am–5pm.*

4 ★★★ **Necropolis of St. Peter's.** A haunting descent beneath the basilica takes you into the ancient level where bones believed to be St. Peter's were found in the 1940s. See also p 47. *45 min. Ufficio Scavi. ☎ 06-69885318. Fax 06-69885518. uffscavi@fabricsp.va. 9€. Tours Mon–Sat 9am–5pm. Book at least 1 month in advance.*

5 ★★ **Vatican Gardens.** An oasis of manicured lawns, quaint fountains, and the occasional nun-driven Vespa exists behind the imposing Vatican fortification walls. *1 hr. ☎ 06-69884466. Fax 06-69885100. 9€. Tours Tues, Thurs–Sat 10am only. Book at least 1 week in advance.*

6 ★★★ **Vatican Museums.** The richest museum in the world is enthralling in its quantity and quality, aggravating in its utter lack of explanatory signage. As a rule, the important stuff is where the crowds are, but try to resist the riptide of tour groups that washes headlong toward the Sistine Chapel, skipping a ton of fabulous art along the way. The museum guidebook—or, better yet, the CD-ROM audioguide—can make your meander through these masterpiece-packed halls vastly more meaningful. (The Museums' website, **http://mv.vatican.va**, is also an excellent source of background information.)

The double-helix spiral staircase in the Vatican Museums.

Start your tour of the Museums in the ★★ **Pinacoteca** (picture gallery), home to Raphael's *Transfiguration* (1520; his last painting), in Room 8; Leonardo's enigmatic *St. Jerome* (1482), in Room 9; and Caravaggio's eerie, green-fleshed *Deposition* (1604), in Room 12. In the Octagonal Courtyard (part of the Pio-Clementine museums of classical statuary), the exquisite marble ★★ **Apollo Belvedere** (a 2nd-c.-A.D. copy of a 5th-c. B.C. original) is a paragon of classical composure. In radical stylistic contrast, the stunning 1st-century-A.D. ★★★ **Laocoon** (Lay-*ah*-koh-on) captures the very height of human vulnerability. The sculpture depicts the fate of a Trojan priest who was suspicious of the Trojan horse and asked his people to "beware of Greeks bearing gifts." The Greek-favoring gods, angered, sentenced him to death by sea serpents. The expressive, though fragmentary, ★ **Belvedere Torso** inspired Michelangelo's rendering of Christ in the *Last Judgment,* in the Sistine Chapel. Upstairs, the ★ **Etruscan Museum** has knockout gold breastplates from a 2,500-year-old tomb. From here, the Vatican Museums morph into fresco heaven.

The Laocoon sculpture in the Vatican Museums is from the 1st century A.D.

The brightly colored frescoes in the ★ **Gallery of the Maps** are a wonderfully detailed cartographical record of 16th-century Italy. Pink-tinged frescoes by Giulio Romano in the ★ **Hall of Constantine** (1522–25) are a tribute to Christianity toppling paganism. In the famed ★★★ **Raphael Rooms** (1506–17), exquisite frescoes like *School of Athens* and *Liberation of St. Peter* display the harmony of color and balance of composition that were the hallmark of High Renaissance classicism and Raphael's mastery.

After the Raphael Rooms, a wrong turn and confusing signs can take you downstairs to the Vatican's dreadful modern art collection; stay to the left for the direct route to the ★★★ **Sistine Chapel,** where Michelangelo's spectacular frescoes very much live up to the hype, and after a restoration in the 1980s and '90s, they're more eye-popping than ever. On the ceiling (1508–12), the stories of creation, Adam and Eve, and Noah are told in nine frames, surrounded by faux architectural elements and medallions. On the altar wall, the swirling *Last Judgment* (1535–41) is much more fire-and-brimstone, reflecting the anger and disappointment of Michelangelo's later years. Exit the museums via the right rear door of the Sistine Chapel to go straight to St. Peter's. Exit via the left door to return any rented audioguides. 🕘 *2 hr. Go after 12:30pm in high season. Viale Vaticano.* ☎ *06-69883333. http://mv.vatican.va. 12€ adults/8€ students. Audioguide 5.50€. Mar–Oct Mon–Fri 8:45am–3:20pm (exit 4:45pm), Sat 8:45am–12:20pm (exit 1:45pm); Nov–Feb Mon–Sat 8:45am–12:20pm (exit by 1:45pm). Closed Catholic holidays—check website for most up-to-date schedule.*

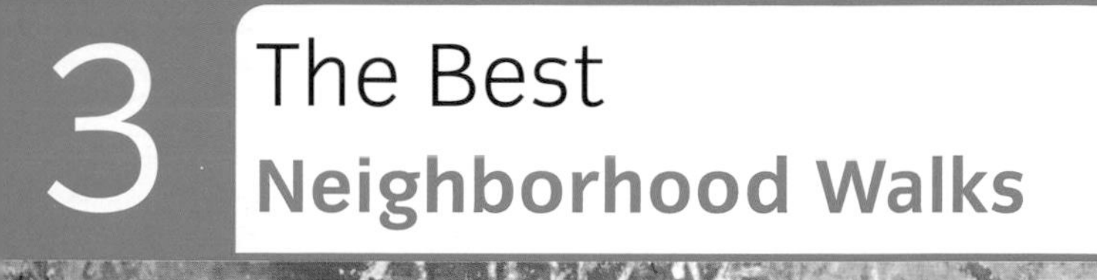

3 The Best Neighborhood Walks

Piazza Navona & the Pantheon

1. Castel Sant'Angelo
2. Ponte Sant'Angelo
3. Via dei Coronari
4. Via della Pace area
5. Bar della Pace
6. Piazza Navona
7. Sant'Agnese in Agone
8. Sant'Agostino
9. San Luigi dei Francesi
10. Sant'Ivo alla Sapienza
11. Pantheon
12. Piazza della Minerva
13. Sant'Ignazio
14. Piazza di Pietra
15. Gran Caffè la Caffettiera
16. Piazza di Montecitorio
17. Galleria Doria Pamphilj
18. Column of Marcus Aurelius

Prepare to switch sightseeing gears quickly in the most central part of the old city—quiet, labyrinth-like alleys abruptly give way to imposing monuments and knockout postcard panoramas, and a slew of nonchalant-looking churches stash away some of the city's most celebrated works of art. **START: Take bus 40, 62, or 74 to Castel Sant'Angelo/Piazza Pia.**

1 ★★★ Castel Sant'Angelo. Rome's hamburger of history started out as Hadrian's mausoleum in the 2nd century A.D. and was converted in the Middle Ages into a fortress for the popes, who then gave themselves apartments here in the Renaissance. Its final incarnation, as a prison, lasted through the end of the 19th century, long enough to inspire Puccini's *Tosca*. Be sure to climb all the way up to the highest terrace—looking straight down over the Tiber is as soaring and dramatic as an operatic finale. ⌚ *1 hr. Lungotevere Castello 50.* ☎ *06-6819111. 5€. Tues–Sun 9am–7pm.*

2 ★★ Ponte Sant'Angelo. *See p 33, bullet 2.*

3 ★ Via dei Coronari. This charming little street was formerly a pilgrim route to the Vatican; today, it's lined with antiquarians' shops and intersected by dozens of quaint alleys, with hidden trattorias and artists' studios.

4 ★ Via della Pace area. Via della Pace bisects the web of streets, known as the "triangle of fun," between Via dei Coronari and Via del Governo Vecchio. By day, motorcycle mechanics rub shoulders with Roman nobility; by night, Roman hipsters flock to the area's countless eateries and *boîtes.*

5 ★ Bar della Pace. The chic and the restless flutter in and out of this eternally fashionable cafe from morning to night, but we recommend you stay a while—it's a prime spot for reading, postcard-writing, and ogling the lovely Santa Maria della Pace, just down the street. *Via della Pace 3–7.* ☎ *06-6861216.*

A close-up view of Ponte Sant'Angelo with the Castel Sant'Angelo in the background.

Travelers taking a break in the Piazza Navona.

❻ ★★★ **Piazza Navona.** Nine meters (30 ft.) below the baroque fountains and churches located here is the site where the ancient *agones* (athletic competitions) were held in the Stadium of Domitian (p 47, bullet ❽). In the medieval period, the Romans called this space *platea in agona* ("place of competition"), which later evolved into the modern appellation, Piazza Navona. ***See p 34, bullet*** ❸.

❼ ★ **Sant'Agnese in Agone.** Borromini's broad, flamboyant facade belies this church's rather small interior. Through a door marked SACRA TESTA to the left of the altar, there's a reliquary holding the chimpanzee-sized skull of St. Agnes, martyred here in the 4th century A.D. ◷ ***15 min. Piazza Navona. No phone. Free admission. Tues–Sun 9am–noon, 4–7pm.***

❽ ★ **Sant'Agostino.** On the left wall, Caravaggio's *Madonna dei Pellegrini* (1604) shocked contemporaries with its frank depiction of dirty-footed pilgrims. On a pillar nearby, Raphael's meaty *Isaiah* (1512) recalls the frescoes of the Sistine Chapel. ◷ ***20 min. Piazza Sant'Agostino.*** ☎ ***06-68801962. Free admission. Daily 8am–noon, 4–7:30pm.***

❾ ★★ **San Luigi dei Francesi.** Revolutionary for their high-keyed emotions and contrived play of light, Caravaggio's three *Life of St. Matthew* altarpieces (1603), displayed here, are some of his greatest masterpieces. ◷ ***20 min. Piazza San Luigi dei Francesi.*** ☎ ***06-688271. Free admission. Daily 8:30am–12:30pm; Mon–Wed, Fri–Sun 3:30–7pm.***

❿ ★★ **Sant'Ivo alla Sapienza.** ***See p 34, bullet*** ❹.

⓫ ★★★ **Pantheon.** Hands-down the most masterful architectural feat of ancient Rome, the Pantheon is almost perfectly preserved. The porch consists of 16 monolithic Egyptian granite columns, weighing 82 tons each. Inside, the 44m-wide (143-ft.) dome—poured in concrete in the 120s A.D. and never structurally modified—is pierced by a 9m-wide (30-ft.) oculus, open to the

Sunlight streams from the oculus in the dome of the Pantheon.

sky. While most ancient buildings lost their marbles to the popes, the Pantheon's brick walls retain their rich revetment of yellow marble and purple porphyry. The tombs of Raphael and the Savoia monarchs are also here. ⌚ ***30 min. Best in early morning or late afternoon, and in the rain.*** *Piazza della Rotonda. ☎ 06-68300230. Free admission. Daily 9am–6pm, until 7:30pm in summer.*

⑫ ★★ Piazza della Minerva. In front of the Gothic church Santa Maria Sopra Minerva (p 43, bullet ⑦), an Egyptian obelisk—one of 13 in Rome—is supported on the back of a plucky elephant, sculpted by Bernini. The neighborhood is also home to most of Rome's religious outfitters, with their fabulous window displays of gem-encrusted chalices and the latest in liturgical couture.

⑬ ★ Sant'Ignazio. The focal point of this tight and tidy baroque square is the Jesuit Church of St. Ignatius, famous for its illusionistic "dome," frescoed on the church's flat roof by Andrea Pozzo in 1626. ⌚ *15 min. Piazza di Sant'Ignazio. ☎ 06-6794406. Free admission. Daily 7:30am–12:15pm, 4–7pm.*

⑭ ★★ Piazza di Pietra. The impressive row of columns here were the north wall of the 2nd-century-A.D. Temple of Hadrian, a plastic model of which can be seen in a showcase window across the square.

⑮ ★ Gran Caffè La Caffettiera. This coffee and snack bar (and outré Internet hot spot) is especially cozy in winter. *Piazza di Pietra 65. ☎ 06-6798147.*

⑯ ★ Piazza di Montecitorio. On this sloping square in front of the Bernini-designed lower house of Parliament, dapper *carabinieri* (army police) survey the scene for terrorists—and eligible foreign women. The 2,600-year-old obelisk, moved here in 1751, was the shadow-casting *gnomon* of Augustus's sundial (9 B.C.), an approximation of which is inlaid in bronze over the square.

The Column of Marcus Aurelius rises from Piazza Colonna.

⑰ ★★ Galleria Doria Pamphilj. This collection, whose audioguide is read (in English) by a living Pamphilj prince, has an enviable array of 16th- and 17th-century canvases, as well as Velázquez's famously soul-exposing portrait of Pope Innocent X Pamphilj. *Piazza del Collegio Romano 2. ☎ 06-6797323. www.doriapamphilj.it. 7.30€. Fri–Wed 10am–5pm.*

⑱ ★ Column of Marcus Aurelius. Dismissed by some art historians as a cheap imitation of Trajan's Column (p 24, bullet ⑤), this 30m-high (100-ft.) marble shaft (180–96 A.D.) depicts Marcus Aurelius's military exploits in Germany. *Piazza Colonna.*

Campo de' Fiori

Unpretentious, workaday, and totally picturesque, the area around Campo de' Fiori is the best place in the *centro storico* to see Roman daily life at its most authentic. Locals far outnumber tourists, and you can't walk a few steps without coming across a coffee bar, wine shop, or neighborhood trattoria. START: **Take bus 30, 40, 62, 64, 70, 87, 116, 492, 571, or 628 to Corso Vittorio Emanuele, or tram 8 to Largo Argentina.**

1 ★★★ Campo de' Fiori. Bustling with energy night and day, and welcoming all, Campo de' Fiori is the beating heart of the *centro storico*. In the morning, the stalls of the city's most famous fruit and vegetable market sell produce to top chefs and local housewives. At night, all and sundry descend on the piazza's cafes and wine bars for the evening *aperitivo*.

2 ★★ Craftsmen's Streets. Many of the streets in the *centro storico* are named for the crafts practiced by artisans there throughout the ages; the best examples of these lie north of the Campo. On Via dei Cappellari, medieval hatmakers have been replaced by furniture workshops, where old men (and some young) make table legs on lathes powered by foot pedals. Off Via del Pellegrino, tiny Arco degli Acetari (Vinegar-Makers' Arch) is the ramshackle, ochre-walled corner featured on so many Roman postcards.

3 ★★ Piazza Farnese. Serene Piazza Farnese enjoys the same Renaissance harmony as its

A vendor selling produce in the Campo de' Fiori.

namesake architectural feature, the dignified and imposing 16th-century Palazzo Farnese. The square and its immediate vicinity have recently become some of the most sought-after real estate in the city, with fabulous flats that accommodate visiting film stars on location in Rome.

4 ★★ Via Giulia. The dead-straight path of Via Giulia—for many, the most beautiful street in Rome—was cleared by Pope Julius II in the 1500s to give pilgrims a fail-safe passage to the Vatican. The picturesque ivy-covered arch that spans the street was to be part of a private bridge—never completed—for the Farnese family, connecting Palazzo Farnese with the Villa Farnesina, across the river in Trastevere.

5 ★ Galleria Spada. Private galleries with works by Titian and other Renaissance masters are almost a dime a dozen in Rome; what makes the Spada especially worth a visit is the uncannily deceptive Borromini Corridor, which is only 9m (30 ft.) long but appears to be three times that. *30 min. Piazza Capo di Ferro 3. ☎ 06-6874896. 5€. Tues–Sun 9am–7pm. Bus: 23, 30, 40, 62, 64, 70, 87, 116, 280, or 492. Tram: 8.*

6 ★ Via dei Giubbonari. Shopaholics rejoice—this narrow, cobblestone thoroughfare is bursting with up-and-coming fashion boutiques, gourmet food stores, and street vendors.

7 Via di Grotta Pinta. The inward curve of this hidden road, named for the underlying "painted grotto" of the 55 B.C. Theater of Pompey, corresponds with the *cavea* (seating area) of the ancient theater.

8 ★ Sant'Andrea della Valle. The second highest dome in Rome—after St. Peter's—rests atop this excellent 16th-century basilica, where Puccini set the first act of *Tosca. 15 min. Corso Vittorio Emanuele II 6. ☎ 06-6861339. Free admission. Daily 8am–noon, 4:30–7:30pm.*

9 ★ Area Sacra di Largo Argentina. During the excavation fever of the 1930s, Mussolini evicted hundreds of Romans who were living here and ordered archaeologists to dig. What you see here today, 9m (30 ft.) below street level, are four Republican temple foundations and a much-hyped though visually underwhelming fragment of the Senate house (Curia Pompei) where Julius Caesar was stabbed on the Ides of March, 44 B.C. *Ruins open by appointment only. ☎ 06-67103819. Fax 06-6790795.*

Trastevere

Separated from the rest of the old city by the river, picturesque Trastevere has strived to maintain its own identity since ancient times, when it was dubbed *Trans Tiberim* ("across the Tiber"). Although expatriates have relocated here in droves, the district still has its insular character and village-y appeal. **START: Take bus 23, 271, 280, 780, H, or tram 8 to Piazza G.G. Belli (Lungotevere degli Anguillara/Viale Trastevere).**

---

1 ★ Vicolo dell'Atleta. The "alley of the athlete"—as tiny as streets get in Rome—has a facade of a 13th-century synagogue, now the restaurant Spirito di Vino (p 113).

2 ★★ Santa Cecilia. *See p 15, bullet 1.*

3 ★ San Francesco a Ripa. Home to Bernini's overtly sexual *Beata Ludovica Albertoni* (1674). *15 min. Piazza San Francesco d'Assisi 88. ☎ 06-5819020. Free admission. Daily 7:30am–noon, 4–7pm.*

4 ★★ Frontoni. Fuel up on pizza bread sandwiches, stuffed with deli meats, cheeses, or roasted vegetables. *Viale Trastevere 52. ☎ 06-5812436.*

5 Via dei Fienaroli. Dense ivy blankets the walls of this pretty street, hiding numerous interesting bookshops and cafes.

6 ★★ Piazza and Basilica Santa Maria in Trastevere. The hub of daily life in Trastevere is

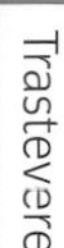

Wining, dining, and being serenaded in a Trastevere cafe.

graced by the magnificent church of Santa Maria in Trastevere, with 22 recycled Roman columns lining the nave and sparkling mosaics adorning the apse. Legend has it the church was built over the spot where a fountain of oil miraculously bubbled up in 38 B.C., apparently heralding the coming of Christ. The piazza's handsome fountain, by Carlo Fontana, is somewhat blighted by omnipresent drunks and their flea-bitten dogs. *See p 39, bullet 8, and p 43, bullet 9.*

7 ★ Via della Scala to Via del Moro. This warren of gnarled streets (Vicolo del Cedro, Vicolo del Bologna, Piazza de' Renzi) is the most charming part of old Trastevere, where clotheslines are strung over narrow alleys, parking jobs reach new heights of ingenuity, and neighbors chat animatedly.

8 ★★ Panificio la Renella. Purveyor of *pane* to all restaurants and households in the vicinity, this bread bakery also has excellent pizza by the slice, bar stools to sit on, and a community message board. ***Via del Moro 15–16. ☎ 06-5817265.***

9 Piazza Trilussa. This is the point of egress for all the tiny streets in the area, and where pedestrian Ponte Sisto leads across the Tiber toward Campo de' Fiori.

10 ★ Caffè Settimiano. In the shadow of the old Septimian Gate (part of the 3rd-C.-A.D. Aurelian Walls), this is a wonderful place to rest your feet, read the paper, and watch *trasteverini* go by. ***Via di Porta Settimiana. ☎ 06-5810468.***

11 ★★★ Gianicolo. The hike to the top of Janiculum Hill—the highest point in central Rome—is steep, but well worth the spectacular views, tree-lined promenades, and clear air. Don't miss the fabulously inviting 17th-century Fontanone dell'Acqua Paola. ***30 min. Take Via Garibaldi to Via di Porta San Pancrazio and climb the steps to the Passeggiata del Gianicolo.***

12 ★ Tempietto and San Pietro in Montorio. In the courtyard of this church is Donato Bramante's round, classically inspired Tempietto (1508), one of Rome's greatest, and most undervisited, architectural masterpieces. ***15 min. Piazza San Pietro in Montorio 2. ☎ 06-5813940. Free admission. Tempietto daily 10am–noon, 2–4pm.***

The Best Neighborhood Walks

Tridente

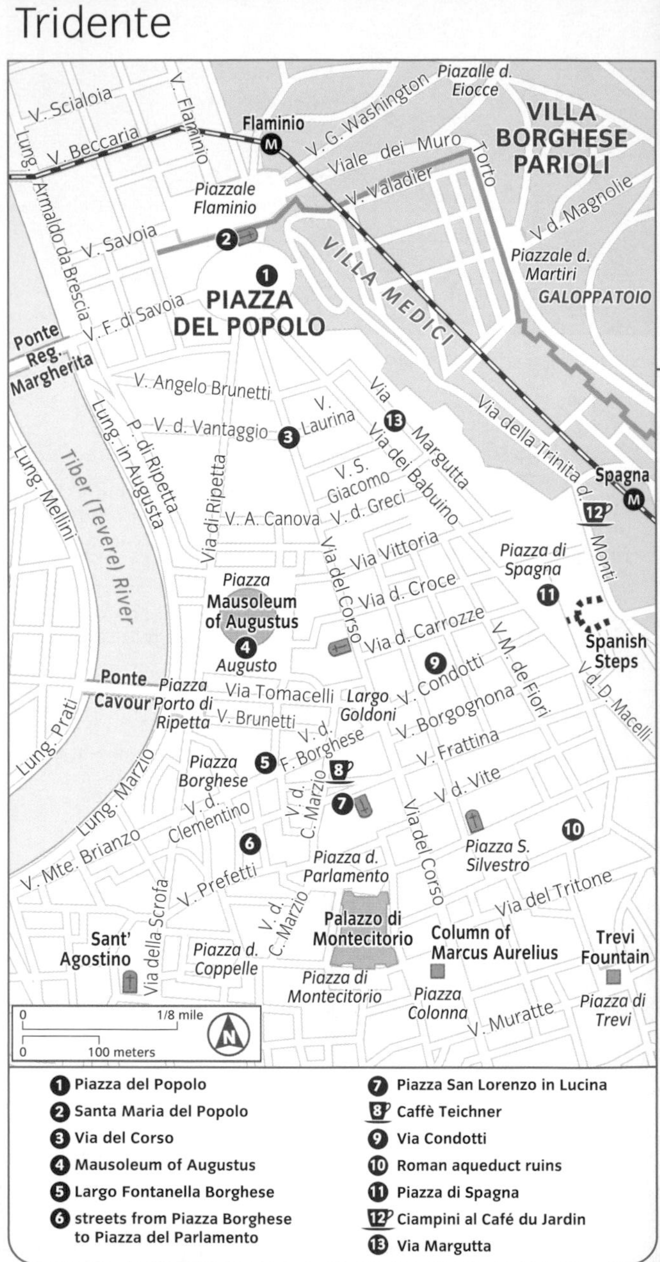
VILLA BORGHESE PARIOLI
PIAZZA DEL POPOLO
VILLA MEDICI
GALOPPATOIO
Flaminio
Spagna
Piazzale Flaminio
Piazzalle d. Eiocce
Piazzale d. Martiri
Piazza Mausoleum of Augustus
Augusto
Piazza Porto di Ripetta
Piazza Borghese
Largo Goldoni
Piazza di Spagna
Spanish Steps
Piazza d. Parlamento
Piazza S. Silvestro
Palazzo di Montecitorio
Piazza di Montecitorio
Column of Marcus Aurelius
Piazza Colonna
Trevi Fountain
Piazza di Trevi
Sant' Agostino
Piazza d. Coppelle
Tiber (Tevere) River
Ponte Reg. Margherita
Ponte Cavour
V. Scialoia
V. Beccaria
V. Flaminio
Lung. Armaldo da Brescia
V. Savoia
V. F. di Savoia
V. G. Washington
Viale dei Muro Torto
V. Valadier
V. d. Magnolie
V. Angelo Brunetti
V. d. Vantaggio
V. Laurina
Via Margutta
Via dei Babuino
Via della Trinita d. Monti
V. S. Giacomo
V. d. Greci
V. A. Canova
Via di Ripetta
Lung. in Augusta
P. di Ripetta
Lung. Mellini
Via Vittoria
Via d. Croce
Via d. Carrozze
Via del Corso
V. M. de Fiori
V. d. D. Macelli
Via Tomacelli
V. Brunetti
V. Condotti
V. Borgognona
V. Frattina
V. d. F. Borghese
V. d. Vite
V. d. C. Marzio
V. d. Clementino
Lung. Prati
Lung. Marzio
V. Mte. Brianzo
V. Prefetti
Via della Scrofa
Via del Tritone
V. Muratte
0 1/8 mile
0 100 meters
N
1 Piazza del Popolo
2 Santa Maria del Popolo
3 Via del Corso
4 Mausoleum of Augustus
5 Largo Fontanella Borghese
6 streets from Piazza Borghese to Piazza del Parlamento
7 Piazza San Lorenzo in Lucina
8 Caffè Teichner
9 Via Condotti
10 Roman aqueduct ruins
11 Piazza di Spagna
12 Ciampini al Café du Jardin
13 Via Margutta

Named for the three-pronged splay of streets (Via Ripetta, Via del Corso, and Via del Babuino) south of Piazza del Popolo, the Tridente is the toniest part of town, where wealthy neighborhood co-ops keep their cobblestone streets swept clean and lined with potted plants. The area east of Via del Corso is a shopper's paradise; to the west, it's darker and quieter, with dog-legging alleys that feel like time warps to the 16th century. Relieved on both sides by open spaces (the Tiber and the Villa Borghese), the air here is jaunty and glamorous. Note that "Tridente" is a term largely made up for the convenience of guidebook writers; locals usually refer to this neighborhood by its principal streets or squares (Piazza di Spagna and Piazza del Popolo). **START: Take Metro Line A to Flaminio, or take bus 62, 85, 95, 116, 175, or 492 to Largo Chigi, and walk.**

1 ★★★ Piazza del Popolo. In the tradition of the grandest Roman piazzas, the vertex of the Tridente is vast, sun-drenched, and obelisked. It was given its present oval shape by neoclassical architect Giuseppe Valadier in 1818 and made traffic-free in 1998. The piazza is bounded to the east by the glorious green terraces of the Pincio gardens, one of the most romantic spots in the city. *See p 38, bullet 4.*

2 ★★ Santa Maria del Popolo. In 1099, a church was built on this spot to "expel the demons"—tradition holds that the detested emperor Nero was secretly buried here by his mistress, Poppaea Sabina, in 68 A.D. The low-ceilinged interior is at first unremarkable, but look closely and you'll find works by Bramante, Pinturicchio, Raphael, and Bernini, as well as two masterpieces by Caravaggio—the tipsy *Martyrdom of St. Peter* (1600) and *Conversion of St. Paul* (1601) with its prominent horse's butt. *30 min. Piazza del Popolo 12. ☎ 06-3610836. Mon–Sat 7am–noon, 4–7pm; Sun 8am–1pm, 4:30–7:30pm.*

3 Via del Corso. Named for the barbaric riderless horse races *(corse)* that took place here during *Carnevale,* Via del Corso is the main north-south thoroughfare in the *centro storico* and packed with

A rainbow rises over the rooftops of Piazza del Popolo.

The Valentino shop on stylish Via Condotti.

mid-range boutiques. The pedestrianized northern half is the favorite stomping ground of obnoxious Roman teens and best avoided if you're looking for a pleasant place to stroll.

4 ★★ Mausoleum of Augustus. This crumbling though still massive brick cylinder, the 28 B.C. tomb of the first Roman emperor, was once clad with marble and planted with elegant rings of cypress trees. Mussolini had designs on making the mausoleum his own family tomb, so he built the surrounding iceberglike travertine buildings to give the area an appropriately harsh Fascist aesthetic. In fact, the Duce had plans to enshrine all the ruins of Rome with such austere honorific architecture—had he remained in power longer, similarly stark facades would appear all over the *centro* today. *15 min. Piazza Augusto Imperatore. Ruins open by appointment only. ☎ 06-67103819. Fax 06-6790795.*

5 Largo della Fontanella Borghese. Home to the Mercato delle Stampe antique books market. *See p 86.*

6 ★ Streets from Piazza Borghese to Piazza del Parlamento. These dark and narrow alleys seem to breathe ancient intrigue. Indeed, Vicolo del Divino Amore is where the short-tempered painter Caravaggio threw rocks at his landlord's window after a rent dispute. Nearby, Palazzo Firenze is home to the Società Dante Alighieri, the city's most venerable school of Italian for foreigners *(www.dantealighieri-roma.it).*

7 ★ Piazza San Lorenzo in Lucina. This cafe-equipped refuge for weary shoppers is home of the eponymous church, where the very grill on which St. Lawrence was barbecued is kept in a side chapel. *15 min. Church open daily 9am–noon, 5–7:30pm.*

8 Caffè Teichner. Coffee, beer, and light sandwiches are served. Caffè Ciampini, adjacent, is its virtual twin. *Piazza San Lorenzo in Lucina 17. ☎ 06-6790612.*

9 Via Condotti. Aided by its deputies, Via Borgognona, Via Bocca di Leone, Via Mario de' Fiori, and Via Belsiana, high-end retail artery Via Condotti spearheads an effort to bring financial ruin on all who dare to carry a credit card near the Spanish Steps.

10 ★ Roman aqueduct ruins. Hidden behind an iron gate are some arches of the 13 B.C. Aqua Virgo, the only aqueduct never severed by the Goths, and restored in the 17th century. Due to the rise in ground level since antiquity, the water pressure isn't great, but the cool and sweet "virgin water" still feeds the drinking spigots at the Trevi Fountain (p 34, bullet 5) and the *Barcaccia* fountain, at the base of the Spanish Steps (bullet 11 below). *Via del Bufalo.*

This Roman aqueduct, on the outside of town, is typical of the aqueduct ruins found in and around Rome.

⓫ ★★★ **Piazza di Spagna.** De rigueur on any tourist's itinerary, but prepare to contend with perpetual mobs of gelato-wielding tourists and Casanovas trawling the square for naïve foreign females. Luckily, neither taints the overall beauty of the glamorously upsweeping Spanish Steps (which were actually designed and funded by the French). At the base of the 18th-century stairs, the sunken *Barcaccia* ("bad boat") fountain is by Pietro Bernini (Gian Lorenzo's father) and fed by the ancient Aqua Virgo (bullet ❿ above). Crowning the top of the stairs is the graceful Trinità dei Monti Church. ◷ *20 min. Piazza di Spagna. Best in early am or late evening.*

12 ★ **Ciampini al Café du Jardin.** An open-air, panoramic cafe at the top of the Spanish Steps? You'd think it would have "tourist trap" written all over it, but somehow, Ciampini manages to preserve its dignity—and romance, especially at sunset. *Viale Trinità dei Monti.* ☎ *06-6785678.*

⓭ ★★ **Via Margutta.** This impossibly gorgeous lane, nestled between the Pincio and Via del Babuino and lined with artists' ateliers, has sparked many a visitor's fantasy about dropping everything and moving to Rome.

The Margutta Art Fair, on Via Margutta.

Aventine Hill

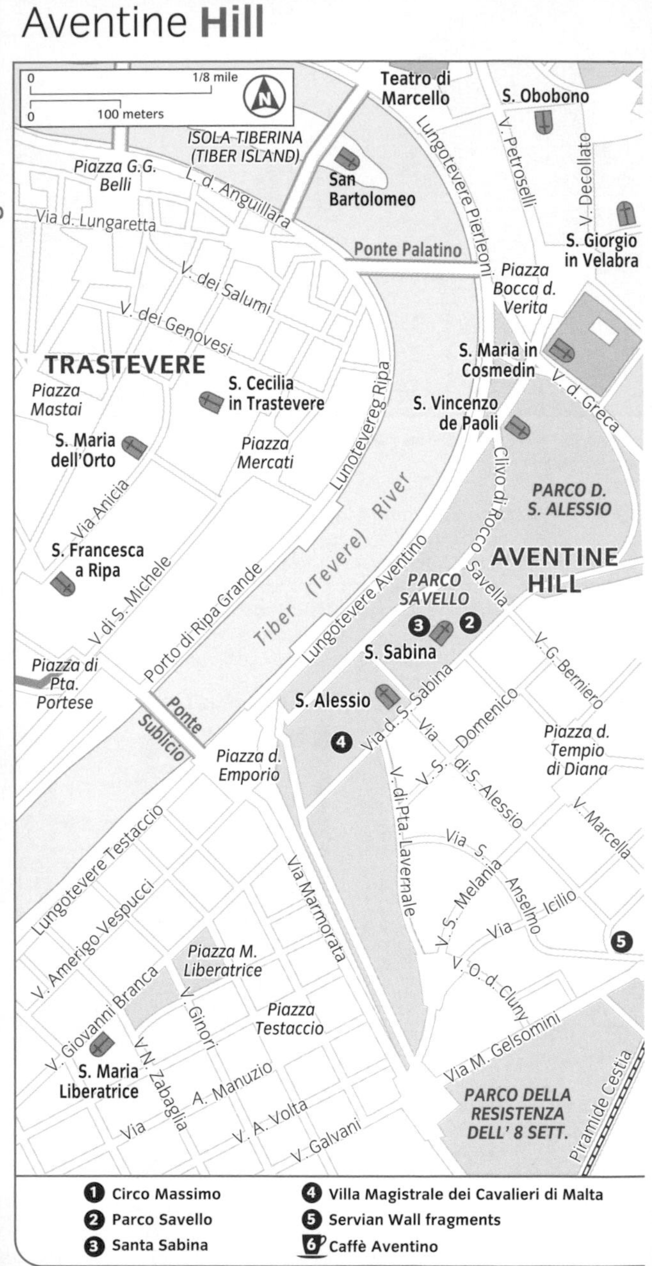

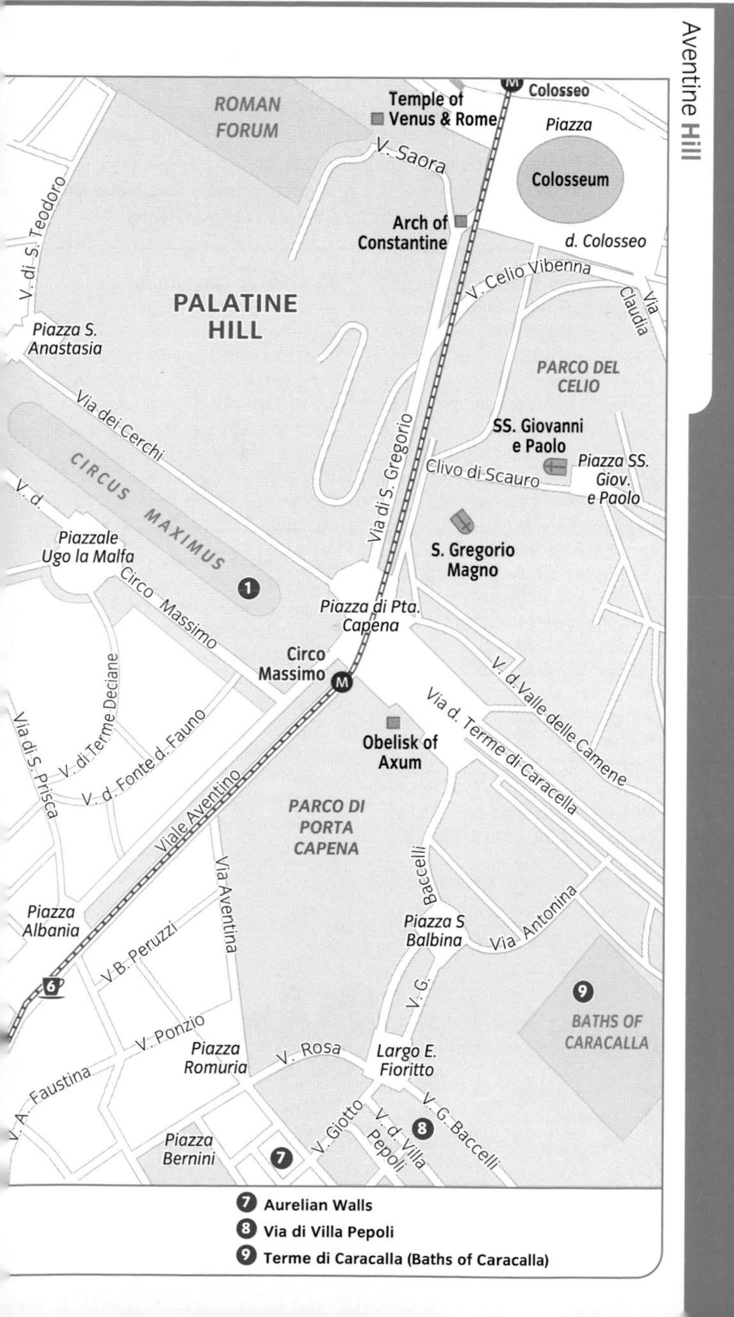

7 Aurelian Walls
8 Via di Villa Pepoli
9 Terme di Caracalla (Baths of Caracalla)

Rising steeply to the east of the Tiber, the Aventine is the most exclusive of Rome's seven hills—today as in antiquity. The leafy heights of Aventine Hill offer a convenient escape from the bustle of the *centro,* with quiet churches, elegant villas, and spectacular vistas. The rustic stretch of archaeological park running along the Aventine's low, eastern edge is home to such dramatic ancient monuments as the Circus Maximus and the Baths of Caracalla. **START: Take Metro Line B, bus 30, 75, 95, 170, 175, or 628, or tram 3 to Circo Massimo.**

1 ★★ Circo Massimo. Nothing remains of ancient Rome's chariot-racing venue but its incredibly vast, 640×229m (700×250 yard) footprint. Where the track used to be, the sun-baked dirt is strewn with broken bottles, and the grassy central ridge, where obelisks and other war trophies stood, is now a favorite haunt of hash-smoking slackers and their dogs. Nevertheless, it's still possible to imagine the thunder of the *quadrigae* (four-horse rigs), fighting for their lives and victory through seven harrowing laps, to the roaring excitement of 300,000 Romans in the stands. From the umbrella pines of Via del Circo Massimo, the awesome panorama across the valley to the red-brick ruins of Palatine Hill cannot help but stir up nostalgia for Roman days of glory. ◷ ***30 min. Metro Circo Massimo. Bus: 30, 60, 75, 95, 118, 170, or 175. Tram: 3.***

2 ★ Parco Savello. Neighborhood families and tourists-in-the-know frequent this garden of orange trees and oleanders. The stone parapets that hem in the western boundary of the park offer a great place to catch some sun, as well as spectacular views over the *centro storico* and Trastevere. ◷ ***30 min. Via di Santa Sabina. Daily dawn–dusk. Bus: 30, 60, 75, 95, 118, 170, or 175. Tram: 3.***

3 ★ Santa Sabina. One of the first Christian churches to be built in Rome, somber Santa Sabina dates back to the 5th century A.D. Before *basilica* came to be synonymous with "church," the word denoted a rectangular hall that ancient Romans used for legal and other official meetings. The architecture of Santa Sabina—an arcaded main nave flanked by two side aisles, terminating in a semi-domed apse

The ruins of the Circus Maximus (Circo Massimo).

An 1870 black-and-white photograph of the ancient Aurelian walls during the oxcart days.

with a triumphal arch; clerestory windows bathing the space with diffused sunlight—is a direct interpretation of the ancient Roman basilical plan and gives visitors an excellent sense of what many of the ruined structures in the Forum used to look and feel like. *20 min. Piazza Pietro d'Illiria 1. Daily 6:30am–12:45pm, 3:30–7pm. Bus: 30, 60, 75, 95, 118, 170, or 175. Tram: 3.*

4 ★ Villa Magistrale dei Cavalieri di Malta. Famous for its delightful keyhole, through which you can view St. Peter's Basilica across town, this property belongs to the Sovereign Order of the Knights of Malta. *15 min. Piazza dei Cavalieri di Malta.*

5 Servian Wall Fragments. On Via di Sant'Anselmo and in Piazza Albania, the brown tufa blocks of Rome's first fortification circuit—the 4th-century-B.C. Servian Walls—survive in fragments, cheek-by-jowl with modern condominiums.

6 Caffè Aventino. This is your basic Roman bar, with snacks, drinks, and a sophisticated clientele of well-heeled locals and employees of the U.N. Food and Agriculture Organization, just down the street. *Piazza Albania 1–2. Metro: Circo Massimo.*

7 ★ Aurelian Walls. Long stretches of the brick-faced Aurelian Walls are preserved along Viale Giotto and Via dei Guerrieri. Built in the 270s (and completed in 5 years) to fend off barbarian creep, the fortifications—Rome's second, after the 5th-century-B.C. Servian walls—circumscribed the city with a total length of 18km (11 miles) and 18 gates, through which all the roads that led to Rome actually entered Rome. The walls are 8m (26 ft.) tall and 4m (13 ft.) thick. Despite their builders' best-laid plans, the fortifications yielded to the invasion of Alaric the Goth in 410 A.D. Other formidable sections of the Aurelian Walls survive along Viale del Muro Torto ("avenue of the crooked wall"), on the southern edge of the Villa Borghese.

8 Via di Villa Pepoli. This exclusive, shady lane is home to some of the most sought-after villas in the city.

9 ★★ Baths of Caracalla. The shady ruins of this enormous 3rd-century bathing complex—a sort of country club for the ancients—are fun to explore and delightfully crowd-free. The main bathing block, where Romans took the waters of the *caldarium* (hot bath), *tepidarium,* and *frigidarium,* has great black-and-white mosaics and brick niches where marble statues used to stand. When you're finished touring, you can picnic, read, or nap against one of the fallen columns in the rear garden. *1 hr. Viale delle Terme di Caracalla 52. 06-5758626. 5€. Mon 9am–1pm, Tues–Sun 9am–1 hr before sunset. Metro: Circo Massimo. Bus: 30, 60, 75, 95, 118, or 170. Tram: 3.*

Jewish Ghetto & Tiber Island

1. Piazza Mattei
2. Piazza Margana
3. Via del Portico d'Ottavia
4. Forno del Ghetto
5. Zi' Fenizia
6. Synagogue
7. Portico d'Ottavia
8. Largo 16 Ottobre
9. Teatro di Marcello
10. Tiber Island
11. Ponte Rotto
12. Cloaca Maxima
13. Temples of Hercules and Portunus
14. Mouth of Truth

Packed with monuments from every era of Roman history, the Jewish Ghetto has left its dark days behind and become a vibrant, rewarding place to explore. Tiber Island and the riverbank here offer rustic charm and some of the city's most interesting, unsung sights. START: **Take bus 30, 40, 62, 64, 70, 87, 116, 492, 571, or 628, or tram 8 to Largo Argentina.**

❶ ★★ **Piazza Mattei.** One of Rome's most prized possessions, the Fontana delle Tartarughe (Tortoise Fountain) lies tucked away in this gem of a square, where you'll often find film crews shooting and art students sketching its picturesquely patinated centerpiece.

❷ ★ **Piazza Margana.** This textbook example of a charming Italian square is complete with geraniums spilling out of window boxes, a pretty alfresco cafe/restaurant—and, if you look carefully down tiny Via di Tor Margana, a gun-barrel view of Trajan's Column, .5km (⅓ mile) away.

❸ ★ **Via del Portico d'Ottavia.** Formerly the eastern boundary of the Jewish Ghetto, this bumpy, busy street is now the principal thoroughfare of the modern neighborhood, with shop signs in Hebrew alluding to the community's heritage.

4 ★ **Forno del Ghetto.** It's hard to resist the sweet smells of almonds, cinnamon, and ricotta emanating from this tiny Ghetto bakery, run by three gruff matrons. Cookies and candied cakes are sold by the kilo and are best eaten fresh out of the oven. *Via del Portico d'Ottavia 1.* ☎ *06-6878637.*

5 ★ **Zi' Fenizia.** Delicious—and kosher—pizza by the slice, and a few stools to sit on while you scarf it down. *Via Santa Maria del Pianto 64.* ☎ *06-6896976.*

❻ ★★ **Synagogue.** Rome's gorgeous, palm-treed *Sinagoga* is a particularly triumphant edifice in this part of town. It was built in the 1890s over land that was once the most squalid part of the Ghetto, shortly after the decree that ended the Jewish segregation. Inside the temple is

A block of colorful houses in the Jewish Ghetto.

The ceiling of the neo-Babylonian Synagogue of Rome is decorated with ornate metalwork and frescoed palm trees.

the Museo d'Arte Ebraica, with vivid exhibits documenting the persecution of the Jews in Rome from 1555—when the papal bull, *Cum nimis absurdum,* established the Ghetto laws—through the Nazi occupation of the 1940s. ⌚ ***30 min. Lungotevere Cenci 15. ☎ 06-68400661. 6€. Sun–Thurs 9am–4:30pm (until 7pm May–Aug), Fri 9am–1:30pm.***

7 ★ Portico d'Ottavia. Poking up from the ancient level at the end of Via del Portico d'Ottavia are the impressive remains of a propylaeum (gate to a temple precinct) built by Augustus, and named for his sister, in 23 B.C. Today, the portico is the monumental entry to the modest medieval Church of Sant'Angelo in Pescheria, where Jews were forced to attend Catholic Mass during the Ghetto period. The pavement outside was the site of Rome's fish market *(pescheria)* for centuries, hence the name of the church. ⌚ ***15 min. Free admission. Excavations daily 9am–5pm.***

8 ★ Largo 16 Ottobre. In front of the Portico d'Ottavia ruins, a plaque on the wall commemorates the place where, on the night of October 16, 1943, Roman Jews were rounded up by Nazi troops and deported to the concentration camps of Auschwitz and Birkenau. Of the 3,091 men, women, and children deported, only 15 survived.

9 ★★ Teatro di Marcello (Theater of Marcellus). With a 15,000-spectator capacity, this 13 B.C. theater was the main ancient Roman venue for plays, concerts, and the occasional public execution. In the 1300s, the Savelli family built a fortress on top of the ponderous ruins, which they then converted into a palace during the Renaissance. Above the ancient travertine arches, the apartments are still inhabited by modern princes and *contessas.* ⌚ ***15 min. Free admission. Excavations daily 9am–5pm.***

10 ★★ Tiber Island. In 391 B.C., a snake slithered onto the shores of Tiber Island; at the same time, a decade-long plague in Rome ended. Ever since, the river island has been a sanctuary of medicine, with the

Fatebenefratelli hospital today occupying the majority of the real estate here. The ancient Romans, in a moment of fancy, sculpted the island to look like a ship; part of the "hull" (a fragment of carved travertine) can still be seen on the lower esplanade, a favorite sunning spot of Romans on their lunch breaks. ***Stairs to the lower esplanade are located west of the main entrance to the hospital.*** *30 min.*

⓫ ★ Ponte Rotto. Stranded in the middle of the river below Tiber Island is the single arch of the 142 B.C. Ponte Rotto, or "broken bridge," which fell and was rebuilt so many times that the city finally abandoned it when it collapsed in 1598. From the neighboring modern bridge, Ponte Palatino, wheel ruts can still be seen on the Ponte Rotto's roadway. *No access.*

⓬ Cloaca Maxima. A gaping arch in the riverbank walls, under the eastern end of the Ponte Palatino, is the mouth of the 6th-century-B.C. "great sewer," constructed to drain the moisture from the swampy valley of the Roman Forum. According to some archaeologists, the underground waterway is still navigable, with secret access hatches in unlikely parts of the city. *No access.*

⓭ ★ Temples of Hercules and Portunus. In a beautiful setting, among oleanders and fountains on a grassy rise near the riverbank, these two Republican-era temples survive because of their reconsecration as churches. For centuries, the round temple (of Hercules) was known as the Temple of Vesta because the only other known round temple was that of Vesta in the Roman Forum. The rectangular temple was dedicated to Portunus, god of port activity; in antiquity, the most important cargo coming to Rome, like columns for the Forum, or lions for the Colosseum, was unloaded from river barges here. *No access.*

⓮ ★ Mouth of Truth. Propped up at the end of the portico of the Church of Santa Maria in Cosmedin (which has a fantastic Romanesque bell tower and unusual Greek Orthodox interior) is an ancient sewer cover known as the Bocca della Verità (Mouth of Truth), which is supposed to bite off the hands of liars. All day, tourists line up to take pictures of themselves with their hands in the mouth slot—cheesy, but a Roman rite of passage. *15 min. Queue shortest before 1pm. Piazza della Bocca della Verita. ☎ 06-6781419. Free admission. Daily 9am–5pm.*

The bridge to Tiber Island.

Testaccio

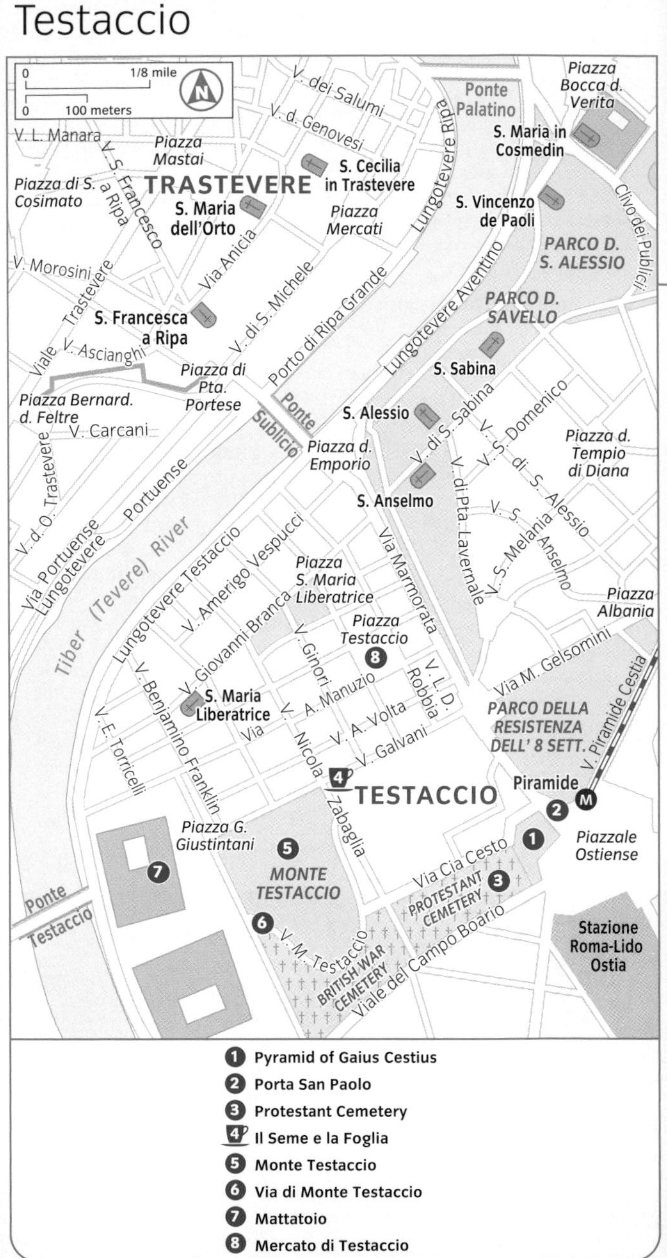
0
1/8 mile
0
100 meters
N
TRASTEVERE
TESTACCIO
Piazza Mastai
Piazza di S. Cosimato
S. Maria dell'Orto
S. Cecilia in Trastevere
Piazza Mercati
S. Francesca a Ripa
Piazza di Pta. Portese
Piazza Bernard. d. Feltre
Piazza Bocca d. Verita
S. Maria in Cosmedin
S. Vincenzo de Paoli
PARCO D. S. ALESSIO
PARCO D. SAVELLO
S. Sabina
S. Alessio
S. Anselmo
Piazza d. Emporio
Piazza d. Tempio di Diana
Piazza Albania
Piazza S. Maria Liberatrice
Piazza Testaccio
S. Maria Liberatrice
PARCO DELLA RESISTENZA DELL' 8 SETT.
Piramide
Piazzale Ostiense
Piazza G. Giustintani
MONTE TESTACCIO
PROTESTANT CEMETERY
BRITISH WAR CEMETERY
Stazione Roma-Lido Ostia
Ponte Palatino
Ponte Sublicio
Ponte Testaccio
Tiber (Tevere) River
V. dei Salumi
V. d. Genovesi
V. L. Manara
V. S. Francesco a Ripa
V. Morosini
Viale Trastevere
V. Ascianghi
V. Carcani
V. d. O. Trastevere
Via Portuense
Portuense
Lungotevere
Via Anicia
V. di S. Michele
Porto di Ripa Grande
Lungotevere Ripa
Lungotevere Aventino
Clivo dei Publici
V. di S. Sabina
V. S. Domenico
V. di S. Alessio
V. di Pta. Lavernale
V. S. Melania
V. S. Anselmo
Via Marmorata
Lungotevere Testaccio
V. Amerigo Vespucci
V. Giovanni Branca
V. Ginori
V. L. D. Robbia
Via M. Gelsomini
V. Piramide Cestia
V. Benjamino Franklin
V. E. Torricelli
Via A. Manuzio
V. A. Volta
V. Galvani
V. Nicola Zabaglia
Via Cia Cesto
V. M. Testaccio
Viale del Campo Boario
1 Pyramid of Gaius Cestius
2 Porta San Paolo
3 Protestant Cemetery
4 Il Seme e la Foglia
5 Monte Testaccio
6 Via di Monte Testaccio
7 Mattatoio
8 Mercato di Testaccio

Testaccio, whose most salient physical features are a defunct slaughterhouse, an ancient rubbish heap, and a slew of nightclubs, has long been a working-class bastion of real Romans and average architecture. Lately, it has become Rome's shabby-chic *quartiere du jour,* but with housing prices skyrocketing and the salt-of-the-earth flavor of the neighborhood changing, residents would prefer to keep the hipsters and health-food stores at bay. **START: Take Metro Line B, bus 23, 30, 170, 271, or 280, or tram 3 to Piramide/Piazzale Ostiense. Transportation: Metro Piramide. Bus: 23, 30, 75, 95, 170, or 280. Tram: 3.**

1 ★ Pyramid of Gaius Cestius. Egyptomania was all the rage in 1st-century-B.C. Rome, and though none would mistake this rather incongruous spike of white marble for the pyramids of Giza, the Roman magistrate who had it built as his tomb probably intended to have it taken just as seriously. *Open by appointment only.* ☎ *06-67103819. Fax 06-6790795.*

2 ★ Porta San Paolo. One of the best-preserved gateways from the 3rd-century-A.D. Aurelian Walls, this is home to the small Museo di Via Ostiense, with interesting artifacts relating to Roman roads. *20 min. Piazzale Ostiense/Via R. Persichetti 3.* ☎ *06-5743193. Free admission. Opening hours vary.*

The Pyramid of Gaius Cestius.

3 ★ Protestant Cemetery. Just beyond a ruined stretch of the Aurelian Walls, the charming *Cimitero Acattolico* complies with the ancient mandate that all burials be outside the city limits. Its peaceful, totally unexpected grounds are home to the graves of John Keats and Antonio Gramsci, founder of the Italian Communist Party, among others. *Via Caio Cestio 6.* ☎ *06-5741900. Donation expected. Tues–Sun 9am–4:30pm.*

4 ★ Il Seme e la Foglia. Opposite Monte Testaccio, this cafe offers monstrous salads, beers on tap, and great local flavor. *Via Galvani 18.* ☎ *06-5743008.*

5 ★★ Monte Testaccio. One of the ancient Romans' most remarkable creations, the "Monte dei Cocci" (Hill of Shards) is an artificial mountain, 30m high (100 ft.), made entirely of broken amphorae (slender vessels used to transport oil and wine) that were discarded here over centuries of importation. There's a good view of the red clay shards through the gates at the corner of Via Galvani and Via Zabaglia, and through the back walls of many of the clubs and bars built against the hill. *Via Zabaglia 24. Open by appointment only.* ☎ *06-67103819. Fax 06-6790795.*

6 ★ Via di Monte Testaccio. Only in Rome: On the road that skirts the base of the hill, see goats grazing above *discotecas* where, hours before, Romans partied to blaring dance music.

7 ★ Il Mattatoio. Rome's decommissioned abattoir—still recognizable by the statue of a naked hero slaughtering a hapless ox atop its neoclassical facade—is now an exhibition space for a variety of contemporary cultural endeavors, under the aegis of MACRO (Museo d'Arte Contemporaneo di Roma). ***Piazza O.*** *Giustiniani. No phone. Hours and prices depend on exhibition.*

8 ★★ Mercato di Testaccio. Mingle with local matrons decked out in their finest housedresses and bedroom slippers at the lively covered market at Piazza Testaccio (Mon–Sat 7am–1pm). Then, take a walk on Via di Monte Testaccio, the circular road that skirts the base of the "mountain made of pottery." By night, this is disco central; by day, livestock bleat happily in their pens on the hillside, directly above the shuttered nightclubs where techno beats blared hours earlier. ●

Grapes for sale in the Mercato di Testaccio.

4 The Best Shopping

Shopping Best Bets

Best **Multi-Label Boutique**
★★★ Gente, *Via del Babuino 81 (p 83)*

Best **Stylish & Affordable Shoes**
★★★ Martina Novelli, *Piazza Risorgimento 38 (p 88);* and ★★ Posto Italiano, *Via Giubbonari 37A (p 88)*

Best **Wine Shop**
★★★ Trimani, *Via Goito 20 (p 86)*

Best **Designer (Men's)**
★★★ Salvatore Ferragamo, *Via Condotti 65*

Best **Designer (Women's)**
★★★ Alberta Ferretti, *Via Condotti 34*

Best **Insanely Expensive Leather Goods**
★★★ Bottega Veneta, *Piazza San Lorenzo in Lucina 8 (p 81)*

Best **Clothing for Edgy Chicks**
★★ Pinko, *Via Giubbonari 76–77 (p 83)*

Best **Clothing for Hip Cats**
★ Prototype, *Via Giubbonari 50 (p 83)*

Best **Accessories at Good Prices**
★ COIN, *Via Cola di Rienzo 173 (p 84);* and ★ La Rinascente, *Largo Chigi 20 (p 84)*

Most **Unique Sneakers**
★★★ Loco, *Via dei Baullari 22 (p 88)*

Best **Teen Fashions**
★★ Energie, *Via del Corso 408–409 (p 82)*

Best **Papal Vestments**
★★ Ghezzi, *Via de' Cestari 32/33 (p 87)*

Best **Gourmet Foods**
★★★ Franchi, *Via Cola di Rienzo 204 (p 86);* and ★★ Castroni, *Via Cola di Rienzo 196–198 (p 86)*

Best **Local Market**
★★★ Piazza Testaccio *(p 86)*

Best **Gifts**
★★★ Modigliani, *Via Condotti 24 (p 85)*

High Fashion Boutiques

All roads lead to Rome; the roads around the Spanish Steps lead to credit card debt. Leading the luxury retail pack is Via Condotti, which boasts the boutiques of **Alberta Ferretti, Armani, Dior, Dolce & Gabbana, Ferragamo, Gucci, Hermès, La Perla, Louis Vuitton, Max Mara, Prada, Valentino,** and **YSL.** Piazza di Spagna weighs in with **Roberto Cavalli, D&G, Escada, Frette, Missoni,** and **Sergio Rossi;** while Via Babuino has **Chanel, Etro, Giuseppe Zanotti,** and **Prada Sport.** Nearby Via Borgognona is graced by the doors of **Fendi, Givenchy, Loro Piana, Tod's,** and **Versace;** and Via Belsiana features **Moschino.**

Centro Storico Shopping

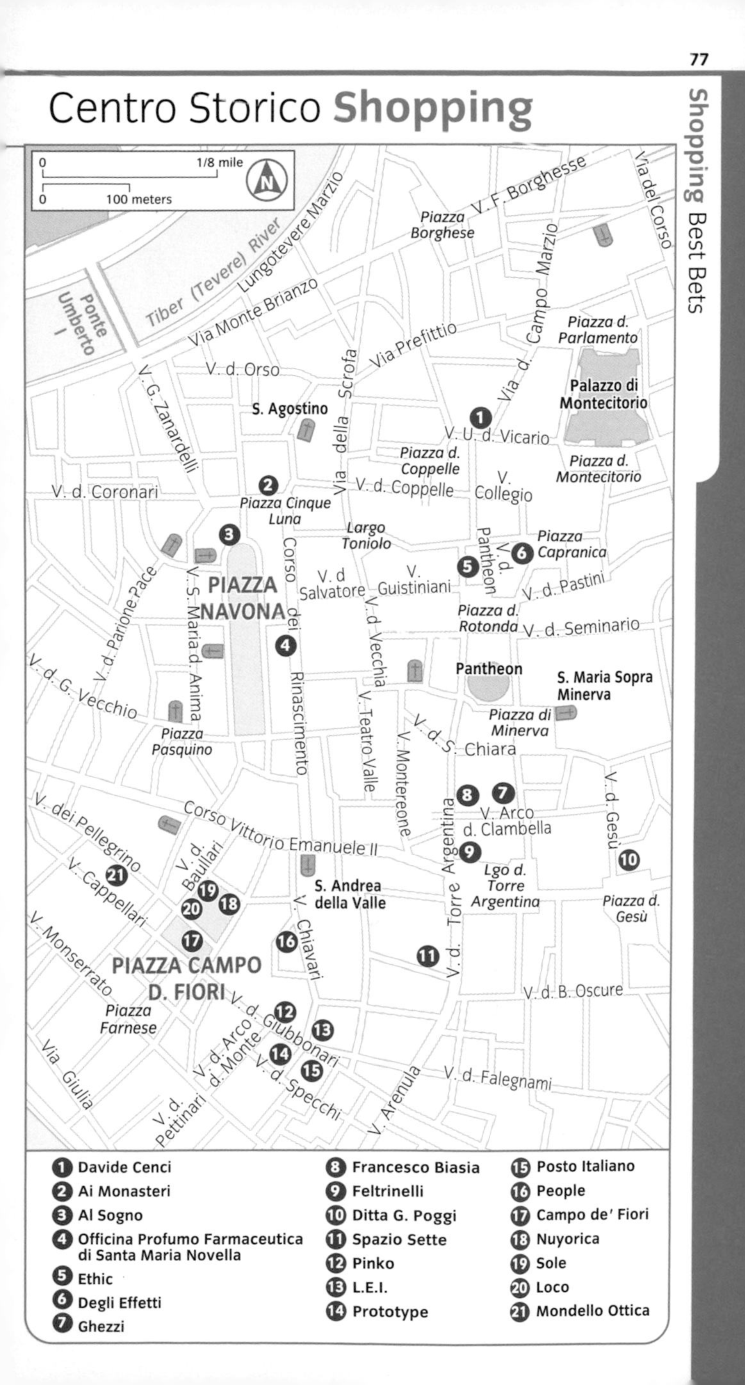

Rome **Shopping**

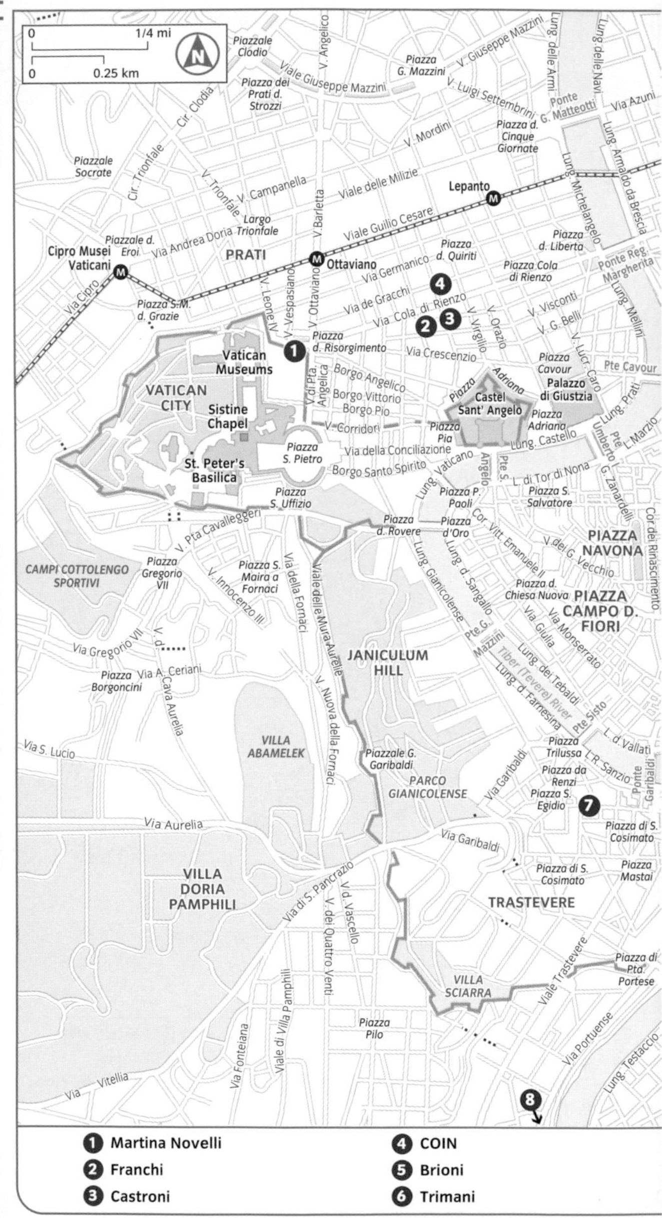

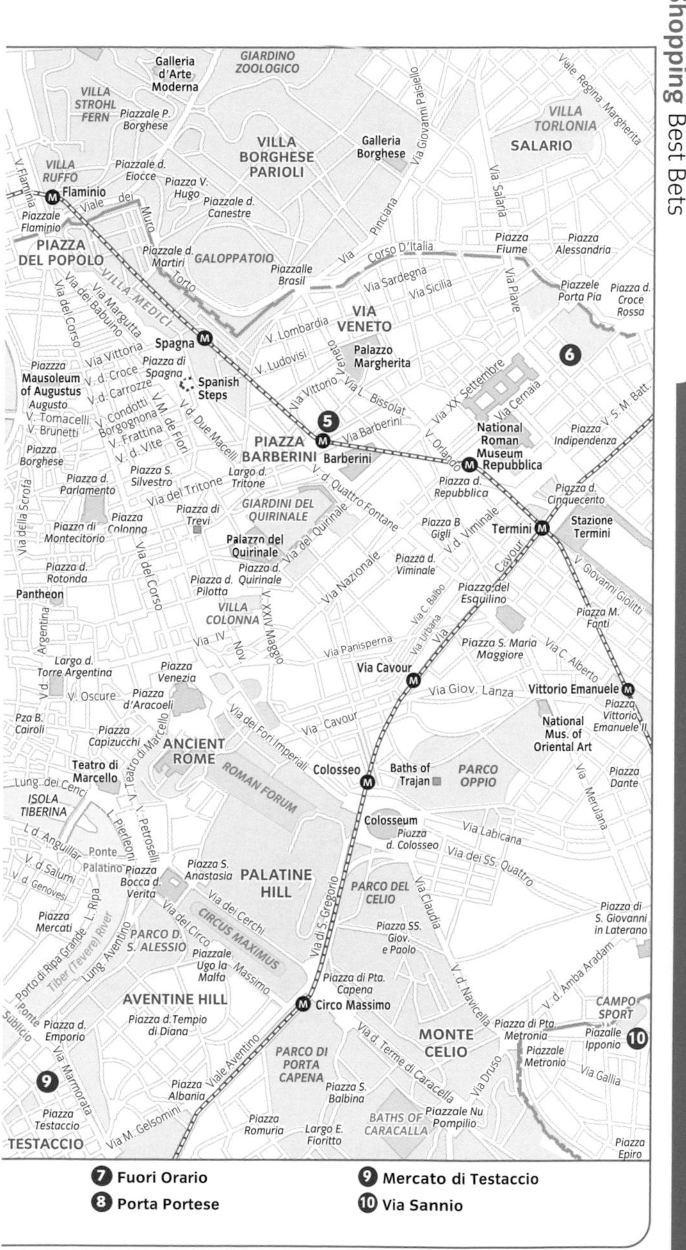

7 Fuori Orario
8 Porta Portese
9 Mercato di Testaccio
10 Via Sannio

Spanish Steps Shopping

1. Energie
2. Simona
3. TAD
4. Eleonora
5. Gente
6. Frette
7. C.U.C.I.N.A
8. Armani Jeans
9. Mercato delle Stampe
10. Campo Marzio Design
11. Bottega Veneta
12. Furla
13. Modigliani
14. Brighenti
15. Anglo-American Book Co.
16. La Rinascente

Rome Shopping, A to Z

Apparel & Accessories

★ **Armani Jeans** SPANISH STEPS Armani for the rest of us: fun, well-cut clothes in cotton and denim for men and women at humane prices. *Via Tomacelli 137 (at Largo degli Schiavoni). ☎ 06-3222249. www.armani.com. AE, DC, MC, V. Metro: Spagna. Bus: 492 or 628. Map p 80.*

★★★ **Bottega Veneta** SPANISH STEPS Buttery soft and exquisitely crafted luggage, handbags, and change-purses from this famed leather-goods maker will handily vanquish your shopping budget in one fell swoop. *Piazza San Lorenzo in Lucina 8 (at Via Campo Marzio). ☎ 06-68809713. AE, DC, MC, V. Bus: 62, 85, 95, 116, or 492. Map p 80.*

★★ **Brioni** PIAZZA BARBERINI You're in excellent (if expensive) hands at this custom men's clothier—the same sartorial masters who have tailored the suits of every dashing 007 from Connery to Brosnan. *Via Barberini 79–81 (at Piazza Barberini). ☎ 06-485855. AE, MC, V. Metro: Barberini. Map p 78.*

★★ **Davide Cenci** PANTHEON At this Roman emporium of classic men's and women's wear, Ralph Lauren sweaters, Burberry coats, Pucci dresses, and Cenci's own label shirts will make country clubbers feel right at home. *Via Campo Marzio 1–7 (at Via Uffici del Vicario). ☎ 06-6990681. AE, DC, MC, V. Bus: 62, 85, 95, 175, or 492. Map p 77.*

A couple shopping on Via Borgogna.

VAT Refund

If you're a non-EU citizen and spend 151€ or more at any one retailer, you're entitled to the VAT refund, which knocks 11% to 13% off your bill. (This is handy if you, like me, are always trying to find ways to rationalize extravagant purchases.) In order to get your refund, you must 1) obtain a **completed tax-free** form from the store, and 2) present your **unused purchases** for inspection at the airport (in Rome or last European port). The inspector will stamp your form, which then enables you to pick up a **cash refund** on the spot at the airport, or to file for a **credit card adjustment,** which can take up to 90 days to process.

The Gucci store on fashionable Via Condotti.

★ **Degli Effetti** PANTHEON From the funky to the classic, this designer boutique stocks labels like Miu Miu and Jil Sander that don't have their own stand-alone stores in Rome. *Piazza Capranica 93–94.* ☎ *06-6790202. AE, DC, MC, V. Bus: 62, 85, 95, 116, 175, or 492. Map p 77.*

★ **Eleonora** SPANISH STEPS Hard-boiled hipsters visit this vibrant boutique for avant-garde, even aggressive fashions by John Galliano, Alexander McQueen, and co. *Via del Babuino 97 (at Via Vittoria).* ☎ *06-6793173. www.eleonoraboutique.it. AE, DC, MC, V. Metro: Spagna. Map p 80.*

★★ **Energie** PIAZZA DEL POPOLO With labels like Miss Sixty and Killah, the brash and bright fashions here are meant for teens, but you'll find many a Roman mom in here buying something for herself along with jeans for her 15-year-old son. *Via del Corso 408–409 (at Via del Vantaggio).* ☎ *06-6871258. AE, DC, MC, V. Metro: Flaminio. Map p 80.*

Shoppers display their Energie shopping bag.

★ **Ethic** PANTHEON Reasonably priced boho-chic pieces in saturated colors and adherent cuts. *Via del Pantheon 46–47 (at Piazza della Maddalena).* ☎ *06-68803167. (Branch at Piazza Cairoli 11–12, at Via Giubbonari.* ☎ *06-68301063.) AE, DC, MC, V. Bus: 30, 40, 62, 64, 70, 85, 87, 95, 116, 175, or 492. Map p 77.*

★★ **Francesco Biasia** PANTHEON Cheaper here than in the U.S., Biasia's fashionable and roomy bags come in a wide array of colors and interesting leather finishes, from pony to patent. *Via di Torre Argentina 7 (at Via dell'Arco della Ciambella).* ☎ *06-6865098. AE, DC, MC, V. Bus: 30, 40, 62, 64, 70, 87, 116, or 492. Map p 77.*

★ **Fuori Orario** TRASTEVERE This tiny corner shop has a kaleidoscopic array of leather jackets, plus inexpensive, trendy apparel by French designers. Discounts for cash payment are often available. *Via del Moro 29 (at Via della Pelliccia).* ☎ *06-5817181. MC, V. Bus: 23, 271, or 280. Map p 78.*

★★ **Furla** SPANISH STEPS These ubiquitous mid-range accessories boutiques specialize in colorful, polished-looking handbags. *Via del Corso 481 (at Via Tomacelli). ☎ 06-36003619. Branches citywide. AE, DC, MC, V. Metro: Spagna. Map p 80.*

★★★ **Gente** SPANISH STEPS A microcosm of the Via Condotti boutiques, with more affordable denim and accessories. *Via del Babuino 81 (at Piazza di Spagna). ☎ 06-3207671. AE, DC, MC, V. Metro: Spagna. (Branch at Via Cola di Rienzo 277, Vatican area.) Map p 80.*

★★★ **L.E.I.** CAMPO DE' FIORI Should one of Rome's remaining princes invite you to the ball, come here first for a feast of frocks, in all shapes and all price ranges. *Via Giubbonari 103 (at Via dei Chiavari). ☎ 06-6875432. AE, DC, MC, V. Bus: 30, 40, 62, 64, 70, 87, or 492. (Branch at Via Nazionale 88.) Map p 77.*

★★ **Nuyorica** CAMPO DE' FIORI With carefully selected clothes, bags, and shoes by such A-list designers as Marni and Balenciaga, this startlingly hip boutique shows just how far the Campo de' Fiori area has come from its humble roots. *Piazza Pollarola 36–37 (at Via del Biscione). ☎ 06 68891243. www.nuyorica.it. AE, DC, MC, V. Bus: 30, 40, 62, 64, 70, 87, or 492. Map p 77.*

★★ **People** CAMPO DE' FIORI By far the best vintage clothing store in town. For those who can't deal with that pre-owned smell, the boutique also sells new clothing with retro styling—think dresses that look like 1960s Pucci. *Piazza Teatro di Pompeo 4A (at Via dei Chiavari). ☎ 06-6874040. AE, DC, MC, V. Bus: 30, 40, 62, 64, 70, 87, 116, or 492. Map p 77.*

★★ **Pinko** CAMPO DE' FIORI Embellished knits, deconstructed denim, and great pants in mineral tones are the hallmark of this Northern Italian women's label. *Via Giubbonari 76–77 (at Campo de' Fiori). ☎ 06-68309116. www.pinko.it. AE, DC, MC, V. Bus: 30, 40, 62, 64, 70, 87, or 492. Map p 77.*

★ **Prototype** CAMPO DE' FIORI The owners of this unisex boutique scour the land to bring hip and colorful casual wear and sneakers to Roman 20- and 30-somethings. *Via*

Sale Season

If you come to Rome in late January and late July, you might not find the best weather, but if you're a shopper, your timing is perfect. All stores in Italy have two annual liquidation periods *(saldi)*, during which there are serious deals to be had. Discounts start at 30% (though most are 50%) and can go as deep as 75% off regular retail. The best part is that these sale items are not chartreuse raincoats or other fashion faux pas; we're talking regular, desirable merchandise, yours for the taking at two magical times per year. Without waiting in long lines, traveling to suburban outlets, or pawing through piles of cast-offs, we've made off with Dolce & Gabbana pumps, Pucci sandals, and Max Mara jackets for proverbial pennies.

Giubbonari 50 (at Campo de' Fiori). ☎ 06-68300330. AE, MC, V. Bus: 30, 40, 62, 64, 70, 87, or 492. Tram: 8. Map p 77.

★★ **Sole** CAMPO DE' FIORI Glam women's accessories and clothing with Italian attitude—think sassy, bejeweled handbags; snug-fitting fur-trimmed trenches—make for fabulous I-picked-this-up-in-Rome purchases. *Via dei Baullari 21 (at Piazza della Cancelleria). ☎ 06-68806987. Bus: 30, 40, 62, 64, 70, 87, 116, or 492. Map p 77.*

★★ **TAD** SPANISH STEPS Everything in this lifestyle "concept" boutique, which looks like a lush, glossy magazine spread, is for sale, from the Lucite Rochas pumps to the bamboo trees. The in-store cafe and hair salon give you even more ways to spend your euros. *Via del Babuino 155A (at Via dei Greci). ☎ 06-32695122. www.taditaly.com. AE, DC, MC, V. Metro: Spagna. Map p 80.*

Books

★★ **Anglo-American Book Co.** SPANISH STEPS English-language titles of all kinds are sold here, but the selection is particularly strong on art and architecture. *Via della Vite 102 (at Via Mario de' Fiori). ☎ 06-6795222. AE, DC, MC, V. Metro: Spagna. Map p 80.*

★★ **Feltrinelli Libri e Musica** PANTHEON With bar-code-scanning CD listening stations and a great travel section, Rome has its answer to Borders in this renovated branch of a national book chain. Quite novel for Italy, there's also an in-store cafe. *Largo di Torre Argentina 5A–6 (at Corso Vittorio Emanuele II). ☎ 06-68803248. AE, DC, MC, V. Bus: 30, 40, 62, 64, 70, 87, or 492. Map p 77.*

Department Stores

★ **COIN** VATICAN It's underwhelming if you're used to the U.S. or U.K. department store standard, but COIN does have some great finds in its accessories section, where the latest looks in handbags and belts are very budget-friendly. *Via Cola di Rienzo 173 (at Via Paolo Emilio). ☎ 06-700020. AE, DC, MC, V. Metro: Ottaviano. Map p 78.*

★ **La Rinascente** SPANISH STEPS Similar to COIN but larger and more central, Rinascente is a good bet when you need to buy a last-minute leather wallet or silk scarf for someone back home. No need to go upstairs: The clothing floors are

The colorful entranceway to the TAD lifestyle "concept" boutique.

The bold facade of the COIN department store.

Frumpsville. *Largo Chigi 20 (at Via del Corso). ☎ 06-6797691. AE, DC, MC, V. Bus: 62, 63, 85, 95, 175, or 492. Map p 80.*

Design & Home Furnishings

★★ **C.U.C.I.N.A.** SPANISH STEPS At this shrine to stainless-steel cookware and kitchen gadgets, you can pick up authentic Bialetti stove-top coffeemakers, mini-parmigiano graters, and all gauges of ravioli-cutters. *Via Mario de' Fiori 65 (at Via delle Carrozze). ☎ 06-6791275. www.cucinastore.com. AE, DC, MC, V. Metro: Spagna. Map p 80.*

★★★ **Frette** SPANISH STEPS For those who can't bear to bed down with anything less than 600 thread-count, Frette has luxurious linens for the home—not to mention a full line of terries perfect for your yacht. *Piazza di Spagna 11 (at Via S. Sebastianello). ☎ 06-6790673. AE, DC, MC, V. Map p 80.*

★★★ **Modigliani** SPANISH STEPS From Murano wineglasses to hand-painted Tuscan platters, the fine (but not fussy) merchandise at this four-story tabletop-goods store makes great gifts that can be shipped anywhere in the world. *Via Condotti 24 (at Via Bocca di Leone). ☎ 06-6785653. www.modigliani.it. AE, DC, MC, V. Metro: Spagna. Map p 80.*

★★ **Spazio Sette** CAMPO DE' FIORI The hottest Italian design, in everything from sofas to picture frames, reigns supreme at this three-floor housewares emporium. *Via dei Barbieri 7 (at Largo Argentina). ☎ 06-68804261. AE, DC, MC, V. Bus: 30, 40, 62, 64, 70, 87, or 492. Map p 77.*

Eyewear

★★ **Mondello Ottica** CAMPO DE' FIORI Quick, friendly service and a dizzying selection of sunglasses and prescription frames make this optician's shop one of the best in Rome. *Via del Pellegrino 97–98 (at Campo de' Fiori). ☎ 06-6861955. AE, DC, MC, V. Bus: 40, 62, or 64. Map p 77.*

Food & Wine

★★ **Castroni** VATICAN This coffee bar extraordinaire has olive pâtés, caviar, fine wines, and all manner of oils and vinegars. A godsend for many expats, Castroni also stocks hard-to-get foreign foodstuffs like Bisquick and Vegemite. *Via Cola di Rienzo 196–198 (at Via Terenzio). ☎ 06-6874383. AE, MC, V. Metro: Ottaviano. Map p 78.*

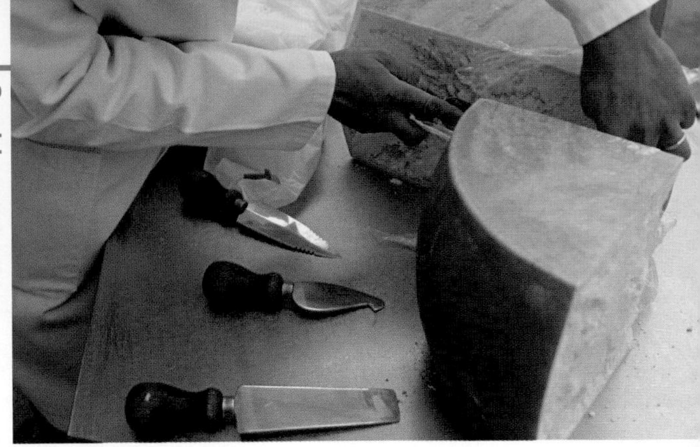

Blocks of Parmesan cheese.

★★★ **Franchi** VATICAN The best gourmet deli in town, Franchi has every cheese and cured meat under the sun. At lunch, prepared food (including heavenly *suppli*) is available to go. *Via Cola di Rienzo 204 (at Via Terenzio). ☎ 06-6874651. AE, MC, V. Metro: Ottaviano. Map p 78.*

★★★ **Trimani** TERMINI Founded in 1821 and still run by the same family, this is Rome's best wine shop. The knowledgeable owners can help you navigate the overwhelming selection. *Via Goito 20 (at Via Cernaia). ☎ 06-4469661. AE, DC, MC, V. Metro: Castro Pretorio. Bus: 60, 75, or 492. Map p 78.*

Lingerie

★★ **Brighenti** SPANISH STEPS Even if you're not one of the film stars who frequent this shop, the pastel interiors and luxurious lingerie offerings will make you feel as glamorous as Marilyn Monroe. *Via Frattina 7 (at Via Mario de' Fiori). ☎ 06-6791484. AE, DC, MC, V. Map p 80.*

★ **Simona** SPANISH STEPS This tiny shop is bursting with lacy bras, skimpy underwear, and bikinis. The no-nonsense sales staff are also bursting . . . into your dressing room to check out the fit of that underwire. *Via del Corso 82–83 (at Via Vittoria). ☎ 06-3613742. AE, DC, MC, V. Map p 80.*

Markets

★★ **Campo de' Fiori** This historic produce market is still a Roman institution and well worth a visit, though kitschy souvenir aprons and all manner of kitchen tools have begun to take over what used to be the city's most authentic fruit-and-veg bazaar. *Mon–Sat 7am–2pm. No credit cards. Bus: 30, 40, 62, 64, 70, 87, or 492. Map p 77.*

★ **Mercato delle Stampe** PIAZZA DEL POPOLO Here you'll find wonderfully worn antique books, old engravings, vintage magazines, and their loving dealers. To get the best price, feign some sort of expertise in the print market. *Largo della Fontanella Borghese. No credit cards. Metro: Spagna. Bus: 81. Map p 80.*

★★★ **Piazza Testaccio** In salt-of-the-earth Testaccio, this covered market is the real deal. Women in housedresses greet everyone by name as they shuffle from butchers' stalls to produce stands, where their inevitable laments over the rising cost of zucchini blossoms are pure theater. *Mon–Sat 7am–1pm. No credit cards. Metro: Piramide. Bus: 23, 75, or 170. Tram: 3.*

★★ Porta Portese TRASTEVERE Unless you're in the market for a Turkish casino ashtray or a dot-matrix printer, you'll find Rome's biggest flea market more spectacle than working shopping experience. *Via Portuense (from Piazza Porta Portese to Via Ettore Rolli). Sun only 7am–2pm. No credit cards. Bus: 23, 271, or 280. Tram: 3 or 8. Map p 78.*

★ Via Sannio SAN GIOVANNI Good for new and used clothes, leather jackets, and shoes. *Via Sannio. Mon–Sat 10am–2pm. No credit cards. Metro: San Giovanni. Map p 78.*

Perfumeries

★ Ai Monasteri PIAZZA NAVONA In a space that recalls a medieval apothecary, choose from potions, elixirs, candles, and sweets—all made by Italian monks. *Corso Rinascimento 72 (at Piazza Cinque Lune). ☎ 06-68802783. AE, DC, MC, V. Bus: 30, 70, 87, 492, or 628. Map p 77.*

★ Officina Profumo Farmaceutica di Santa Maria Novella PIAZZA NAVONA The Roman outpost of the famed Florentine perfumery. *Corso Rinascimento 47 (at Piazza Madama). ☎ 06-6879608. AE, DC, MC, V. Bus: 30, 70, 87, 492, or 628. Map p 77.*

Religious Goods

★★ Ghezzi PANTHEON Couture cassocks, fab fonts, and marvelous monstrances. Unlike other liturgical outfitters, Ghezzi welcomes even laypeople to scope (but not buy) its glorious inventory of all things relating to Catholic ceremony. *Via de' Cestari 32–33 (at Via dell'Arco della Ciambella). ☎ 06-6869744. www.arredi-sacri.it. Bus: 30, 40, 62, 64, 70, 87, 116, or 492. Map p 77.*

A nun admires the flowers on display in the Campo de' Fiori market.

A clerk displays a bottle of elixir from Ai Monasteri.

Shoes

★★★ Loco CAMPO DE' FIORI If Dorothy lived in Rome, she might well find her ruby slippers at this wild and wonderful (and pricey) shoe boutique. Classy, unique men's styles available, too. *Via dei Baullari 22 (at Campo de' Fiori). ☎ 06-68808216. AE, DC, MC, V. Bus: 30, 40, 62, 64, 70, 87, 116, 492, or 571. Map p 77.*

★★★ Martina Novelli VATICAN Delightfully opinionated shop girls will help women choose the right pair at this hip, mostly affordable shoe store near the Vatican. *Piazza Risorgimento 38 (at Via Ottaviano). ☎ 06-39737247. AE, DC, MC, V. Bus: 23, 81, 271, or 492. Tram: 19. Map p 78.*

★★ Posto Italiano CAMPO DE' FIORI This friendly "Italian place" stocks well-priced and current shoes and boots for men and women. *Via Giubbonari 37A (at Campo de' Fiori). ☎ 06-6869373. (Branch: Viale Trastevere 111. ☎ 06-58334820). AE, DC, MC, V. Bus: 30, 40, 62, 64, 70, 87, or 492. Map p 77.*

Stationers

★ Campo Marzio Design PANTHEON These colorful leather-bound notebooks and pens worthy of Dante himself might just inspire you to keep a journal of your visit to Rome. *Via Campo Marzio 41 (at Piazza San Lorenzo in Lucina). ☎ 06-68807877. www.campomarziodesign.it. AE, DC, MC, V. Bus: 62, 63, 85, 116, or 492. Map p 77.*

★★★ Ditta G. Poggi PANTHEON Allow plenty of time to peruse the shelves at this 180-year-old art supplies store. Amid tubes of oil paint and stencils, you might stumble across charming 1950s composition books (at 1950s prices) and the odd Italian BEWARE OF DOG sign. *Via del Gesù 74–75 (at Via Plebiscito). ☎ 06-6784477. www.poggi1825.it. AE, MC, V. Bus: 30, 40, 62, 64, 70, 87, or 492. Map p 77.*

Toys

★★ Al Sogno PIAZZA NAVONA What Santa's workshop must have looked like 50 years ago—this fantastic high-end toyshop amazes young and old alike with its collectible gnomes, life-sized stuffed animals, and themed chess sets. *Piazza Navona 53 (at north end). ☎ 06-6864198. AE, DC, MC, V. Bus: 30, 70, 87, 492, or 628. Map p 77.* ●

"Bambola," one of the amazingly lifelike dolls sold at Al Sogno.

5 The Great **Outdoors**

Villa **Borghese**

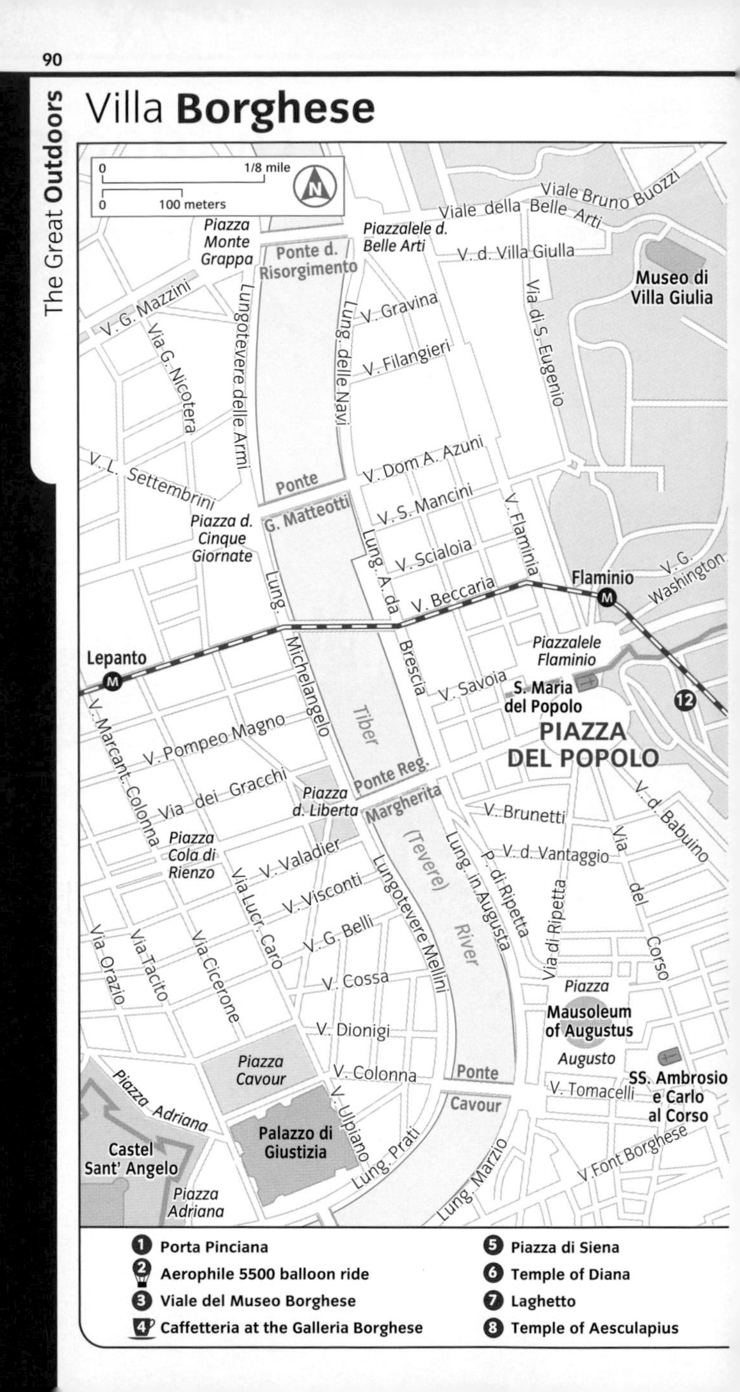

1. Porta Pinciana
2. Aerophile 5500 balloon ride
3. Viale del Museo Borghese
4. Caffetteria at the Galleria Borghese
5. Piazza di Siena
6. Temple of Diana
7. Laghetto
8. Temple of Aesculapius

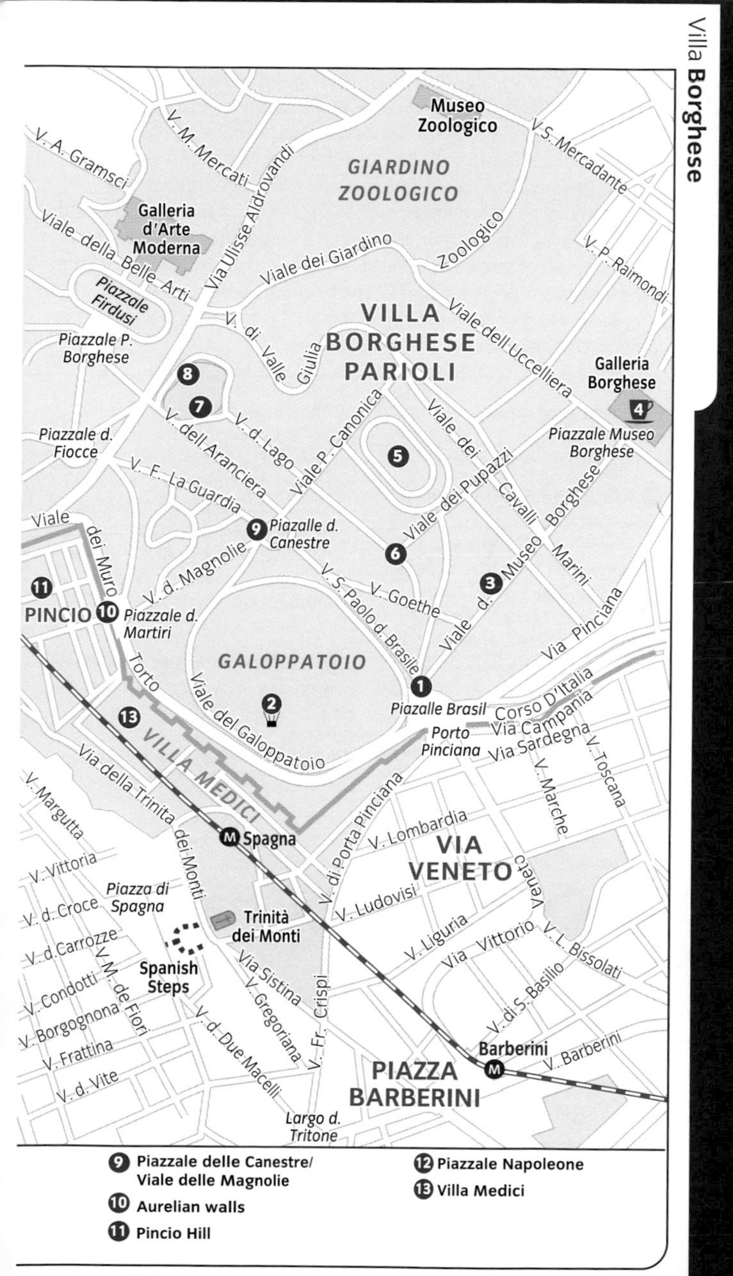

9 Piazzale delle Canestre/ Viale delle Magnolie
10 Aurelian walls
11 Pincio Hill
12 Piazzale Napoleone
13 Villa Medici

Other Roman parks are larger, wilder, and less crowded, but none is as treasured by the city as the gorgeous, glamorous Villa Borghese. Gracing the higher ground directly above the *centro storico,* the Villa Borghese became public property in 1901, when the once-powerful Borghese family ran into financial trouble and sold their estate, complete with its museums, fountains, and faux temples, to the city. The park offers myriad recreation opportunities, with shady lanes, open fields, a lake, a zoo, even a balloon ride; and bikes, *risciò* (rickshaws that you pedal), in-line skates, and rowboats can be rented at several facilities in the park. Bordering some of the city's wealthiest neighborhoods, the Villa Borghese is also the preferred jogging ground—groomed and level—of the Roman rich and famous. **Daily 6am–sunset. Bus: 116 or 490.**

❶ **Porta Pinciana.** Enter the park here, at the top of Via Veneto, just beyond the ancient walls.

❷ **Aerophile 5500 Balloon Ride.** Rising 150m (492 ft.), this big blue tethered balloon takes passengers on 15-minute flights for thrilling views of the city. Galoppatoio. ☎ *06-32111511. 15€ adult, 11€ ages 13–17, 6€ ages 6–12, 3€ ages 6 and under; weekends cost more. Daily 9:30am–sunset (weather permitting; call in advance).*

Shady, hedge-lined ❸ **Viale del Museo Borghese** leads to **the Galleria Borghese** (p 30). When the Borghese family sold their estate to the city, they insisted on a proviso that would preserve the integrity of their magnificent collection of baroque and ancient art in the *galleria.* On either side of the road are grassy fields, popular with picnickers, sunbathers, and lovers.

❹ **Caffetteria at the Galleria Borghese** This efficient little cafe on the museum's lower level (free access) has simple sandwiches, drinks, and sweets. On a nice day, ask for your order *da portare via*

Roman General Furio Camilo Breaks Treaty with the Gauls, *a fresco by Mariano Rossi on display in the Villa Borghese.*

Glide over the Villa in the big blue Aerophile 5500 Balloon.

(to go) and picnic in the handsome gardens nearby. *Piazzale Scipione Borghese. Tues–Sun 9am–7pm.*

Skip the moroseness of the outdated zoo and head west down Viale dei Pupazzi past the elegant ❺ **Piazza di Siena,** where joggers plod (and, in May, horses jump) around a track rimmed with umbrella pines.

At the ❻ **Temple of Diana** (a 17th-c. faux temple to the ancient goddess of the hunt), turn right, and go north to the man-made ❼ **Laghetto,** whose northern shore is graced by the picturesque 17th-century ❽ **Temple of Aesculapius,** the pagan god of medicine. Rent a boat (daily 9am–sunset) and enjoy a relaxing row around the lake.

Head south to ❾ **Piazzale delle Canestre** and **Viale delle Magnolie.** This pedestrianized avenue is often tricked out with low-lying obstacle courses for skaters and bladers, so be careful of Coke-can slaloms underfoot.

Continue to the bridge that crosses Viale del Muro Torto ("Street of the Crooked Wall") and its namesake, the 3rd-century-A.D. ❿ **Aurelian Walls,** behind which lies ⓫ **Pincio Hill,** whose primary attraction is the knockout vista at ⓬ **Piazzale Napoleone.** Gaze past the terrace parapets to the ochre rooftops of Rome and the dome of St. Peter's. *See p 67, bullet* ❼.

Open Sunday only (10am–2pm), the Renaissance ⓭ **Gardens at Villa Medici** comprise the open-air home of priceless works of ancient sculpture. In his *Italian Hours,* Henry James called the exclusive gardens "the most enchanting place." Walk back to Porta Pinciana.

Boating nearby a faux-classical temple in the gardens of the Villa Borghese.

Appia Antica (Appian Way)

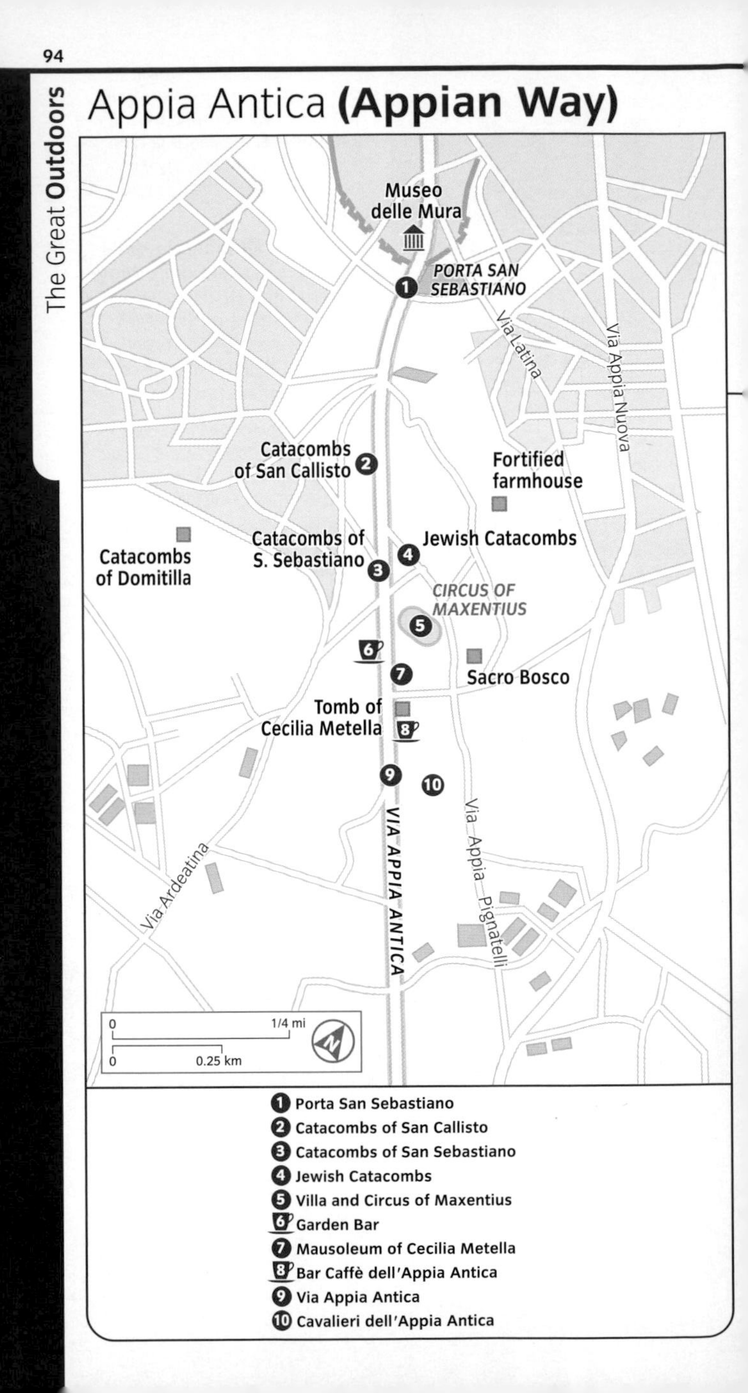

The most important of Rome's famous ancient roads, the rustic Appian Way (Via Appia Antica) is home to most of the city's catacombs and a world away from the bustle of the *centro*. Visit the catacombs for a fascinating descent into the ancient tufa tunnels where Roman Christians were buried, then continue south to the Circus of Maxentius and Tomb of Cecilia Metella, where a landscape steeped in antiquity should leave you spellbound. **Bus: 118 (from Metro Circo Massimo or Metro Piramide) to the second catacombe di san callisto stop. (The first stop will leave you 1km/⅔ mile from the entrance to the catacombs.) Or take a taxi (10–15 min. from the city center, about 12€–15€). Allow 3 to 4 hours for the trip.**

The massive ❶ **Porta San Sebastiano,** a brick gateway left over from Rome's 3rd-century-A.D. fortification, marks the start of Via Appia Antica's southbound route. The first mile is visually underwhelming and plagued with traffic; start your tour of the Appian Way at the catacombs, about a mile south. Farther south, the landscape is greener and quieter.

Enjoy Rome offers a 3-hour bus and walking tour of the Appia Antica, including the stupendous aqueduct park, otherwise hard to reach. *Call for tour times. ☎ 06-4451843.*

Skip the package-tour-infested catacombs of Domitilla and make for San Callisto or San Sebastiano instead (below). Admission to each catacomb (5€ adults, 3€ ages 3–15) includes a 35-minute guided tour, offered in English every 15 minutes or so. The tours can be quite large and guides' accents difficult to understand, so try to stay close to the front of the group.

❷ **Catacombs of San Callisto.** Once home to 500,000 tombs, these are by far the most impressive and extensive of Rome's catacombs. *Via Appia Antica 110–126. Thurs–Tues 8:30am–noon, 2:30–5pm. Closed Feb.*

❸ **Catacombs of San Sebastiano.** A 5-minute walk from San Callisto, and more intimate than San Callisto, with better-preserved tomb decorations, this cluster of pagan tombs offers a fascinating look at

Funerary containers in the Catacombs of San Sebastian.

The Circus of Maxentius.

the typically Roman practice of layering architectures and faiths. *Via Appia Antica 136. Mon–Sat 8:30am–noon, 2:30–5pm. Closed mid-Nov to mid-Dec.*

While catacombs are most often associated with Christianity, the Jews of ancient Rome also buried their dead in the same kinds of underground networks. The ❹ **Jewish Catacombs** at Via Appia Antica 119A can be visited only with prior permission from the Cultural Heritage Department. ☎ *06-67103819. Fax 06-6892115.*

❺ **Villa and Circus of Maxentius.** A 5-minute walk south of San Sebastiano, the ruins of a 4th-century imperial country estate (poorly preserved) and circus (chariot racetrack, which held 10,000 spectators) lie in a field on the east side of the ancient road. Pay the small entrance fee here for awe-inspiring views of Cecilia Metella among the umbrella pines, and for a closer look at the circus's construction. *Via Appia Antica 153. Tues–Fri, Sun 9am–1:30pm; Sat 9am–1 hr. before sunset.*

6 **Garden Bar.** It doesn't get much more civilized than this—a full-service snack bar attached to a lovely *vivaio* (nursery), where Romans stop in for a cappuccino or cypress sapling. *Via Appia Antica 172. Call* ☎ *06-7840911 for hours.*

❼ **Mausoleum of Cecilia Metella.** The best view of this cylindrical tomb of a 1st-century-B.C. socialite is from the middle of the Circus of Maxentius (above) or the road. (The entrance fee here does not gain you access to the tomb's interior but to a courtyard cluttered with ancient marble pieces.) The Appian Way was the Rodeo Drive of tombs in antiquity, and Cecilia Metella's was only one of hundreds of marble-clad sepulchers that used to crowd the roadside. The other tombs, dismantled by the popes and barbarians in the Middle Ages for their valuable materials, are now little more than brick stumps. *Via Appia Antica 161. Tues–Sun 9am–1 hr. before sunset.*

8 **Bar Caffè dell'Appia Antica.** A bike ride can be a very pleasant way to see the Appia Antica, provided you start here and ride south, where vehicle traffic is light to nonexistent. This informal coffee bar rents bikes by the hour. The Appian Way's flagstones can get very uneven at times, meaning you'll have to get off and walk a bit, but you can travel as far as 3km (2 miles) on the ancient road, viewing ruins and rural life, and not worry about getting lost—the Appia's path is due south and dead-straight. *Via Appia Antica 175.*

Visiting the Catacombs

Ancient Roman law forbade burials, regardless of religion, inside the city walls. Of the more than 60 catacombs that have been discovered on the roads leading out of Rome, the most famous are San Callisto and San Sebastiano on the Appian Way. On your guided visit, you'll descend through multiple levels of 1,900-year-old hand-dug corridors, past a mind-boggling number of tomb niches. (To protect them from looters, the bones have been removed.) Christian-themed inscriptions and frescoes, often endearingly simplistic but carrying strong messages of faith, are everywhere in the catacombs.

9 Via Appia Antica. The leafy, 3km (2-mile) segment beginning at Cecilia Metella is the Appia at its most evocative. Here, the road is 4m (14 ft.) wide (the Roman standard), with ancient basalt flagstones still in place. Private villas on either side of the road eventually give way to ruins-strewn fields and the occasional flock of sheep. You'll need to walk for at least 500m (⅓ mile) to appreciate the change of scenery; beyond that, it's somewhat repetitive—umbrella pines, tomb stumps—but still wonderfully soaked in history. *Public transportation is spotty at the southern end of the road; return by foot or bike to 8. From there, catch bus no. 660 to Metro San Giovanni, or have the bar staff call a taxi for you.*

10 Cavalieri dell'Appia Antica. If you really want to do as the Romans did on the "Queen of Roads," get a horse! This small, friendly stable offers an alternative to biking and walking on the Appia Antica. Scenic rides (for all skill levels) take you past the most important ruins. *Via dei Cerceni 15. ☎ 06-7801214. 15€ per 1-hr. ride. Owners speak almost no English, so have your hotel make reservations for you. Tues–Sun 10am–6pm. Bus: 118.*

Travelers stroll or take a break on the pastoral Appian Way.

Other Rome **Parks to Explore**

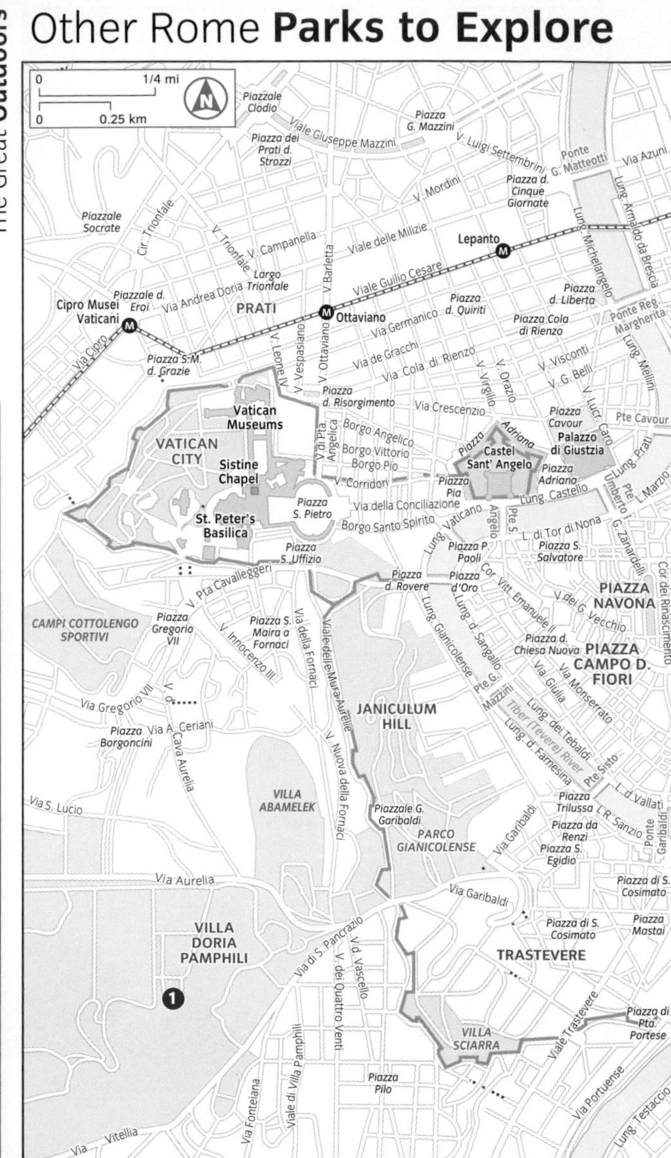

❶ **Villa Pamphilj**
❷ **Villa Celimontana**

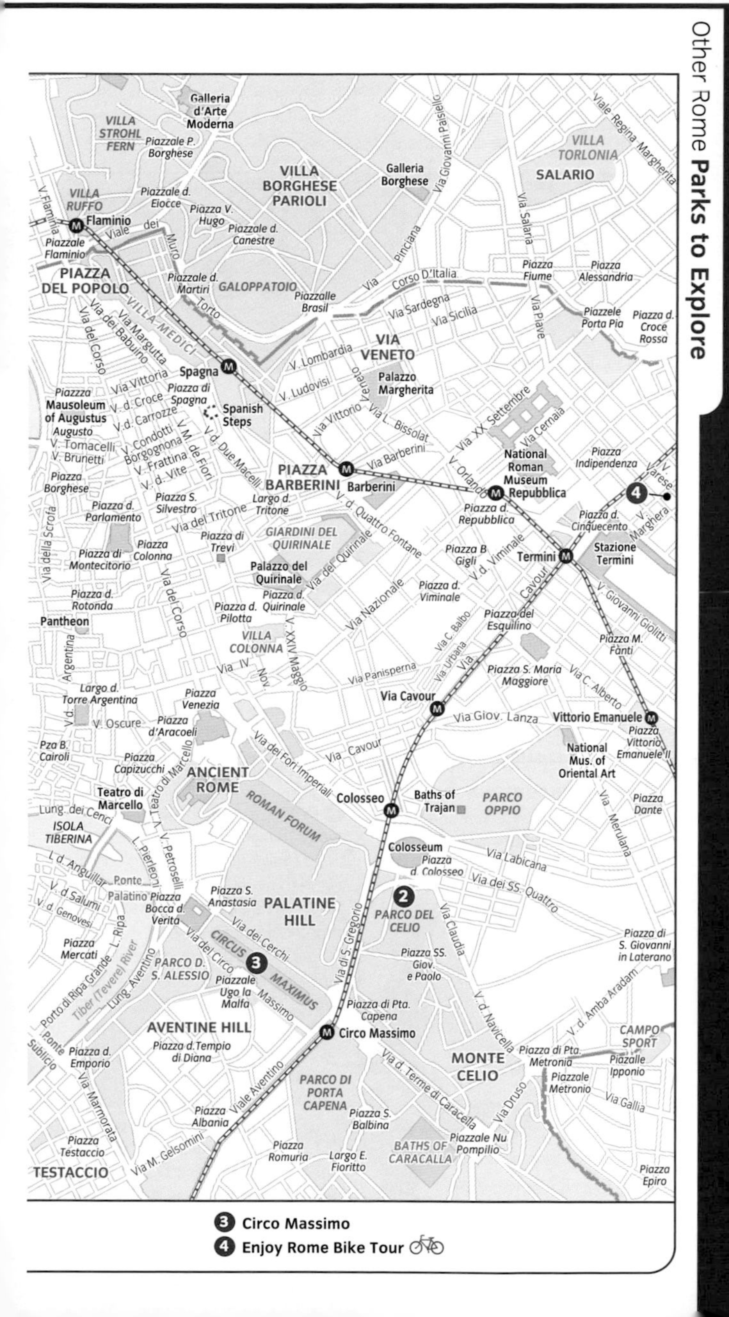
Galleria d'Arte Moderna
VILLA STROHL FERN
Piazzale P. Borghese
VILLA BORGHESE PARIOLI
Galleria Borghese
Via Giovanni Paisiello
Viale Regina Margherita
VILLA TORLONIA
SALARIO
VILLA RUFFO
Piazzale d. Eiocce
Piazza V. Hugo
Piazzale d. Canestre
V. Flaminia
Flaminio
Viale dei Muro Torto
Piazzale Flaminio
Via Pinciana
Via Salaria
PIAZZA DEL POPOLO
Piazzale d. Martiri
GALOPPATOIO
Piazzalle Brasil
Via Corso D'Italia
Piazza Fiume
Piazza Alessandria
VILLA MEDICI
Via del Babuino
Via del Corso
Via Margutta
Via Sardegna
Via Sicilia
Via Piave
Piazzele Porta Pia
Piazza d. Croce Rossa
V. Lombardia
VIA VENETO
Spagna
Via Vittoria
Piazzza
Mausoleum of Augustus
Augusto
Piazza di Spagna
V. d. Croce
V. d. Carrozze
Spanish Steps
V. Ludovisi
Palazzo Margherita
Via Vittorio Veneto
Via L. Bissolat
Via XX Settembre
Via Cernaia
V. Tomacelli
V. Brunetti
V. Condotti
Borgognona
V. Frattina
V. d. Vite
V. M. de Fiori
V. d. Due Macelli
PIAZZA BARBERINI
Barberini
Via Barberini
V. Orlando
National Roman Museum
Repubblica
Piazza Indipendenza
V. Varese
Piazza Borghese
Piazza d. Parlamento
Piazza S. Silvestro
Via del Tritone
Largo d. Tritone
V. d. Quattro Fontane
Piazza d. Repubblica
Piazza d. Cinquecento
V. Marghera
Via della Scrofa
Piazza di Trevi
GIARDINI DEL QUIRINALE
Piazza Colonna
Piazza di Montecitorio
Via del Corso
Palazzo del Quirinale
Via del Quirinale
Piazza B. Gigli
V. d. Viminale
Termini
Stazione Termini
Piazza d. Rotonda
Piazza d. Quirinale
Via Nazionale
Piazza d. Viminale
Cavour
V. Giovanni Giolitti
Pantheon
Piazza d. Pilotta
V. XXIV Maggio
Piazza del Esquilino
VILLA COLONNA
Via C. Balbo
Piazza M. Fanti
Argentina
Via IV Nov.
Via Panisperna
Via Urbana
Via
Piazza S. Maria Maggiore
Via C. Alberto
Largo d. Torre Argentina
Piazza Venezia
Via Cavour
V. d.
V. Oscure
Piazza d'Aracoeli
Via Giov. Lanza
Vittorio Emanuele
Piazza Vittorio Emanuele II
Pza B. Cairoli
Via dei Fori Imperiali
Via Cavour
National Mus. of Oriental Art
Piazza Capizucchi
V. Teatro di Marcello
ANCIENT ROME
Teatro di Marcello
ROMAN FORUM
Colosseo
Baths of Trajan
PARCO OPPIO
Via Merulana
Piazza Dante
Lung. dei Cenci
ISOLA TIBERINA
L. Pierleoni
V. Petroselli
Colosseum
Piazza d. Colosseo
Via Labicana
L. d. Anguillara
Ponte Palatino
Via dei SS. Quattro
V. d. Salumi
V. d. Genovesi
Piazza Bocca d. Verita
Piazza S. Anastasia
PALATINE HILL
PARCO DEL CELIO
Via Claudia
Via dei Cerchi
Via di S. Gregorio
Piazza di S. Giovanni in Laterano
Piazza Mercati
L. Ripa
CIRCUS MAXIMUS
Via del Circo
PARCO D. S. ALESSIO
Piazza SS. Giov. e Paolo
Porto di Ripa Grande
Tiber (Tevere) River
Lung. Aventino
Piazzale Ugo la Malfa
Massimo
V. d. Navicella
V. d. Amba Aradam
Piazza di Pta. Capena
AVENTINE HILL
Circo Massimo
CAMPO SPORT
Ponte Sublicio
Piazza d. Emporio
Piazza d. Tempio di Diana
Via d. Terme di Caracella
MONTE CELIO
Piazza di Pta. Metronia
Piazzalle Ipponio
Viale Aventino
PARCO DI PORTA CAPENA
Piazzale Metronio
Via Gallia
Via Marmorata
Piazza Albania
Piazza S. Balbina
Via Druso
Piazza Testaccio
Via M. Gelsomini
Piazza Romuria
Largo E. Fioritto
BATHS OF CARACALLA
Piazzale Nu Pompilio
TESTACCIO
Piazza Epiro
3 Circo Massimo
4 Enjoy Rome Bike Tour

In addition to the parks and green areas we've mentioned so far in this chapter, other parks we love are Villa Pamphilj, a tourist-free and gargantuan sprawl of woods, lawns, and manicured gardens west of Trastevere; and Villa Celimontana, a beautiful hilltop park a stone's throw from the Colosseum.

Rome's ancient chariot racetrack, the Circo Massimo.

❶ **Villa Pamphilj.** This huge swath of green (455 acres/184 hectares) is where Romans come when they don't want to slum it with tourists at Villa Borghese. Its hilly topography is best suited for serious joggers, but Villa Pamphilj has no shortage of scenic trails for walkers in search of *bel respiro* ("good breathing," the original name of the 17th-c. park). Locals love to bring full-spread picnics here on weekends. A delightful pond teeming with turtles awaits the leftovers. ***Bus: 44, 175, or 870.***

❷ **Villa Celimontana.** Perched atop Celio Hill, just a 5-minute walk south of the Colosseum, the Villa Celimontana park has a bustling kids' play area, limited jogging paths, and a fabulous nighttime jazz festival in summer, where the setting is straight out of *La Dolce Vita*. ***Metro: Colosseo. Bus: 60, 75, 81, or 175. Tram: 3.***

❸ **Circo Massimo.** Everyone loves to ridicule the derelict state of the Circus Maximus, Rome's old chariot racetrack, but there's still something glorious about treading the same earth where chariots once thundered, to the deafening cheers of 300,000 Roman spectators, under the imperial auspices of Palatine Hill. Palatine Hill is where the emperors lived, and the slope you see from here is the spot from which the emperors watched the races at the circus. See how fast you can complete seven laps (one lap is 1,200m/¾ mile), the standard distance for all ancient races. There's no shade, however, and you'll need to watch out for broken beer bottles. ***Metro: Circo Massimo. Bus: 30, 60, 75, 170, or 175. Tram: 3.***

❹ **Enjoy Rome Bike Tour.** If you're thinking about renting a bicycle to tour Rome, keep in mind that trying to figure out where you're going, while also trying to steer clear of potholes and mercurial Roman drivers, is stressful. A great alternative is the bike tour offered by **Enjoy Rome.** They provide bikes, helmets, and an expert guide who will lead you on a scenic route, along the safest streets, to all the important sights. *Via Marghera 8a.* ☎ *06-4451843. www.enjoyrome.com. Call for tour times. Ages 18–40 only. 25€ ages 27–40, 20€ ages 18–26.* ●

The Snake Fountain at Villa Pamphilj.

6 The Best Dining

Dining Best Bets

Best **Lazy Lunch**
★★★ Osteria del Gallo $$ *Vicolo del Montevecchio 27 (p 112)*

Best **Pizza**
★★★ Dar Poeta $ *Vicolo del Bologna 45 (p 110);* and ★★★ La Montecarlo $ *Vicolo Savelli 11 (p 111)*

Best **People-Watching**
★★★ Taverna del Campo $ *Campo de' Fiori 16 (p 114)*

Best **Gourmet Splurge**
★★★ La Pergola $$$$ *Via Cadlolo 101 (p 111)*

Best **Pasta**
★★★ Isidoro $$ *Via di San Giovanni in Laterano 59–63 (p 111)*

Best **Place to Dine with Boozy, Boisterous Locals**
★★ Osteria der Belli $$ *Piazza Sant'Apollonia 9–11 (p 113)*

Best **Paparazzi Haunt**
★★ Due Ladroni $$$ *Piazza Nicosia 24 (p 110)*

Best **Museum Cafe**
★ Caffè delle Arti $$ *Via Gramsci 73–65 (p 108)*

Best **Coffee**
★★★ Bar Sant'Eustachio $ *Piazza di Sant'Eustachio 82 (p 108)*

Best **Gelato**
★★★ San Crispino $ *Via della Panetteria 42 (p 113)*

Best **Value for Quality & Atmosphere**
★★ Maccheroni $$ *Via delle Coppelle 44 (p 112)*

Most **Trendy Scene**
★★★ Supper Club $$$$ *Via de' Nari 14 (p 114)*

Best **Seafood**
★★★ Quinzi e Gabrieli $$$$ *Via delle Coppelle 5 (p 113)*

Dining Tips

In this chapter, we've given you our top recommendations for different cuisine types, price ranges, and levels of formality. However, should you strike out on your own, keep these guidelines in mind:

1. Don't eat at any restaurant where the menu is translated into five languages (or, worse yet, where the menu is simply photographs of spaghetti drowning in red sauce).
2. Avoid restaurants where waitstaff is overly solicitous of passersby. If their restaurant is so great, why do they need to hustle you in off the street?
3. Most restaurants located right on the main piazzas are big-time tourist traps. Stick to the smaller squares and side streets.
4. Do as the Romans do. If you follow the locals (they're the ones who go out after 8pm), you'll be in good shape.

Centro Storico Dining

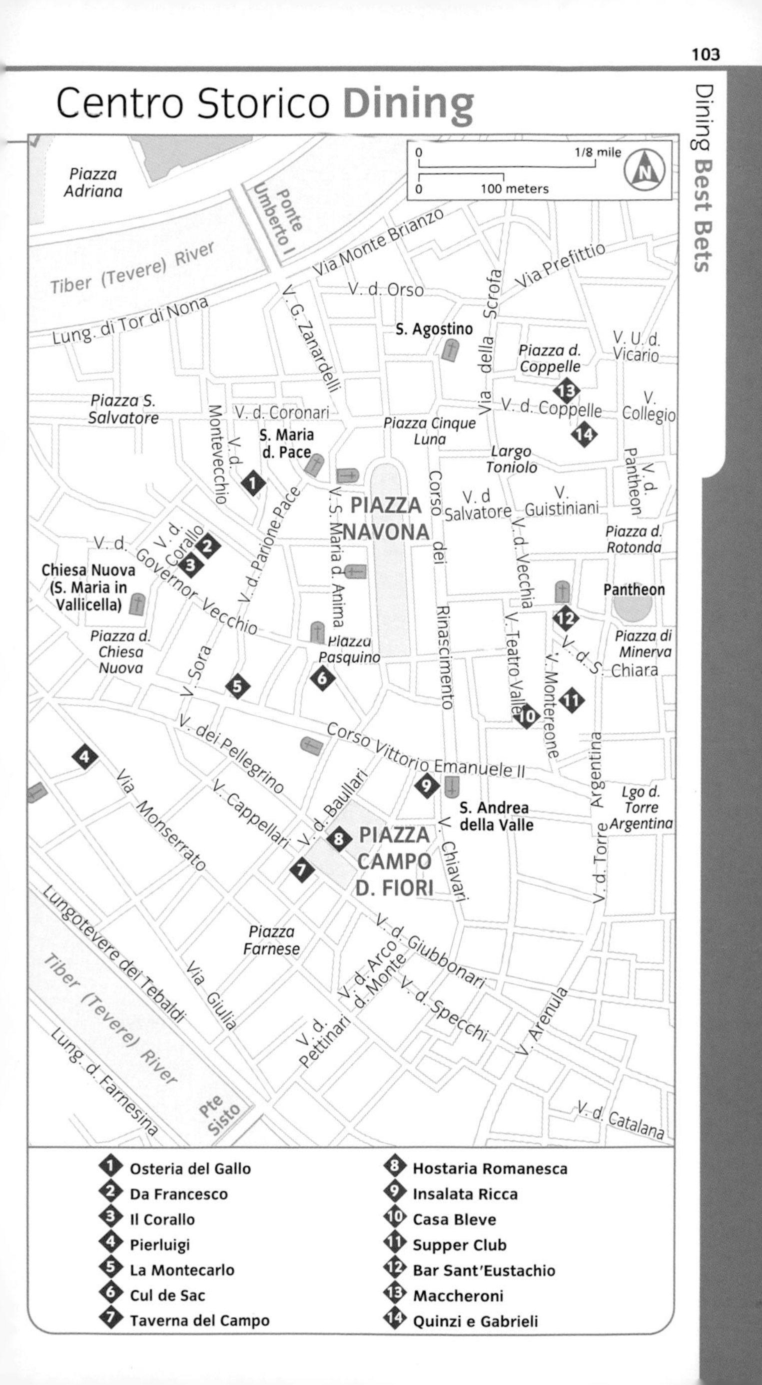

Rome Dining

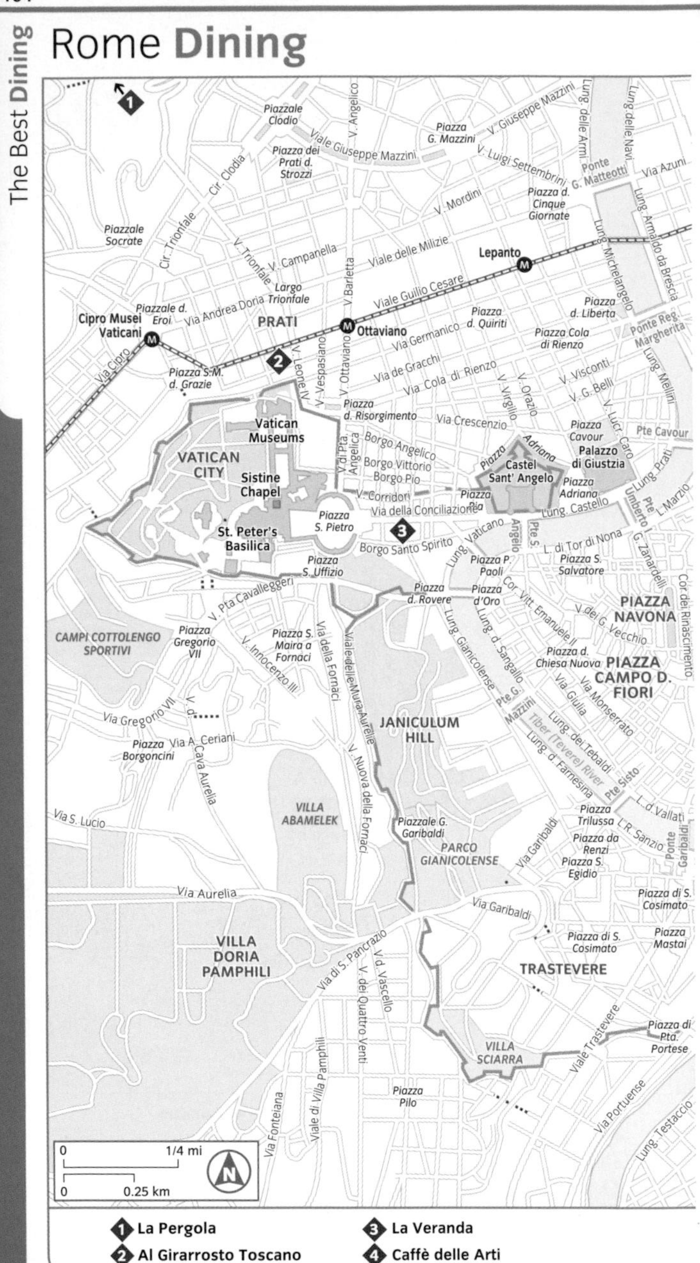

1 La Pergola
2 Al Girarrosto Toscano
3 La Veranda
4 Caffè delle Arti

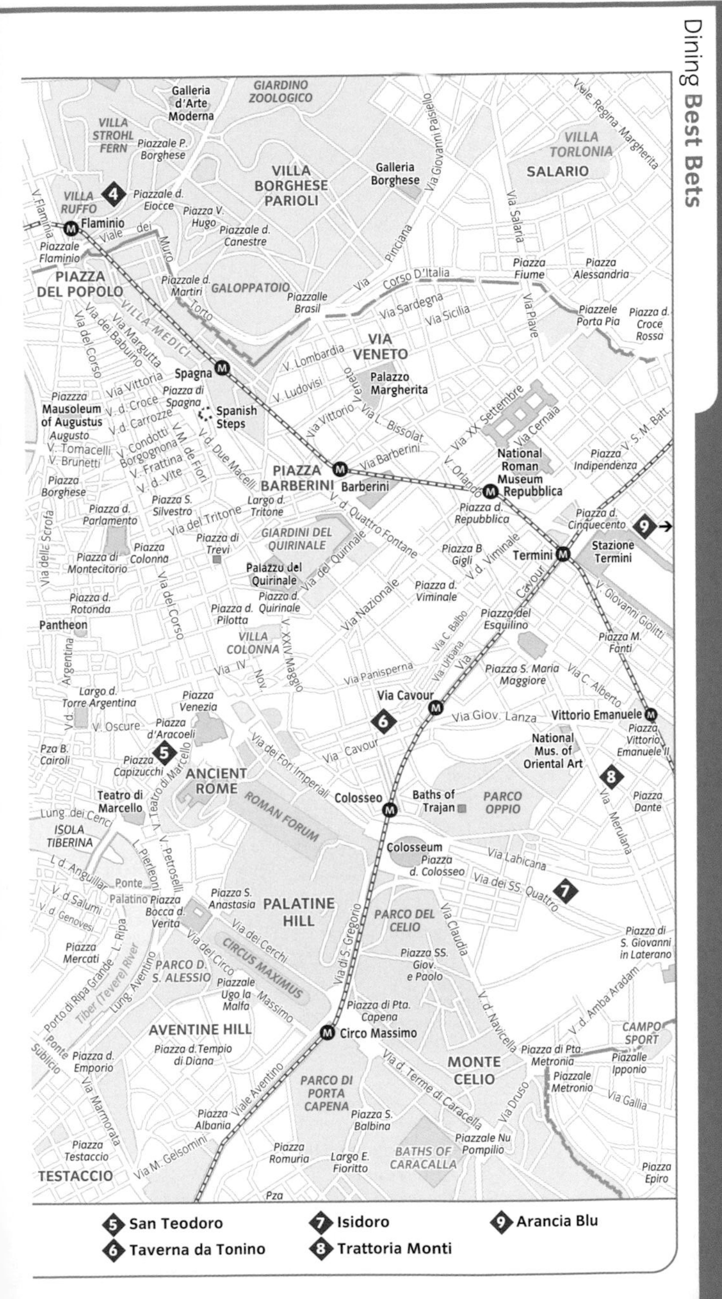
Galleria d'Arte Moderna
GIARDINO ZOOLOGICO
VILLA STROHL FERN
Piazzale P. Borghese
VILLA BORGHESE PARIOLI
Galleria Borghese
Via Giovanni Paisiello
Viale Regina Margherita
VILLA TORLONIA
SALARIO
VILLA RUFFO
Piazzale d. Eiocce
Piazza V. Hugo
Piazzale d. Canestre
Flaminio
V. Flaminia
Viale dei Muro
Piazzale Flaminio
PIAZZA DEL POPOLO
Piazzale d. Martiri
GALOPPATOIO
Torto
Piazzalle Brasil
Via Pinciana
Via Salaria
Piazza Fiume
Piazza Alessandria
Via Corso D'Italia
Via Sardegna
Via Sicilia
Via Piave
Piazzele Porta Pia
Piazza d. Croce Rossa
VILLA MEDICI
Via del Babuino
Via Margutta
Via del Corso
VIA VENETO
V. Lombardia
Spagna
Palazzo Margherita
V. Ludovisi
Via Veneto
Via Vittoria
Piazza di Spagna
Piazzza Mausoleum of Augustus Augusto
V. d. Croce
V. d. Carrozze
Spanish Steps
Via Vittorio
Via L. Bissolat
Via XX Settembre
Via Cernaia
V. Tomacelli
V. Brunetti
V. Condotti
Borgognona
V. Frattina
V. d. Vite
V.M. de Fiori
V. d. Due Macelli
Via Barberini
PIAZZA BARBERINI
Barberini
National Roman Museum
Repubblica
V. Orlando
Piazza Indipendenza
V. S. M. Batt.
Piazza Borghese
Piazza d. Parlamento
Piazza S. Silvestro
Via del Tritone
Largo d. Tritone
V. d. Quattro Fontane
Piazza d. Repubblica
Piazza d. Cinquecento
Via della Scrofa
Piazza di Montecitorio
Piazza Colonna
Piazza di Trevi
GIARDINI DEL QUIRINALE
Via del Quirinale
Piazza B Gigli
V. d. Viminale
Termini
Stazione Termini
Palazzo del Quirinale
Piazza d. Quirinale
Via Nazionale
Piazza d. Viminale
Cavour
V. Giovanni Giolitti
Piazza d. Rotonda
Pantheon
Via del Corso
Piazza d. Pilotta
VILLA COLONNA
V. XXIV Maggio
Via C. Balbo
Via Urbana
Piazza del Esquilino
Piazza M. Fanti
Argentina
Via IV Nov.
Via Panisperna
Piazza S. Maria Maggiore
Via C. Alberto
Largo d. Torre Argentina
Piazza Venezia
Via Cavour
Via Giov. Lanza
Vittorio Emanuele
Piazza Vittorio Emanuele II
V. Oscure
Piazza d'Aracoeli
Via dei Fori Imperiali
National Mus. of Oriental Art
Pza B. Cairoli
Piazza Capizucchi
Via Teatro di Marcello
ANCIENT ROME
Colosseo
Baths of Trajan
PARCO OPPIO
Piazza Dante
Teatro di Marcello
ROMAN FORUM
Via Merulana
Lung. dei Cenci
ISOLA TIBERINA
L. Pierleoni
V. Petroselli
Colosseum
Piazza d. Colosseo
Via Labicana
L. d. Anguillara
Ponte Palatino
Piazza Bocca d. Verita
Via dei SS. Quattro
V. d. Salumi
V. d. Genovesi
Piazza S. Anastasia
PALATINE HILL
PARCO DEL CELIO
Via Claudia
Via dei Cerchi
Piazza di S. Giovanni in Laterano
Piazza Mercati
L. Ripa
Tiber (Tevere) River
Porto di Ripa Grande
Lung. Aventino
PARCO D. S. ALESSIO
Via del Circo Massimo
CIRCUS MAXIMUS
Piazzale Ugo la Malfa
Via di S. Gregorio
Piazza SS. Giov. e Paolo
V. d. Amba Aradam
V. d. Navicella
Piazza di Pta. Capena
AVENTINE HILL
Circo Massimo
CAMPO SPORT
Ponte Sublicio
Piazza d. Emporio
Piazza d. Tempio di Diana
MONTE CELIO
Piazza di Pta. Metronia
Pizalle Ipponio
Piazzale Metronio
Via d. Terme di Caracalla
PARCO DI PORTA CAPENA
Via Gallia
Via Marmorata
Viale Aventino
Piazza Albania
Piazza S. Balbina
Via Druso
Piazzale Nu Pompilio
Piazza Testaccio
Via M. Gelsomini
Piazza Romuria
Largo E. Fioritto
BATHS OF CARACALLA
Piazza Epiro
TESTACCIO
Pza
4
5
6
7
8
9
5 San Teodoro
6 Taverna da Tonino
7 Isidoro
8 Trattoria Monti
9 Arancia Blu

Tridente/Via Veneto Dining

Via Flaminia
Flaminio
V. Washington
Viale dei Muro Torto
Vle Valadier
Piazza V. Hugo
Piazzale d. Canestre
V. d. Magnolie
V. S. Paolo d. Brasile
VILLA BORGHESE PARIOLI
Piazzale Flaminio
PIAZZA DEL POPOLO
GALOPPATOIO
Viale del Galoppatoio
Piazzale Brasil
Porto Pinciana
VILLA MEDICI
Via della Trinita dei Monti
V. Brunetti
Via Margutta
Via dei Babuino
Via del Corso
Via di Ripetta
V. d. P. Pinciana
V. Lombardia
Spagna
VIA VENETO
V. Ludovisi
Via Vittoria
Piazza di Spagna
Trinità dei Monti
Mausoleum of Augustus
Via d. Croce
Via d. Carrozze
Spanish Steps
Via Sistina
V. Liguria
V. Vittorio Veneto
Ponte Cavour
Piazza Augusto
Via Tomacelli
V. Condotti
V. M. de Fiori
V. Brunetti
V. Borgognona
V. d. Due Macelli
V. Fr. Crispi
Piazza Borghese
V. Frattina
PIAZZA BARBERINI
V. d. Clementino
V. d. Leone
V. d. Vite
V. d. Scrofa
Piazza S. Silvestro
Largo d. Tritone
Piazza d. Parlamento
Via del Tritone
V Rasella
V. d. Giardini
V Panetteria
Palazzo di Montecitorio
Trevi Fountain
GIARDINI DEL QUIRINALE
Piazza Colonna
Piazza di Montecitorio
V. Muratte
Piazza di Trevi
Palazzo del Quirinale
V. d. Dataria
V. d. Vergini
Piazza d. Rotonda
Sant' Ignazio
Via del Corso
Piazza d. Quirinale
V. Seminario
Piazza d. Pilotta
V. d. Consulta
Pantheon
S. Maria Sopra Minerva
Piazza di Minerva
Piazza d. Coll. Romano
0 1/8 mile
0 100 meters
N

1. 'Gusto
2. Osteria della Frezza
3. Due Ladroni
4. Opera Unica
5. San Crispino
6. La Terrazza dell'Eden

Trastevere Dining

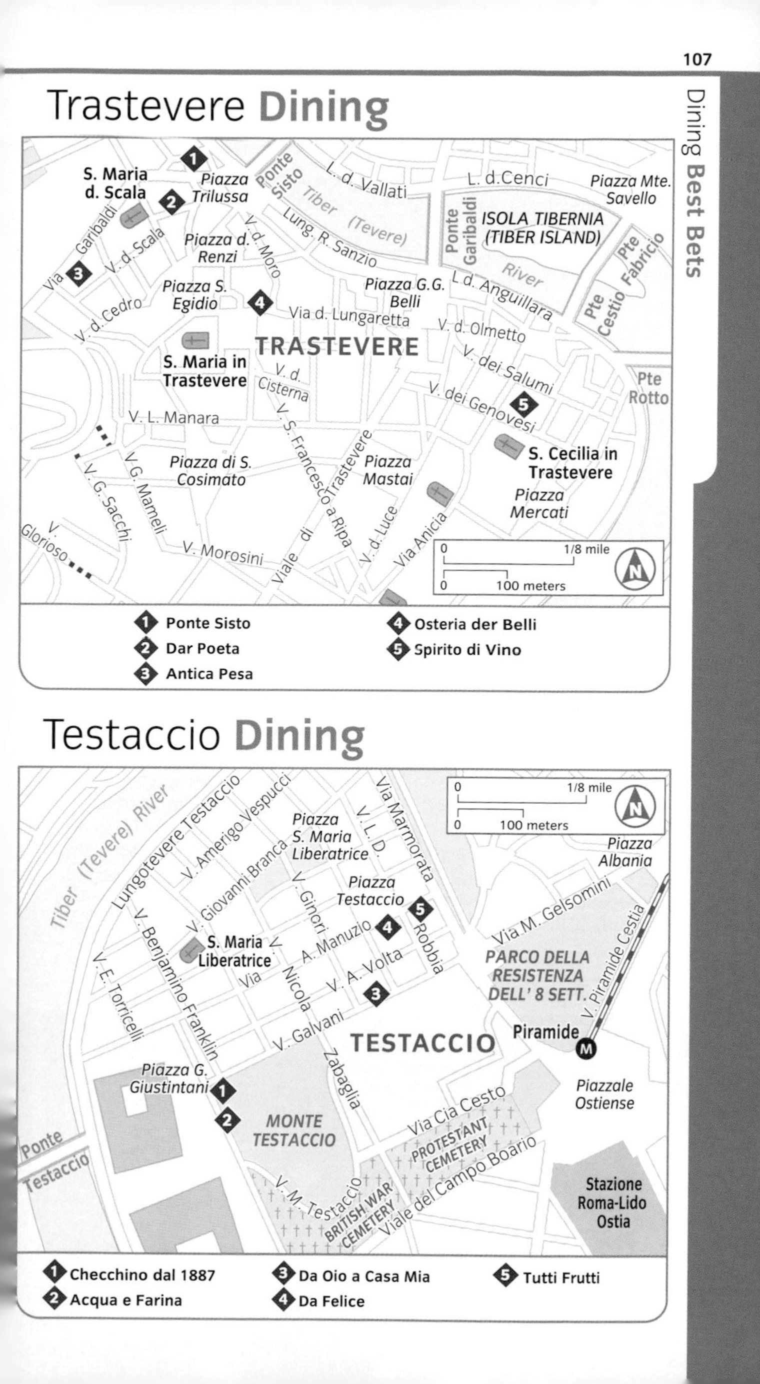

Rome Restaurants, A to Z

★ **Acqua e Farina** TESTACCIO *PIZZA* The dough at this happening nouvelle pizzeria is cut and twisted in creative ways and topped with delicious combos like Gorgonzola and walnuts, or sun-dried tomatoes and goat cheese. *Piazza O. Giustiniani 2 (at Via Galvani).* ☎ *06-5741382. Pizzas 6€–11€. AE, DC, MC, V. Open daily, dinner only. Metro: Piramide. Bus: 23, 75, 95, 170, or 280. Tram: 3. Map p 107.*

★★ **Al Girarrosto Toscano** VATICAN *GRILL* Carnivores go wild for the succulent perfection of these Tuscan-style grilled meats. *Via Germanico 58–60 (at Via Vespasiano).* ☎ *06-39723373. Entrees 8€–18€. AE, DC, MC, V. Open Tues–Sun lunch and dinner. Metro: Ottaviano. Bus: 23 or 492. Tram: 19. Map p 104.*

★★ **Antica Pesa** TRASTEVERE *ROMAN* Refined *signori e signore* trek halfway up the Gianicolo Hill to this charmer with a reliable traditional menu and lovely interior garden, a converted bocce court. *Via Garibaldi 18 (at Via del Mattonato).* ☎ *06-5809236. Entrees 10€–17€. AE, DC, MC, V. Open Mon–Sat 7:30–11pm. Bus: 23, 271, or 280. Map p 107.*

★★ **Arancia Blu** SAN LORENZO *VEGETARIAN* Exquisite, delicious, gourmet preparations (that also happen to be meat-free) are served in a handsome Italian dining room of dark wood furniture, exposed-brick arches, and wine racks galore. *Via dei Latini 55-65 (at Via Arunci).* ☎ *06-4454105. Entrees 10€–18€. No credit cards. Open daily for dinner. Bus: 71 or 492. Map p 104.*

★★★ **Bar Sant'Eustachio** PANTHEON *COFFEE* Its blue, Art Deco neon sign is a beacon for coffee snobs in search of the richest, creamiest brew in the city. *Piazza Sant'Eustachio 82 (south side of square).* ☎ *06-6561309. Coffee 1.50€–3€. No credit cards. Open daily 8:30am–1am. Bus: 30, 40, 62, 64, 70, 87, 116, or 492. Map p 103.*

★ **Caffè delle Arti** VILLA BORGHESE *ITALIAN* Surrounded by trees and the white marble of the modern art gallery, these alfresco tables are perfect for a romantic interlude. The lunch menu ranges from light salads to hearty meat dishes; stop in any time for a coffee, beer, or cocktail. *Via Gramsci 73–75 (off Viale delle Belle Arti).* ☎ *06-32651236. Entrees 9€–18€. AE, DC, MC, V. Open*

A waiter holding a platter of typically colorful Roman fare.

Tues–Sun noon–3pm, 7pm–12:30am; Mon noon–3pm. Tram: 3 or 19. Map p 104.

★★ Casa Bleve PANTHEON *WINE BAR* Lavish spreads of cheeses, meats, olives, and other delicacies at this ambitious *enoteca*-and-more resemble a Renaissance feast. *Via del Teatro Valle 48–49 (off Corso Vittorio Emanuele II). ☎ 06-6865970. Entrees 7€–15€. AE, DC, MC, V. Open Mon–Sat for lunch, Thurs–Sat for dinner. Bus: 30, 40, 62, 64, 70, 87, 116, or 492. Tram: 8. Map p 103.*

★★★ Checchino dal 1887 TESTACCIO *ROMAN* Often mischaracterized as an offal-only joint, this 108-year-old establishment across from Rome's now-defunct abattoir serves wonderful *bucatini all'amatriciana* and veal saltimbocca—as well as hearty plates of, er, heart and other slaughterhouse cast-offs. *Via di Monte Testaccio 30 (at Via Galvani). ☎ 06-5746318. Entrees 16€–30€. AE, DC, MC, V. Open Tues–Sat for dinner. Metro: Piramide. Bus: 23, 95, 170, or 280. Tram: 3. Map p 107.*

★★ Cul de Sac PIAZZA NAVONA *WINE BAR* Cozy and lively, this popular *enoteca* has a mind-boggling selection of cheeses and cold cuts, savory Mediterranean salads and hors d'oeuvres, and wines by the glass or bottle. *Piazza Pasquino 73 (at Via del Governo Vecchio). ☎ 06-68801094. Entrees 6€–13€. MC, V. Open Tues–Sun for lunch, daily for dinner. Bus: 40, 62, 64, 70, 87, or 492. Map p 103.*

★ Da Felice TESTACCIO *ROMAN* Often compared with *Seinfeld*'s "soup Nazi" for his arbitrary refusal to seat some, Felice has now put his kinder, gentler son in charge of the no-frills dining room at this hearty trat. If you can get a table, you won't leave hungry. *Via Mastro Giorgio 29 (at Piazza Testaccio). ☎ 06-5745800. Entrees 6€–13€. No credit cards. Open Mon–Sat for lunch and dinner. Bus: 23, 75, 95, 170, or 280. Tram: 3. Map p 107.*

★★ Da Francesco PIAZZA NAVONA *PIZZA* As popular as La Montecarlo (see below) but with an older clientele and fewer tables, cozy Francesco has great pizza and low prices—and often excruciatingly long waits. *Piazza del Fico 29 (at Via del Corallo). ☎ 06-6864009. Pizzas 5€–9€. No credit cards. Open daily for dinner, Wed–Mon for lunch. Bus: 40, 62, or 64. Map p 103.*

★ Da Oio a Casa Mia TESTACCIO *ROMAN* *Cucina romana* at its most authentic—affable service, nonexistent decor, and heavy fare. Watch for nightly specials of *coratella* (lamb heart, liver, and spleen) and *animelle* (mixed calf glands). *Via Galvani 43–45 (at Via Mastro Giorgio). ☎ 06-5782680. Entrees 7€–14€. No credit cards. Open Mon–Sat for dinner. Bus: 23, 75, 170, or 280. Tram: 3. Map p 107.*

★★★ Dar Poeta TRASTEVERE *PIZZA* Throw carb-caution to the wind at this hard-to-find, eternally packed pizzeria. Gorge yourself on flavor-packed bruschette and pizzas, but save room for the heavenly

The charming facade of the restaurant Checchino dal 1887.

Platter of traditional Roman antipasto.

Nutella-and-ricotta dessert calzone. *Vicolo del Bologna 45 (at Piazza della Scala). ☎ 06-5880516. Pizzas 7€–11€. AE, MC, V. Open daily for dinner only. Bus: 23, 271, or 280. Map p 107.*

★★ **Due Ladroni** PIAZZA DEL POPOLO *ITALIAN* Italian gossip mags always feature a few grainy photos of celebs dining at this upscale but unpretentious restaurant, where standard fare is solid, and waiters have the tip-enhancing quality of treating you as if you might be famous. *Piazza Nicosia 24 (off Via di Ripetta). ☎ 06-6896299. Entrees 12€–22€. AE, DC, MC, V. Open Mon–Sat for lunch and dinner. Bus: 87, 280, 492, or 628. Map p 106.*

Patrons enjoying pizza and drinks at Dar Poeta in Trastevere.

★★ **'Gusto** PIAZZA DEL POPOLO *CREATIVE ITALIAN/PIZZA* There's always a crowd of well-groomed Roman scenesters at this modern, warehouse-y eatery in a Fascist-era building. The ristorante requires reservations and is more expensive than the equally buzzing pizzeria. *Piazza Augusto Imperatore 9. ☎ 06-3226273. Entrees 9€–22€. AE, DC, MC, V. Open Tues–Sun for lunch and dinner. Metro: Flaminio or Spagna. Bus: 913. Map p 106.*

★ **Hostaria Romanesca** CAMPO DE' FIORI *ROMAN* Recommended mostly for its ringside seats on the piazza, Romanesca does dependable Roman fare, including a gloriously fatty *pollo ai peperoni* (stewed chicken with peppers). *Campo de' Fiori 40 (east side of square). ☎ 06-6864024. Entrees 8€–14€. No credit cards. Open Tues–Sun for lunch and dinner. Bus: 30, 40, 62, 64, 70, 87, 116, 492, or 571. Tram: 8. Map p 103.*

★ **Il Corallo** PIAZZA NAVONA *ITALIAN/PIZZA* The excellent pizza and pasta at this straightforward *osteria* are a blessed bargain, attracting more locals than tourists. In warm weather, go for a table outside on the cobblestones. *Via del Corallo 10 (at Via del Governo Vecchio). ☎ 06-68307703. Entrees 6€–12€. AE, MC, V. Open daily for lunch and dinner. Bus: 40, 62, or 64. Map p 103.*

★★ **Insalata Ricca** CAMPO DE' FIORI *SALADS* The "rich salads" at this wildly popular lunch spot are laden with everything from lobster meat to hearts of palm to fresh mozzarella. Other branches around town are no match for the original. *Largo Chiavari 85 (at Corso Vittorio Emanuele II). ☎ 06-68803656. Entrees 7€–15€. AE, DC, MC, V. Open daily for lunch and dinner. Bus: 30, 40, 62, 64, 70, 87, 116, 492, or 571. Tram: 8. Map p 103.*

★★★ **Isidoro** ANCIENT ROME *PASTA* We can't think of a more triumphant place to fall off the Atkins wagon than at this friendly *osteria*, whose fantastic *assaggini misti* (pasta sampling menu) is the stuff of Roman legend. *Via di San Giovanni in Laterano 59–63 (at Piazza San Clemente). ☎ 06-7008266. Entrees 8€–14€. Open daily for lunch and dinner. Metro: Colosseo. Bus: 60, 85, 87, 175, 271, or 571. Tram: 3. Map p 104.*

★★★ **La Montecarlo** PIAZZA NAVONA *PIZZA* Dirt-cheap and immensely popular with young Romans, Montecarlo feels like a big party: Efficient, flirtatious servers sling piping-hot, thin-crusted pies on metal pans, and the wine and beer flow freely. *Vicolo Savelli 11 (at Corso Vittorio Emanuele II). ☎ 06-6861877. Pizzas 5€–8.50€. AE, DC, MC, V. Open Tues–Sun for lunch and dinner. Bus: 40, 64, or 571. Map p 103.*

★★★ **La Pergola** MONTE MARIO/WESTERN SUBURBS *MEDITERRANEAN* Celebrity chef Heinz Beck's always-perfect, creative cuisine employs the full bounty of the region, from fish to seasonal vegetables to rare fowl and game. With dramatic views, good-looking staff, and two Michelin stars, this is one of the best meals you'll have in your life—and it's priced accordingly. Jacket required. *Via Cadlolo 101 (at the Cavalieri Hilton). ☎ 06-35092211. Reserve at least 1 month in advance. 85€ and up per person. AE, DC, MC, V. Open Tues–Sat for dinner only; closed part of Jan and Aug. Map p 104.*

★★★ **La Terrazza dell'Eden** VIA VENETO *MEDITERRANEAN* Chef Adriano Cavagnini's haute

Typical Roman formaggio *(cheese) shop.*

Mediterranean *cucina moderna* and Michelin star attract gourmands; the swank setting and fab views attract the jet set. ***Via Ludovisi 49 (at the Hotel Eden). ☎ 06-478121. Entrees 35€–50€. AE, DC, MC, V. Open daily 12:30–2:30pm, 7:30–10:30pm. Metro: Spagna. Bus: 52, 53, 63, or 116. Map p 106.***

★★ **La Veranda** VATICAN *CREATIVE ITALIAN* With exquisite dishes like *tonnarelli* with ricotta and cinnamon, this upscale, frescoed trat is a favorite of the Vatican press corps and visiting cardinals. ***Borgo Santo Spirito 73 (at the Hotel Columbus). ☎ 06-6872973. Entrees 13€–28€. AE, DC, MC, V. Open daily for lunch and dinner. Bus: 23, 40, 62, 64, or 271. Map p 106.***

★★ **Maccheroni** PANTHEON *ITALIAN* Popular with Roman scenesters, this is also one of the best dining values in Rome, offering simple but perfectly executed dishes (like pasta *all'amatriciana* and chicken *alla cacciatora*) at humane prices. ***Via delle Coppelle 44 (at Via degli Spagnoli). ☎ 06-68307895. Entrees 8€–14€. AE, DC, MC, V. Open Tues–Sun for dinner only. Bus: 30, 62, 70, 81, 87, 116, or 492. Map p 103.***

★ **Opera Unica** SPANISH STEPS *PIZZA* *Mozzarella di bufala* adds the Midas touch to almost everything on the menu at this intimate and refined bi-level joint. The *fiori di zucca* pizza is especially nice. ***Via del Leone 23 (at Largo Fontanella Borghese). ☎ 06-68809927. Pizzas 6€–11€. AE, DC, MC, V. Open daily for lunch and dinner. Map p 106.***

★★★ **Osteria del Gallo** PIAZZA NAVONA *ITALIAN* This lovely little trat on a quiet *centro storico* alley was made for languorous lunching. Menu standouts include the pecorino cheese plate with fig marmalade, and the ravioli with porcini. ***Vicolo di Montevecchio 27 (at Via della Pace). ☎ 06/687-3781. Entrees 9€–17€. AE, MC, V. Open Mon–Sat for dinner, Tues–Sun for lunch. Bus: 30, 70, 87, or 492. Map p 103.***

★★ **Osteria della Frezza** PIAZZA DEL POPOLO *CREATIVE/ WINE BAR* This hip offshoot of 'Gusto offers *cicchetti* (small plates

Pasta bolognese, pasta with a meat and tomato sauce, with wine.

The classic sauce for pasta carbonara, the quintessential Roman dish, is made with eggs, bacon, and butter.

of hot food), hundreds of cheeses, and top-notch wine. Stick to the front salon—where the action is. ***Via della Frezza 16 (at Via della Corea). ☎ 06-3226273. Entrees 10€–18€. AE, DC, MC, V. Open daily for lunch and dinner. Bus: 81, 87, 280, 492, 628, or 913. Map p 106.***

★★ **Osteria der Belli** TRASTEVERE *SARDINIAN/SEAFOOD* Proprietor Leo keeps us happy with a knockout sauté of clams and mussels, spaghetti *alla pescatora,* and grilled swordfish. The energetic indoor-outdoor spot gets especially lively on Friday nights, when boozy old-timers settle in for their fish fix. ***Piazza Sant'Apollonia 9–11 (at Via della Lungaretta). ☎ 06-5803782. Entrees 8€–13€. AE, MC, V. Open Tues–Sun for lunch and dinner. Bus: 23, 271, 280, 780, or H. Tram: 8. Map p 107.***

★★★ **Quinzi e Gabrieli** PANTHEON *SEAFOOD* Local VIPs and visiting movie stars come here for the best (and most expensive) fish, crustaceans, and shellfish in town. ***Via delle Coppelle 5 (at Via degli Spagnoli). ☎ 06-6879389. Entrees 20€–35€. AE, DC, MC, V. Open Mon–Sat for lunch and dinner. Bus: 30, 70, 87, 116, or 492. Map p 103.***

★★ **Pierluigi** CAMPO DE' FIORI *ITALIAN* Popular with older, well-heeled locals and tourists, this trusty indoor/outdoor trat does a mean octopus *soppressata* and *tagliata di manzo* (tender beef strips on a bed of rucola). ***Piazza de' Ricci 144 (at Via Monserrato). ☎ 06-6861302. Entrees 8€–18€. AE, DC, MC, V. Open Tues–Sun for lunch and dinner. Bus: 23, 40, 64, 116, 271, 280, or 571. Map p 103.***

★ **Ponte Sisto** TRASTEVERE *ROMAN/SEAFOOD* With long, communal tables and red-check tablecloths, this bustling and well-priced joint is great for groups. The seafood pastas are outstanding. ***Via di Ponte Sisto 80 (at Piazza Trilussa). ☎ 06-5883411. Entrees 8€–13€. AE, MC, V. Open daily for lunch and dinner. Bus: 23, 271, or 280. Map p 107.***

★★★ **San Crispino** TREVI FOUNTAIN *GELATO* Seriously yummy, laboratory-like gelateria with a strict no-cone policy. ***Via della Panetteria 42 (at Via del Lavatore). ☎ 06-6793924. 3.50€–7€. No credit cards. Open Wed–Mon noon–12:30am. Metro: Barberini. Bus: 52, 53, 62, 63, 95, 175, or 492. Map p 106.***

★★ **San Teodoro** ANCIENT ROME *ITALIAN/SEAFOOD* The evocative surroundings of the Forum and Palatine are enough to make an outdoor meal here worthwhile; that the cuisine is first-rate only adds to the rapture. ***Via dei Fienili 49–51 (at Piazza della Consolazione). ☎ 06-6780933. Entrees 16€–28€. AE, DC, MC, V. Open daily for lunch and dinner. Bus: 30, 95,or 170. Map p 104.***

★★ **Spirito di Vino** TRASTEVERE *ROMAN* In a medieval synagogue atop a 2nd-century-street, the Catalani family does exceptional modern and ancient Roman cuisine (like *maiale alla mazio,* a favorite pork dish of Julius Caesar's) and other plates as warm and comforting as

Gelato lovers on a Rome street.

the ambience. ***Via dei Genovesi 31 (at Vicolo dell'Atleta). ☎ 06-5896689. Entrees 10€–22€. AE, DC, MC, V. Open Mon–Sat for dinner only. Bus: 23, 271, 280, 780, or H. Tram: 8. Map p 107.***

★★★ **Supper Club** PANTHEON *INTERNATIONAL* Recline and dine among statuesque bare-chested waiters, lounge music, and white interiors, at this fabulously sensual, totally European space. ***Viade' Nari 14. ☎ 06-68807207. Prix fixe 75€. AE, DC, MC, V. Open Tues–Sun for dinner only. Bus: 30, 40, 62, 64, 70, 87, 116, 492, or 57. Tram: 8. Map p 103.***

★ **Taverna da Tonino** ANCIENT ROME *ROMAN* Sink your teeth into succulent roast lamb and other hearty *secondi* at this inexpensive, homey trat near the Forum. Come early or be prepared to wait. ***Via Madonna dei Monti 79 (at Via dell' Agnello). ☎ 06-4745325. Entrees 6€–12€. No credit cards. Open Mon–Sat for lunch and dinner. Metro: Cavour. Bus: 60, 75, 85, 87, or 175. Map p 104.***

★★★ **Taverna del Campo** CAMPO DE' FIORI *CAFE/WINE BAR* This trendy lunch and *aperitivo* spot on Campo de' Fiori has terrific, garlicky sandwiches, cheap cocktails and *vino* by the glass, and free peanuts. Snag a front-row table, don your fashionista sunglasses, and watch the pageant go by. ***Campo de' Fiori 16 (at Via dei Baullari). ☎ 06-6874402. Sandwiches 4.50€–6€. No credit cards. Open Tues–Sun 8am–1am. Bus: 30, 40, 62, 64, 70, 87, 492, or 571. Map p 103.***

★★ **Trattoria Monti** ESQUILINO *REGIONAL/MARCHE* This cozy trat run by the earnest Camerucci family serves outstanding, hearty cuisine from the Marche region—try the rabbit-and-potato casserole and the *flan di parmigiano*. ***Via di San Vito 13A (at Via Merulana). ☎ 06-4466573. Entrees 7€–13€. AE, DC, MC, V. Open Tues–Sat for dinner, Sun lunch only. Metro: Vittorio. Bus: 714. Map p 104.***

★★ **Tutti Frutti** TESTACCIO *CREATIVE ITALIAN* Don't be thrown by the smoothie-joint name—this Southern Italian "food club" with wonderful pizzelles and earnest servers is a treasure. ***Via Luca della Robbia 3A. ☎ 06-5757902. Entrees 9€–15€. MC, V. Closed Mon. Metro: Piramide. Bus: 23, 30, 75, 95, 170, or 280. Tram: 3. Map p 107.*** ●

7 The Best Nightlife

Nightlife Best Bets

Best **Bar for Getting Wasted on 2€ Glasses of Wine**
★★★ Vineria Reggio, *Campo de' Fiori 15 (p 122)*

Best **People-Watching**
★★★ Taverna del Campo, *Campo de' Fiori 16 (p 122)*

Most **Romantic**
★★ La Terrazza dell'Eden, *Via Ludovisi 49 (p 121)*

Best **Pub**
★★ Shamrock, *Via del Colosseo 1 (p 124);* and ★ Fiddler's Elbow, *Via dell'Olmata 43 (p 124)*

Best ***Aperitivo* Scene**
★ BarBar, *Via Crescenzio 18 (p 121)*

Best **Summer Party**
★★★ La Terrazza dell'Eur, *Piazzale Kennedy (p 123)*

Best **Lounge for the In-Crowd**
★★★ Bloom, *Via del Teatro Pace 29–30 (p 121)*

Best **Frat Party alla Romana**
★★ Trinity College, *Via del Collegio Romano 6 (p 124)*

Best **Club for Non-Clubbers**
★★★ La Maison, *Vicolo dei Granari 4 (p 123);* and ★★ Piper, *Via Tagliamento 9 (p 123)*

Best **Live Music**
★★★ Big Mama, *Vicolo di San Francesco a Ripa 18 (p 123)*

Best **Locals' Scene Worth the Trek**
★★ Chioschetto di Ponte Milvio, *Piazzale del Ponte Milvio 44 (p 121)*

Best **Gay Disco**
★★ Alibi, *Via di Monte Testaccio 40–47 (p 123)*

Best **Bar for Aspiring Astronauts**
★★ Etò, *Via Galvani 46 (p 121)*

You can listen to live jazz at the Alexander Platz Jazz Club, near the Vatican.

Centro Storico Nightlife

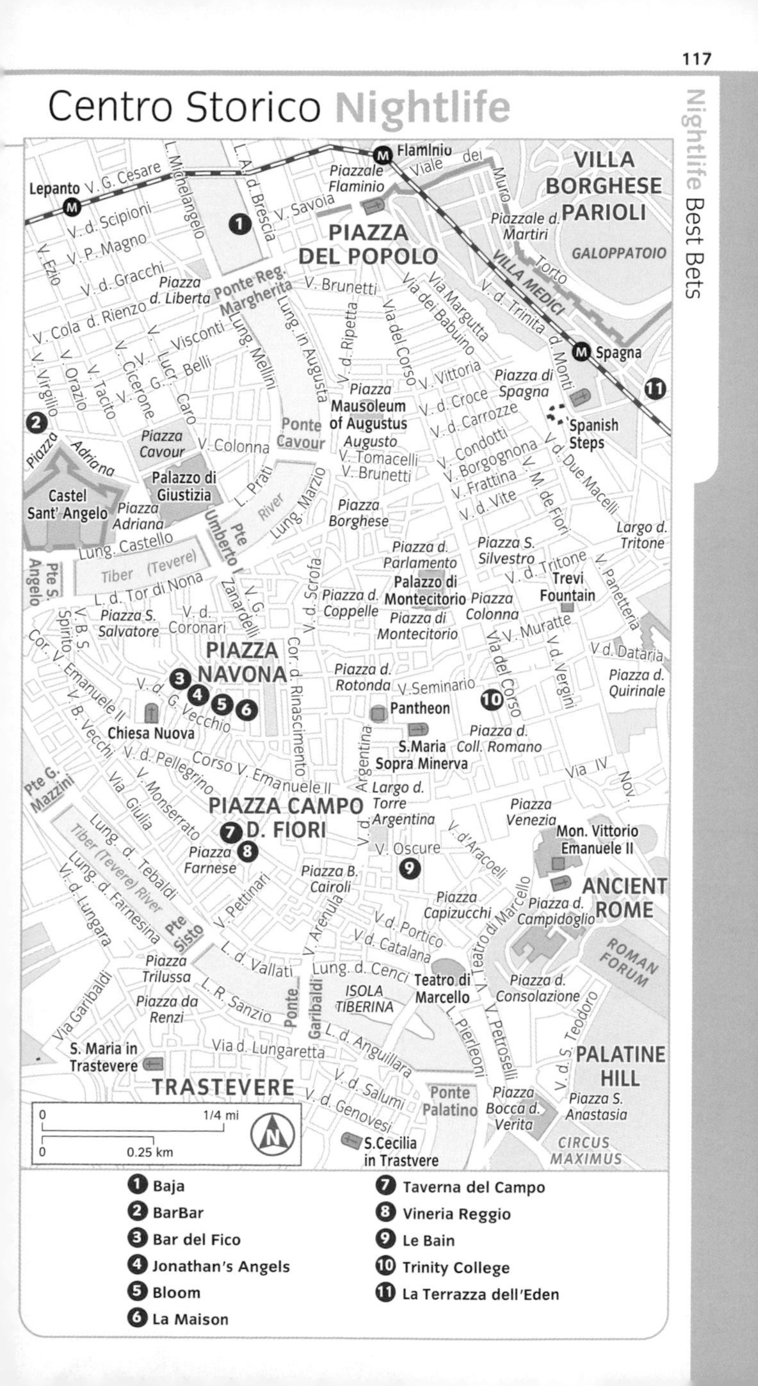

1 Baja
2 BarBar
3 Bar del Fico
4 Jonathan's Angels
5 Bloom
6 La Maison
7 Taverna del Campo
8 Vineria Reggio
9 Le Bain
10 Trinity College
11 La Terrazza dell'Eden

Rome Nightlife

0 1/4 mi
0 0.25 km
N
Piazza d. Fante
L. Oberdan
Viale Tiziano
Piazza Bainsizza
Circo. Clodia
Ponte d. Risorgimento
Lung. delle Armi
Lung. delle Navi
Piazzale Clodio
V. Angelico
Piazza G. Mazzini
V. Giuseppe Mazzini
Viale Giuseppe Mazzini
Piazza dei Prati d. Strozzi
V. Luigi Settembrini
Ponte G. Matteotti
Via Azuni
Cir. Clodia
Piazza d. Cinque Giornate
V. Mordini
Lung. Armaldo da Brescia
Piazzale Socrate
Cir. Trionfale
V. Trionfale
V. Campanella
Viale delle Milizie
Lepanto
Lung. Michelangelo
V. Barletta
Largo Trionfale
Viale Guilio Cesare
Piazza d. Liberta
Piazzale d. Eroi
Via Andrea Doria
Cipro Musei Vaticani
PRATI
Ottaviano
Piazza d. Quiriti
Ponte Reg. Margherita
Via Germanico
Piazza Cola di Rienzo
Via Cipro
V. Leone IV
V. Vespasiano
V. Ottaviano
Via de Gracchi
Lung. Mellini
Piazza S.M. d. Grazie
Via Cola di Rienzo
V. Visconti
V. Virgilio
V. Orazio
V. G. Belli
Piazza d. Risorgimento
Via Crescenzio
V. Lucr. Caro
Vatican Museums
Piazza Cavour
Pte Cavour
VATICAN CITY
V. di Pta. Angelica
Borgo Angelico
Adriana
Palazzo di Giustzia
Borgo Vittorio
Castel Sant' Angelo
Sistine Chapel
Borgo Pio
Piazza Adriana
Lung. Prati
V. Corridori
Piazza Pia
Lung. Castello
Pte Umberto I
L. Marzio
Piazza S. Pietro
Via della Conciliazione
St. Peter's Basilica
Borgo Santo Spirito
Lung. Vaticano
Angelo
Pte S.
L. di Tor di Nona
Piazza P. Paoli
Piazza S. Salvatore
G. Zanardelli
Piazza S. Uffizio
V. Pta Cavalleggeri
Piazza d. Rovere
Piazza d'Oro
Cor. Vitt. Emanuele II
PIAZZA NAVONA
Cor. dei Rinascimento
V. d. G. Vecchio
CAMPI COTTOLENGO SPORTIVI
Piazza Gregorio VII
Piazza S. Maira a Fornaci
Via della Fornaci
Viale delle Mura Aurelie
Lung. Gianicolense
Lung. d. Sangallo
Piazza d. Chiesa Nuova
PIAZZA CAMPO D. FIORI
V. Innocenzo III
Via Giulia
Via Monserrato
Via Gregorio VII
V. d.
Pte G. Mazzini
JANICULUM HILL
Tiber (Tevere) River
Lung. dei Tebaldi
Piazza Borgoncini
Via A. Ceriani
Cava Aurelia
Lung. d. Farnesina
Pte Sisto
V. Nuova della Fornaci
VILLA ABAMELEK
Piazza Trilussa
L. d. Vallati
Via S. Lucio
Piazzale G. Garibaldi
Via Garibaldi
Piazza da Renzi
L. R. Sanzio
Ponte Garibaldi
PARCO GIANICOLENSE
Piazza S. Egidio
Piazza di S. Cosimato
Via Aurelia
Via Garibaldi
VILLA DORIA PAMPHILI
Via di S. Pancrazio
Piazza di S. Cosimato
Piazza Mastai
V. d. Vascello
V. dei Quattro Venti
TRASTEVERE
Pamphili
VILLA SCIARRA
Viale Trastevere
Piazza di Pta. Portese

1. Chioschetto di Ponte Milvio
2. Brunswick Café
3. Piper
4. Alien
5. Alexanderplatz Jazz Club
6. Fonclea

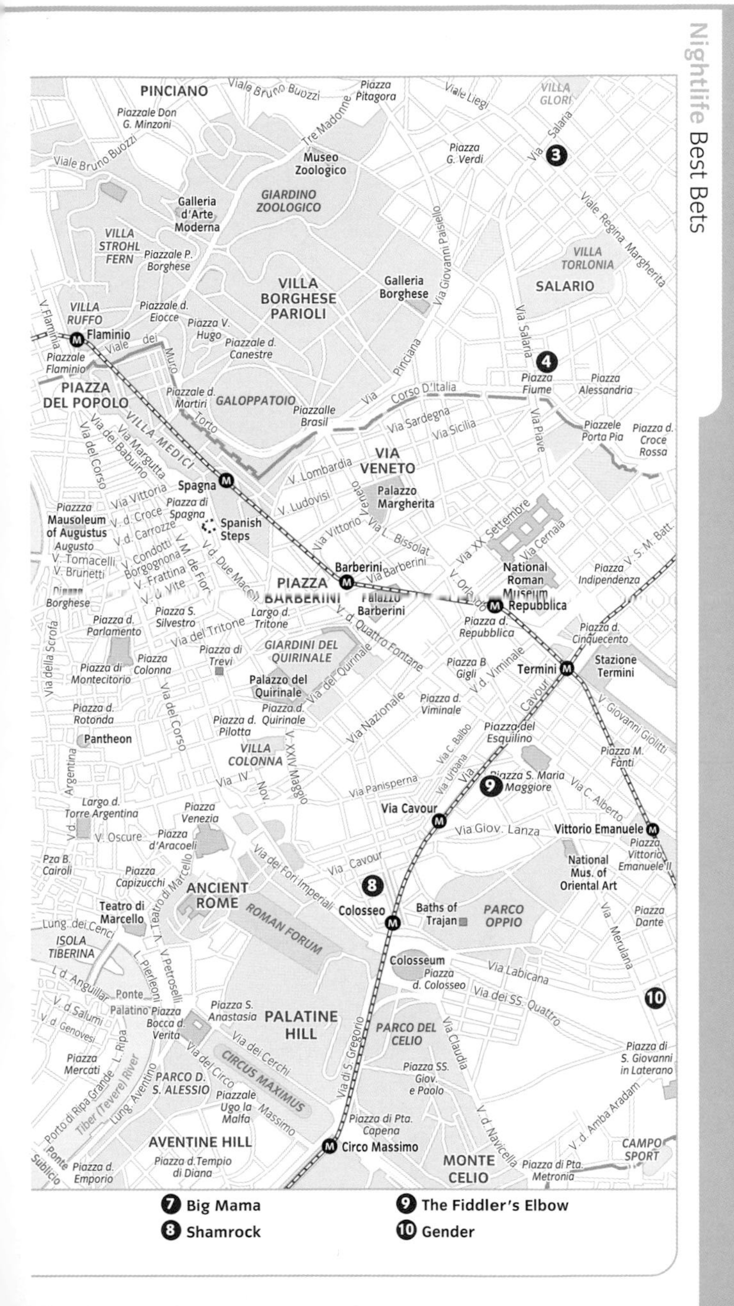

7 Big Mama
8 Shamrock
9 The Fiddler's Elbow
10 Gender

Testaccio/Ostiense Nightlife

Roma di Notte: The city all lit up for the evening.

Bars & Lounges

★ **BarBar** VATICAN The hot spot in Rome for an indoor *aperitivo*—its multiple rooms buzz with people and energy, although Sunday nights can be a bit too crowded. ***Via Ovidio 17 (at Via Crescenzio).*** ☎ ***06-68308435. Bus: 87 or 492. Map p 117.***

★★★ **Bar del Fico** PIAZZA NAVONA *Fico* means fig, but it's also Roman slang for "cool." And, when in doubt, the cool people in Rome make their way here. Snag an outside table below the namesake tree, and you'll be mingling with the eclectic, always stylish crowd in no time. ***Piazza del Fico 26–28 (at Via della Fossa).*** ☎ ***06-6865205. Bus: 30, 40, 62, 64, 70, 87, 492, or 571. Map p 117.***

★★★ **Bloom** PIAZZA NAVONA After dinner, this restaurant morphs into an ultra-cool Art Deco cocktail joint for good-looking 20- and 30-somethings. Bar opens to non-diners after 11:30pm. Cheaper drinks and heartier partyers on Monday. ***Via del Teatro Pace 29–30 (at Via del Governo Vecchio).*** ☎ ***06-68802029. Bus: 30, 40, 62, 64, 70, 87, 492, or 571. Map p 117.***

★★ **Chioschetto di Ponte Milvio** NORTHERN SUBURBS Take a cab to this surprisingly hip, grassy, gravelly riverside spot, where the hot young things of upscale *Roma nord* congress nightly at plastic tables for coffee, beer, or the signature *mojito*. ***Piazzale del Ponte Milvio 44 (at Lungotevere Maresciallo Diaz).*** ☎ ***06-3333461. Tram: 2 from Metro Flaminio. Map p 118.***

★★ **Etò** TESTACCIO If you've ever dreamed of partying in a space shuttle, look no further than this futuristic-feeling bi-level lounge/disco. The Tomorrowland motif is even more fun after a few drinks. ***Via Galvani 46 (at Via Zabaglia).*** ☎ ***06-5748268. Metro: Piramide. Bus: 23, 30, 75, 95, 170, or 280. Tram: 3. Map p 120.***

★ **Jonathan's Angels** PIAZZA NAVONA Fantastically kitschy, frescolike photo collages of owner Nino (aka Jonathan) and his kids (the angels) in motorcycle regalia cover the walls of this mostly touristy cocktail bar, famous for its secret-garden toilets. ***Via della Fossa 16 (at Via di Parione).*** ☎ ***06-6893426. Bus: 30, 40, 62, 64, 70, 87, 492, or 571. Map p 117.***

★★ **La Terrazza dell'Eden** VIA VENETO For lovers only—the view over rooftops and church domes from this old-world bar, on the sixth floor of the elegant Hotel Eden, are especially swoon-worthy at sunset.

An evening of eating and drinking on the Piazza Santa Maria.

Via Ludovisi 49 (at Via di Porta Pinciana). ☎ 06-47812752. Metro: Spagna. Bus: 62, 63, or 116. Map p 117.

★★ **Le Bain** PIAZZA VENEZIA Recline in a plush banquette or armchair, sip a cocktail, and observe the Eurotrash species in its natural habitat—a sexy but nebulous lounge/restaurant/art gallery space with chill-out music. *Via delle Botteghe Oscure 32A–33. ☎ 06-6865673. www.lebain.it. Bus: 30, 40, 62, 64, 70, 87, 492, or 571. Map p 117.*

★ **Ombre Rosse** TRASTEVERE Neighborhood cafe by day, low-key outdoor cocktail spot by night, great for people-watching. *Piazza Sant'Egidio 12 (off Via della Scala). ☎ 06-5884155. Bus: 23, 271, or 280. Tram: 8. Map p 14.*

★★★ **Taverna del Campo** CAMPO DE' FIORI Roman hipsters ebb and flow through its outdoor tables from the *aperitivo* hour (6–7pm) till closing (2am), leaving peanut shells in their wake. *Campo de' Fiori 16 (at Via Baullari). ☎ 06-6874402. Bus: 30, 40, 62, 64, 70, 87, 116, or 492. Tram: 8. Map p 117.*

★★★ **Vineria Reggio** CAMPO DE' FIORI Night after night, this super-cheap, social Campo drinking spot perpetuates *la dolce vita. Campo de' Fiori 15 (at Via Baullari). ☎ 06-68803268. Bus: 30, 40, 62, 64, 70, 87, 116, or 492. Tram: 8. Map p 117.*

Discos & Clubs

★ **Alien** NORTHERN SUBURBS Sophisticated clubbers scoff at this commercial disco with aging decor, but the music is familiar, and the crowd doesn't take itself too seriously. *Via Velletri 13–19 (at Via Savoia). ☎ 06-8412212. Cover varies. Bus: 63. Map p 118.*

The atmospheric Ombre Rosse bar/cafe in Trastevere.

★★ Baja PIAZZA DEL POPOLO The sleek decks at this indoor/outdoor disco-bar—a moored barge on the Tiber—are always festive. What's more, sudden rises of the river's water level occasionally necessitate exciting rescues by Italian firemen. Closed January to February. *Lungotevere Arnaldo da Brescia (between Ponte Margherita and Ponte Matteotti). ☎ 06-32600118. Metro: Flaminio. Bus: 81 or 628. Map p 117.*

★★ Joia TESTACCIO Drunk rich kids go crazy for this Testaccio newcomer, where in-house "paparazzi" make everyone feel like someone. Techno blares downstairs; the VIP room upstairs is less loud, with danceable R&B and '80s sets. *Via Galvani 20–22 (at Via Zabaglia). ☎ 06-5740802. 1-drink minimum. Metro: Piramide. Bus: 23, 30, 75, 95, 170, or 280. Tram: 3. Map p 120.*

★★★ La Maison PIAZZA NAVONA A boon for tourist club-goers, this is the most central *discoteca* in the city—and one of the hippest, where the *bella gente* come to prolong their nights out after Bar del Fico, Bloom, and other places close. *Vicolo dei Granari 4 (at Via del Teatro Pace). ☎ 06-6833312. 15€ cover Sat–Sun. Bus: 30, 40, 62, 64, 70, 87, 116, or 492. Tram: 8. Map p 117.*

★★★ La Terrazza dell'Eur SOUTHERN SUBURBS From June to August, the bronzed, buffed, and well-oiled of Rome party to faint strains of house music on the roof of this office building, in the Fascist-era cityscape of EUR. As fabulous as it is absurd, and worth the cab fare. *Piazzale Kennedy (off Via Cristoforo Colombo). ☎ 06-6833312. Cover varies. Metro: EUR Fermi. Bus: 30, 170, or 714.*

★★ Piper NORTHERN SUBURBS There's a winking, strutting, disco vibe at this historic venue. The multilevel dance floors make for good scoping of potential mates. Saturday nights are gay. *Via Tagliamento 9. ☎ 06-8414459. 20€ cover. Bus: 63. Map p 118.*

★★ Saponeria OSTIENSE At this soap factory turned dance factory, the crowd tends to be squeaky clean and very good-looking—think Italian water polo players in Façonnable shirts and their female groupies. *Via degli Argonauti 20 (at Via Ostiense). ☎ 06-5746999. 15€–20€ cover. Metro: Garbatella. Bus: 23, 271, or 280. Map p 120.*

Gay & Lesbian

★★ Alibi TESTACCIO Consistently good gay disco with an infamously heavy pickup scene; music is a happy mix of house and techno. In summer, the dancing spills out to the club's fabulous rooftop. *Via di Monte Testaccio 40–47 (at Via Galvani). ☎ 06-5743448. www.alibionline.it. Metro: Piramide. Bus: 23, 30, 75, 95, 170, or 280. 12€–15€ cover (Fri–Sat only). Map p 120.*

★ Gender SAN GIOVANNI Intimate, erotic lesbian/gay/transsexual club with strip shows and private cabins—equal opportunity for exhibitionists and voyeurs alike. *Via Faleria 9 (at Via Appia Nuova). ☎ 06-70497638. 10€–15€ cover. Metro: San Giovanni or Re di Roma. Map p 118.*

Live Music

★★ Alexander Platz Jazz Club VATICAN Smooth and classy, this low-ceilinged jazz joint is one of the best in Italy. In summer, the club sponsors the Jazz & Image festival at Villa Celimontana. *Via Ostia 9 (at Via Leone IV). ☎ 06-39742171. 6.50€ cover. Metro: Ottaviano. Map p 118.*

★★★ Big Mama TRASTEVERE With a reassuring reek of smoke and beer, this subterranean blues club is the closest thing in Rome to a honky-tonk. Top-notch blues, rock,

Fiddler's Elbow, a popular Irish pub near the train station.

and soul acts guarantee a good time, so the small, sticky wooden tables go fast. *Vicolo di Francesco a Ripa 18 (at Via San Francesco a Ripa). ☎ 06-5812551. Cover 6€–10€. Bus: 23, 271, 280, 780, or H. Tram: 3 or 8. Map p 118.*

★★ **Fonclea** VATICAN This multi-room, smoke-free, English-style venue has a mellow happy hour and live sets of soul, funk, jazz, and rock. Pub food is served. *Via Crescenzio 82A (at Piazza Risorgimento). ☎ 06-6896302. 10€ food/drink minimum. Metro: Ottaviano. Bus: 23, 81, 271, or 492. Tram: 19. Map p 118.*

Pubs

★ **Fiddler's Elbow** TERMINI The oldest Irish pub in Rome—always packed with a talkative, smoky crowd of locals, resident expats, and travelers. *Via dell'Olmata 43 (at Piazza Santa Maria Maggiore). ☎ 06-4872110. Metro: Cavour or Termini. Bus: 70 or 75. Map p 118.*

★★ **On the Rox** TESTACCIO Open till 5am, this pub/cocktail bar is where you stumble in after all the nearby clubs have closed. Danish owners Anas and Christian indulge ill-advised sambuca orders, and prompt drunken singalongs with their knowingly cheesy music selections. *Via Galvani 54 (at Via Zabaglia). ☎ 328-2852088. Metro: Piramide. Bus: 23, 30, 75, 95, 170, or 280. Tram: 3. Map p 120.*

★★ **Shamrock** ANCIENT ROME Packed with young Romans who know how to drink (there aren't many), this nominally Irish pub near the Colosseum gets especially rowdy when Roman soccer games are on. *Via del Colosseo 1 (at Via Cavour). ☎ 06-6791729. Metro: Colosseo. Bus: 60, 75, 85, or 87. Map p 118.*

★★ **Trinity College** PIAZZA VENEZIA A bit sleazy, a lot cheesy, this pop-music-blaring disco-pub is nevertheless a guilty pleasure and one of the city's most reliable meat-markets for foreign girls and Roman boys. *Via del Collegio Romano 6 (off Via del Corso). ☎ 06-6786472. Bus: 30, 40, 62, 70, 85, 87, 95, 170, 175, or 492. Map p 117.*

Bowling

★ **Brunswick Café** FLAMINIO Bowling (pronounced "bu-ling" here) is always a good time, but Italians' knack for drama over missed splits is especially entertaining. *Lungotevere Acqua Acetosa 10 (off Corso Francia). ☎ 06-8086147. Bus: 92 to Ponte Salario or 910 to Piazzale Euclide. Map p 118.*

8 The Best Arts & Entertainment

A&E Best Bets

Best **Entertainment, Period**
★★★ AS Roma or ★★ SS Lazio, *Stadio Olimpico (p 131)*

Best **Classical Music**
★★ Accademia di Santa Cecilia, *Auditorium (p 129)*

Best **Summer Festival**
★★ Jazz & Image, *Villa Celimontana (p 130)*

Best **for Living La Dolce Vita**
★★★ Baths of Caracalla, *Viale delle Terme di Caracalla (p 130)*

Best **Opera**
★ Teatro dell'Opera, *Via Firenze 72 (p 129)*

Best (and only full-time) **English-Language Cinema**
★ Pasquino, *Piazza Sant'Egidio (p 131)*

Music is everywhere in Rome, from symphony halls to the street, where guitarists like this one offer impromptu entertainment.

Rome Performs

The performing arts do exist in Rome, but they've never been the city's highest priority. Having said that, the symphony is excellent, and summer sees an explosion of cultural offerings, with romantic concerts among ruins, operas in church courtyards, and jazz in the parks. The best tickets in town, however, are to soccer games at the Stadio Olimpico. For the most detailed information about what's on, check out the weekly *Roma C'è* (1€ at newsstands).

Centro Storico **Arts & Entertainment**

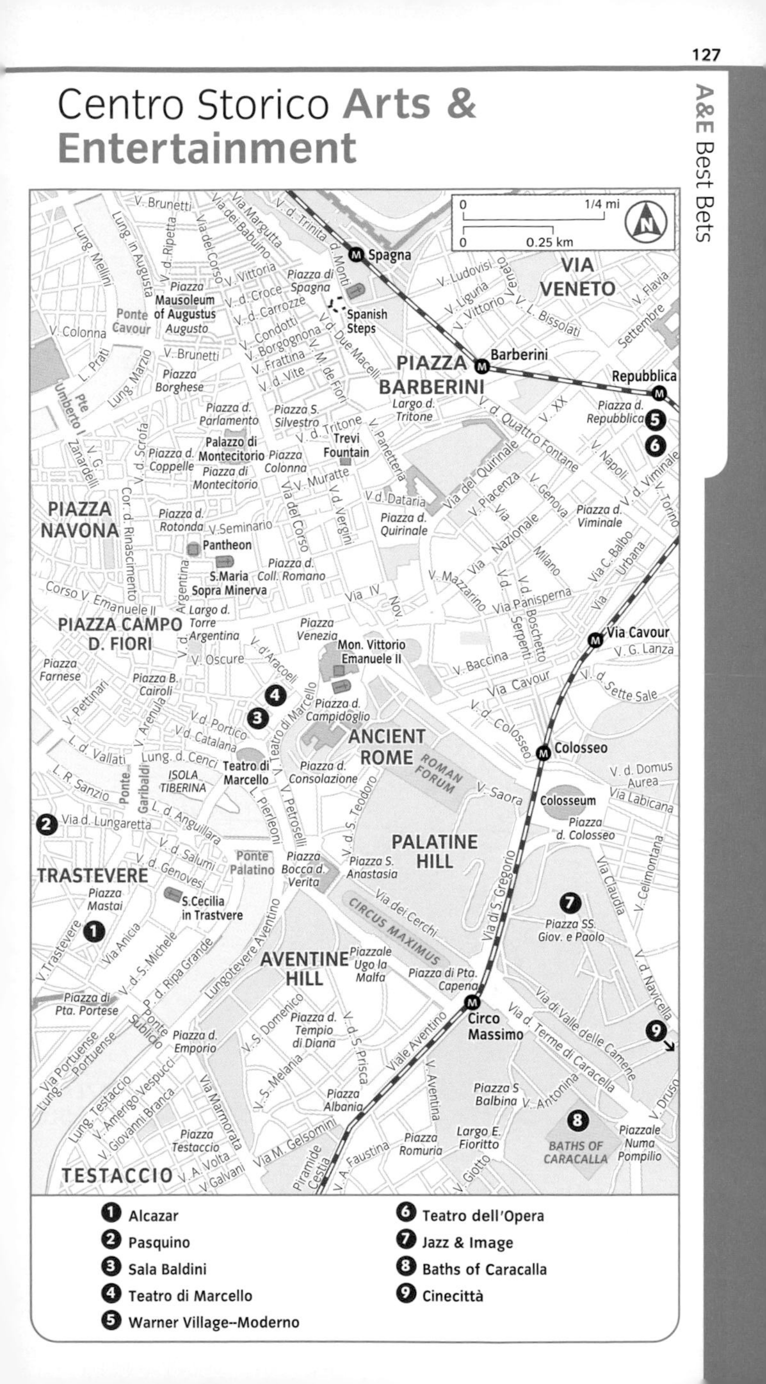

1 Alcazar
2 Pasquino
3 Sala Baldini
4 Teatro di Marcello
5 Warner Village--Moderno
6 Teatro dell'Opera
7 Jazz & Image
8 Baths of Caracalla
9 Cinecittà

Northern Rome Arts & Entertainment

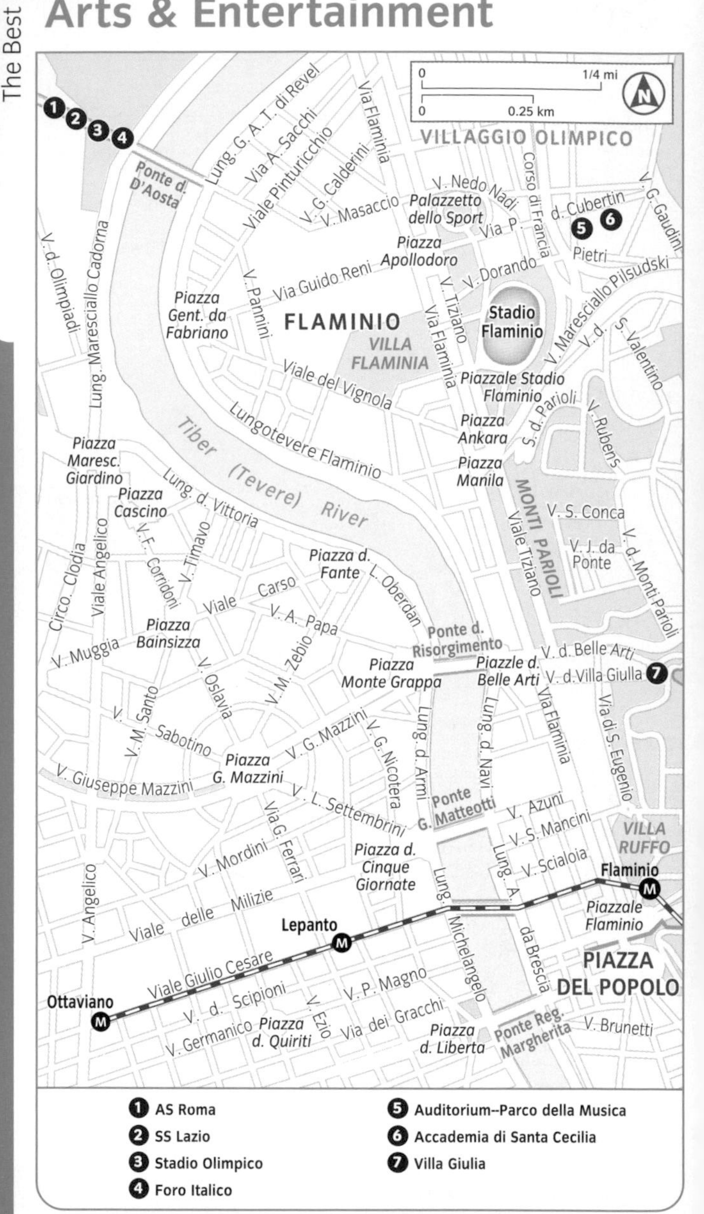

Classical Music

★★ Accademia di Santa Cecilia NORTHERN SUBURBS Rome's premier symphony orchestra, founded by Palestrina in the 16th century, performs in the brand-new concert halls at the Auditorium–Parco della Musica. *Largo Luciano Berio 3 (Auditorium).* ☎ *06-8082058. www.santacecilia.it. Tickets 15€–90€. Bus: M, 53, 217, or 910. Tram: 2. Map p 128.*

★★ Auditorium–Parco della Musica NORTHERN SUBURBS This exciting new multipurpose center for the arts, designed by Renzo Piano, brings a refreshing breath of modernity to Rome. Some say the three lead-roofed concert halls look like giant beetles, but the architecture is undeniably dramatic and the acoustics outstanding. *Viale Pietro di Coubertin (Corso Francia/Viale Tiziano).* ☎ *06-802411. www.auditoriumroma.com. Ticket prices vary. Bus: M, 53, 217, or 910. Tram: 2. Map p 128.*

★ Sala Baldini ANCIENT ROME Home of the Tempietto concert series from November to May, with everything from Strauss to Gershwin. *Piazza Campitelli 9 (at Via del Teatro di Marcello).* ☎ *06-87131590. www.tempietto.it. Tickets 15€. Bus: 23, 30, 63, 95, 170, or 280. Map p 127.*

Posters of upcoming arts attractions are everywhere in Rome, like this one advertising a musical play, Vampiri!.

★ Teatro dell'Opera TERMINI Performances tend to be good, but seldom great, at the financially troubled city opera. Still, the opera house's ornate 19th-century interior is a perfect setting for a sophisticated Roman night out. The 2005 season brings *Turandot, Le Nozze di Figaro,* and *Cavalleria Rusticana. Via Firenze 72 (at Via del Viminale).* ☎ *06-481601. www.opera.roma.it. Tickets 20€–130€. Map p 127.*

The new Auditorium–Parca della Musica is a multipurpose center for the arts.

Classical concerts are held in the nymphaeum, pictured here, at the Villa Giulia.

Summer Venues

★★★ Baths of Caracalla AVENTINE Attend a classical concert or opera here, amid the towering ruins of the 3rd-century-A.D. caldarium, and you'll know the meaning of *la dolce vita*. ***Viale delle Terme di Caracalla. July–Aug only. Ticket prices vary. Metro: Circo Massimo. Bus: 30, 118, or 628. Map p 127.***

★★ Jazz & Image ANCIENT ROME In the gorgeous Villa Celimontana park, a summer-long festival offers nightly jazz, blues, and rock acts, as well as food and drink stands run by some of Rome's top restaurants. ***Piazza della Navicella (at Via Claudia). ☎ 06-5897807. Tickets 15€–25€. Metro: Colosseo. Bus: 60, 75, 81, 87, 175, or 271. Tram: 3. Map p 127.***

★ Teatro di Marcello ANCIENT ROME Part of the music association Il Tempietto concert series, performances at this 13 B.C. theater are atmospheric, but can be hard to hear over the rush of traffic on the busy street above. ***Via del Teatro di Marcello. ☎ 06-87131590. www.tempietto.it. Tickets 15€. Bus: 30, 63, 95, or 170. Map p 127.***

★★ Villa Giulia VILLA BORGHESE It doesn't get much lovelier than an intimate classical concert here, in the nymphaeum (ornamental grotto built as a shrine to water nymphs) of a 16th-century villa. ***Piazza di Villa Giulia (at Viale delle Belle Arti). ☎ 06-39734576. www.musicaeuropa.it. Ticket prices vary. Tram: 3 or 19. Map p 128.***

Cinemas

Alcazar TRASTEVERE Single-screen cinema with films in Versione Originale on Monday. ***Via Cardinale Merry del Val 14 (at Viale Trastevere). ☎ 06-5880099. Tickets 3€–5€. Bus: H or 780. Tram: 3 or 8. Map p 127.***

★ Cinecittà SOUTHERN SUBURBS Rome's legendary film lots had their heyday in the 1950s and '60s. Nowadays, more reality shows than silver-screen classics are shot here, but the sets from such epics as *Ben-Hur* are fascinating. At press time, tours of the film lots were only available to students (free), arranged by calling the central line. **Note:** Cinecittà is developing a theme park to be called **CINECITTÀ WORLD,** a 60-hectare (146-acre) park that will occupy a part of the current studios' premises. It promises to "transport visitors in the fanciest journeys of movie magic and entertainment." Stay tuned. ***Via Tuscolana 1055. ☎ 06-722931. Metro: Cinecittà. Map p 127.***

The Baron von Munchhausen *set at the old Cinecittà film lots.*

★ **Pasquino** TRASTEVERE The only all-original-language cinema in Rome has three screens (and a knack for showing the films you're least interested in seeing). *Piazza Sant'Egidio 10 (off Piazza di Santa Maria in Trastevere). ☎ 06-5803622. Tickets 4.50€–7€. Bus: 23, 271, 280, or H. Tram: 8. Map p 127.*

★ **Warner Village—Moderno** TERMINI One screen at this American-style multiplex is dedicated to films in Versione Originale—usually a big-budget action flick. *Piazza della Repubblica 45. ☎ 06-477791. Tickets 5.50€–7.50€. Metro: Repubblica. Bus: 40, 64, 70, or 170. Map p 127.*

Sports

★★★ **AS Roma** NORTHERN SUBURBS La Roma wears yellow and red *(giallorosso)*, draws fans from the city center and political left, and is Lazio's archrival. Team captain Francesco Totti is a local hero. See Stadio Olimpico, below. ***Tickets can be purchased at the Stadio Olimpico on game day, at Lottomatica stores, or at the official Roma Store at Via Colonna 360.*** *☎ 06-6786514. www.asromacalcio.it. Tickets 15€–90€. Map p 128.*

★ **Foro Italico** NORTHERN SUBURBS This sprawling athletics complex, dotted with umbrella pines and Fascist-era mosaics and statues, is home to soccer games, the Italian Open tennis tournament, and various other sporting events. *Viale del Foro Italico/Viale dei Gladiatori. ☎ 06-36858218. Ticket prices vary by event. Bus: 32, 271, or 280. Tram: 225. Map p 128.*

★★ **SS Lazio** NORTHERN SUBURBS Rome's other *Serie A* soccer team wears light blue and white *(biancoceleste)*; its followers hail from the

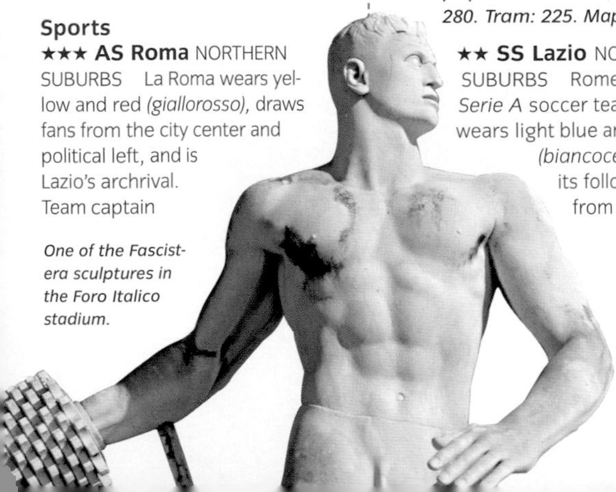

One of the Fascist-era sculptures in the Foro Italico stadium.

GOOOOOOL! Soccer, Rome Style

To experience Roman culture at its most fervent, don't go to Mass—go to a soccer game. Full of pageantry, dramatic tension, and raw emotion, the home games of **Roma** and **Lazio,** the city's two *Serie A* (Italian premier league) teams, can be far more spectacular than any fancy theater event, and certainly more interactive (when was the last time you got beaned in the head by a sandwich, thrown by an irate fan, at *La Bohème?*). *Romanisti* far outnumber *laziali,* but both fan bases pack the Stadio Olimpico, coloring the stands with the red and yellow of Roma or the light blue and white of Lazio, every weekend from September to June. If you go to a game, invest in a team scarf (sold at concession stands outside the stadium), and learn a few stadium choruses—both teams have a few easy ones set to the tune of "The Entertainer" and the march from *Aïda.* To score huge points with the locals, stop by Porta Portese (see chapter 4) before the game and pick up some colored smoke bombs *(fumogeni)* or firecrackers *(petardi)* to set off outside the stadium—true tailgating, Italian-style!

monied suburbs. ***See Stadio Olimpico, below. www.sslazio.it. Tickets can be purchased at the Stadio Olimpico on game day, at Lottomatica stores, or at the Lazio Point on Via Farini 34, ☎ 06-4826768. Tickets 15€–90€. Map p 128.***

★★ **Stadio Olimpico** NORTHERN SUBURBS For better or for worse, there is no better place to soak up modern Roman culture than at the soccer stadium. The Olimpico, Rome's premier venue, is where the AS Roma and SS Lazio *Serie A* (premier league) teams play once a week from September to June. ***Foro Italico/Viale dello Stadio Olimpico. ☎ 06-3237333 (box office). Tickets 15€–90€. Bus: 32, 271, or 280. Tram: 225. Map p 128.*** ●

AS Roma's Antonio Cassano celebrates his third goal against Siena in 2004 at the Stadio Olimpico soccer stadium.

9 The Best **Lodging**

Hotel Best Bets

Best **View**
★★★ Hassler $$$$ *Piazza Trinità dei Monti 6 (p 143)*

Best **Boutique Hotel**
★★ Casa Howard $$ *Via Capo le Case 18 (p 140)*

Best **Cheap & Centrally Located**
★ Sole al Biscione $ *Via del Biscione 76 (p 145);* and ★ Navona $ *Via dei Sediari 8 (p 144)*

Best **for Celebrity-Spotting**
★★ Hotel de Russie $$$$ *Via Babuino 9 (p 143)*

Best **for Discerning Travelers**
★★★ Eden $$$$ *Via Ludovisi 49 (p 142)*

Best **for Families**
★★ Capo d'Africa $$ *Via Capo d'Africa 54 (p 140);* and ★ Aldrovandi Palace $$$ *Via Ulisse Aldrovandi 15 (p 140)*

Best **in an Authentic Roman Neighborhood**
★★ Santa Maria $$ *Vicolo del Piede 2 (p 145)*

Best **Escape from Vespa Drone**
★★ Villa San Pio $$ *Via di S. Melania 19 (p 146)*

Best **Glitz & Glamour**
★★ Excelsior $$$$ *Via Veneto 125 (p 142)*

Best **for Artists & Poets**
★★ Locarno $$ *Via della Penna 22 (p 144)*

Sexiest
★★ Valadier $$$ *Via della Fontanella 15 (p 146)*

Best **for Visiting Cardinals**
★ Columbus $$$ *Via della Conciliazione 33 (p 141)*

Best **for Devils in Disguise**
★★ Aleph $$$ *Via di San Basilio 15 (p 140)*

Best **for Modern Design Buffs**
★ Radisson SAS $$$ *Via Filippo Turati 171 (p 145)*

Best **Cheap Sleep (Minus the Bed Bugs)**
★ Colors $ *Via Boezio 31 (p 141)*

Best **for Early Flights**
Mach 2 $ *Via Portuense 2465 (p 144)*

The handsome facade of the Aldrovandi Palace hotel.

Centro Storico **Lodging**

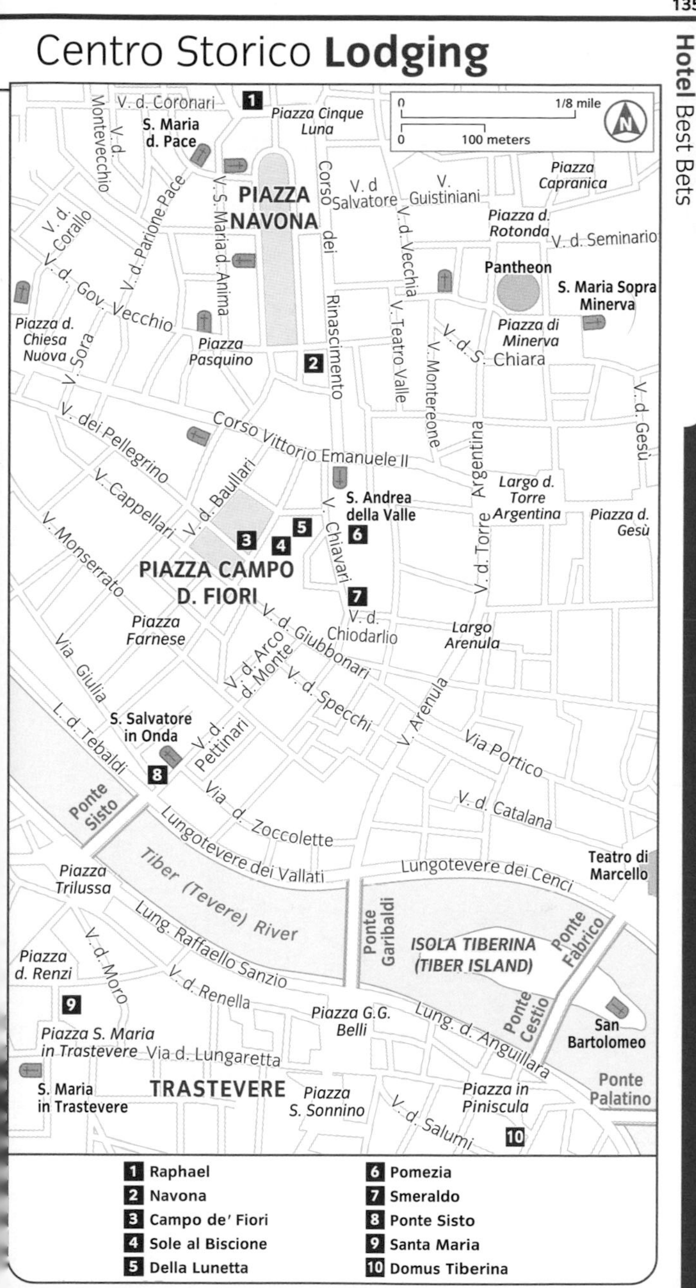

Rome **Lodging**

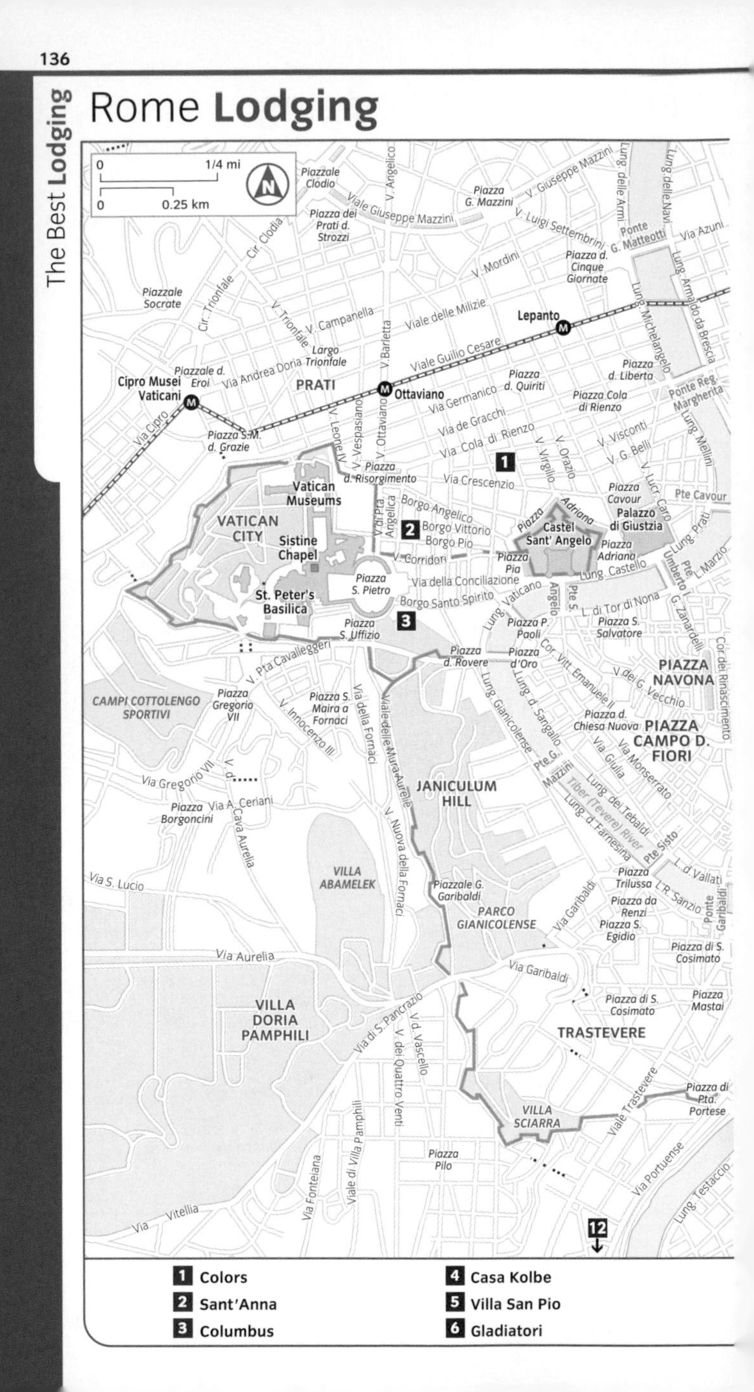

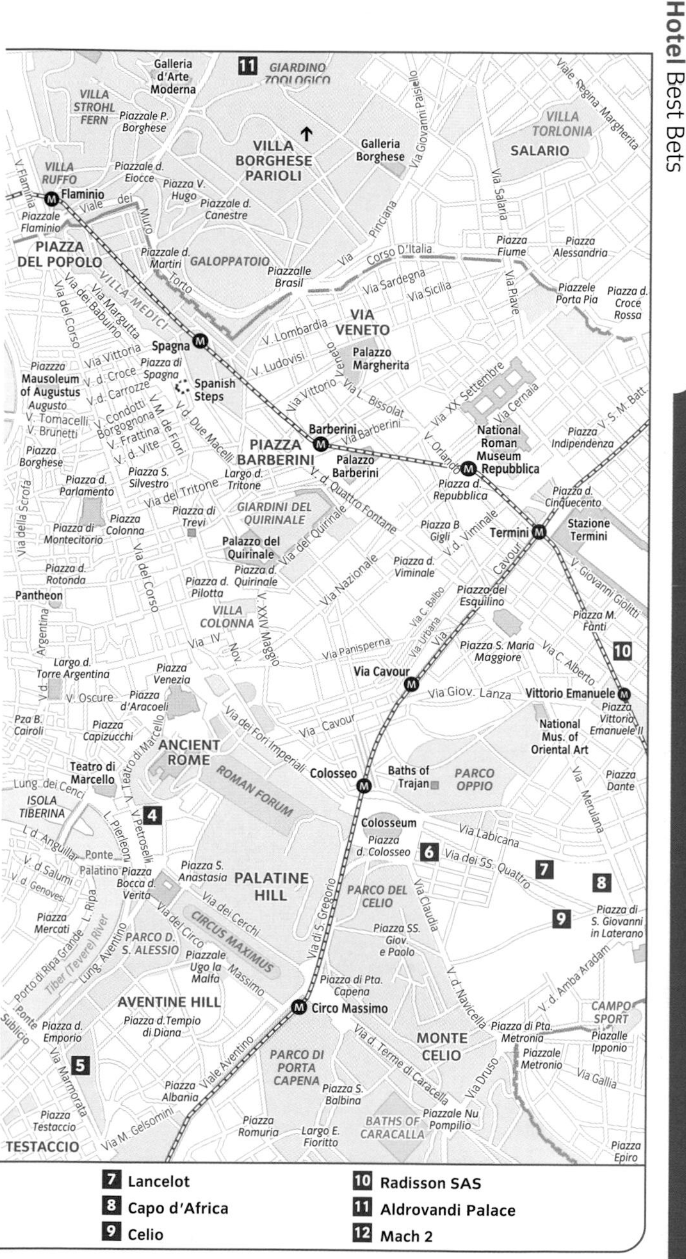
Galleria d'Arte Moderna
GIARDINO ZOOLOGICO
VILLA STROHL FERN
Piazzale P. Borghese
VILLA BORGHESE PARIOLI
Galleria Borghese
VILLA TORLONIA
SALARIO
VILLA RUFFO
Piazzale d. Eiocce
Piazza V. Hugo
Piazzale d. Canestre
Flaminio
Piazzale Flaminio
PIAZZA DEL POPOLO
Piazzale d. Martiri
GALOPPATOIO
Piazzalle Brasil
Corso D'Italia
Piazza Fiume
Piazza Alessandria
Piazzele Porta Pia
Piazza d. Croce Rossa
VILLA MEDICI
VIA VENETO
Palazzo Margherita
Spagna
Piazza di Spagna
Spanish Steps
Mausoleum of Augustus
Barberini
PIAZZA BARBERINI
Palazzo Barberini
National Roman Museum
Repubblica
Piazza d. Repubblica
Piazza Indipendenza
Piazza d. Cinquecento
Stazione Termini
Termini
GIARDINI DEL QUIRINALE
Palazzo del Quirinale
Piazza di Trevi
Piazza Colonna
Piazza di Montecitorio
Piazza d. Rotonda
Pantheon
VILLA COLONNA
Piazza del Esquilino
Piazza S. Maria Maggiore
Via Cavour
Vittorio Emanuele
Piazza Vittorio Emanuele II
National Mus. of Oriental Art
Largo d. Torre Argentina
Piazza Venezia
ANCIENT ROME
ROMAN FORUM
Colosseo
Baths of Trajan
PARCO OPPIO
Teatro di Marcello
ISOLA TIBERINA
Colosseum
Piazza d. Colosseo
PALATINE HILL
PARCO DEL CELIO
Piazza di S. Giovanni in Laterano
CIRCUS MAXIMUS
PARCO D. S. ALESSIO
Tiber (Tevere) River
AVENTINE HILL
Circo Massimo
MONTE CELIO
CAMPO SPORT
PARCO DI PORTA CAPENA
BATHS OF CARACALLA
TESTACCIO
1
2
3
4
5
6
7
8
9
10
11
7 Lancelot
8 Capo d'Africa
9 Celio
10 Radisson SAS
11 Aldrovandi Palace
12 Mach 2

Tridente & Campo Marzio Lodging

Lodging in Via Veneto, Villa Borghese & Termini

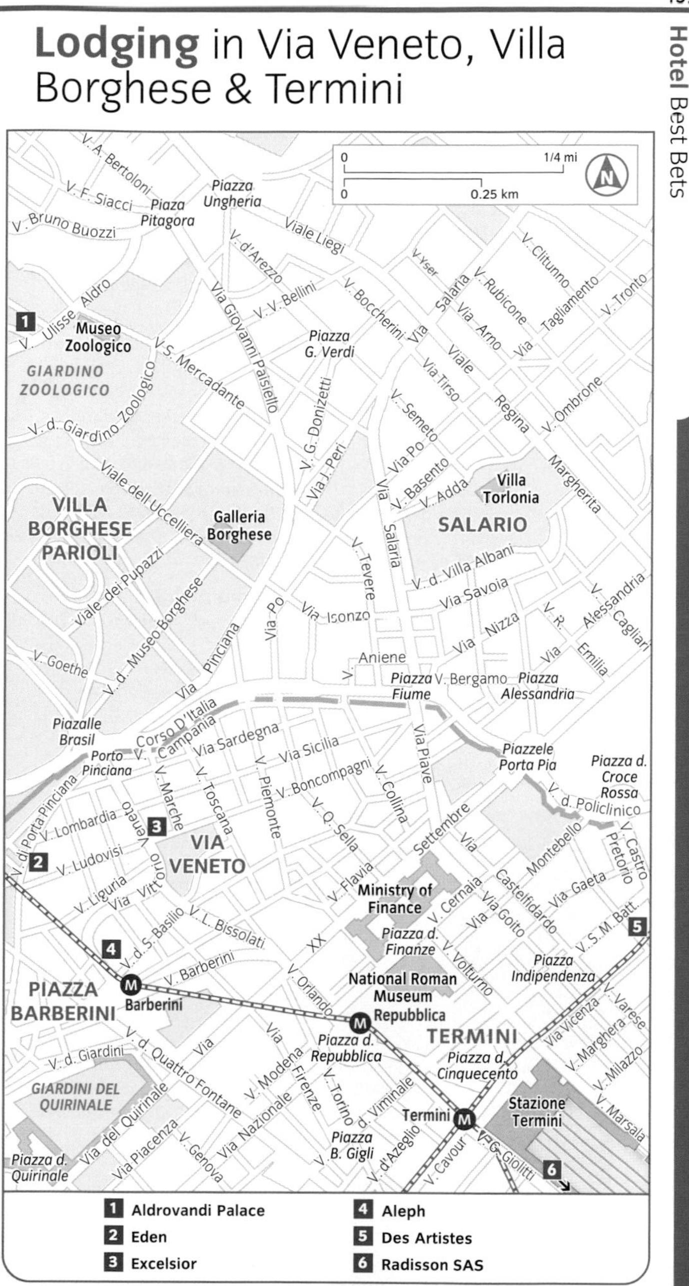

Rome Hotels, A to Z

★ **Aldrovandi Palace** VILLA BORGHESE Occupying some seriously prize real estate in the gorgeous greenery north of Villa Borghese, this classy hotel boasts a swimming pool and all modern amenities. *Via Ulisse Aldrovandi 15. ☎ 06-3223993. www.aldrovandi.com. 135 units. Doubles 350€–430€. AE, DC, MC, V. Bus: 52 or 53. Tram: 3 or 19. Map p 136.*

★★ **Aleph** VIA VENETO The guest rooms are comfortable and quiet, but all who enter must contend with the "red-tinged vortex" of designer Adam Tihany's Dante-inspired interiors. Clientele at the hotel's bars and restaurant is as sexy as the decor. *Via di San Basilio 15. ☎ 06-422901. www.boscolohotels.com. 96 units. Doubles 220€–370€. AE, DC, MC, V. Metro: Barberini. Bus: 62, 95, 116, 175, or 492. Map p 139.*

Art SPANISH STEPS Giant mozzarella-ball reception desks are just one of many wacky design touches at this boutique inn. The entry looks like a Mykonos lane, the lobby is a former chapel, and each floor is awash in a different bright color. *Via Margutta 56. ☎ 06-328711. www.hotelart.it. 46 units. Doubles 390€–490€. AE, DC, MC, V. Metro: Spagna. Map p 138.*

The warmly lighted hallway of the Celio hotel.

Campo de' Fiori CAMPO DE' FIORI From baby blue florals to exposed ancient brick, a grab bag of interiors awaits you at this funky, affordable (and cramped) inn. *Via del Biscione 6. ☎ 06-68806865. www.hotelcampodefiori.com. 28 units. Doubles 90€–140€. AE, MC, V. Bus: 40, 62, 64, 70, 87, 492, or 571. Map p 135.*

★★ **Capo d'Africa** ANCIENT ROME On sunny and rustic Celio Hill, a few blocks from Villa Celimontana park, a big playground, and the Colosseum, this cheerful three-star is a great refuge for families. Immaculate rooms are done up in tasteful Deco brights. *Via Capo d'Africa 54. ☎ 06-772801. www.hotelcapodafrica.com. 65 units. Doubles 220€–290€. AE, DC, MC, V. Metro: Colosseo. Bus: 60, 75, 87, 175, or 271. Tram: 3. Map p 136.*

★★ **Casa Howard** SPANISH STEPS This stylish, intimate guesthouse features luxe fabrics like Toile de Jouy and Shanghai silk, fresh flowers in every room, and a Turkish bath. Such luxury, at these prices, is unheard of in Rome. *Via Capo le Case 18. ☎ 06-69924555. www.casahoward.com. 10 units. Doubles 160€–210€. AE, MC, V. Metro: Spagna. Map p 138.*

Casa Kolbe ANCIENT ROME Book yourself at this former convent only if you can secure one of the rooms with a view; the knockout panorama of the Forum and Palatine more than compensates for the school groups and surly staff. *Via di San Teodoro 44. ☎ 06-6794974. 63 units. Doubles 65€–85€. AE, MC, V. Bus: 30, 95, or 170. Map p 136.*

★ **Celio** ANCIENT ROME Sumptuous decor borders on kitsch, but soft lighting helps tone down the garish rooms at this well-priced Colosseum-area three-star. *Via dei Santissimi Quattro 35/C. ☎ 06-70495333. www.hotelcelio.com. 20 units. Doubles 190€–310€. AE, DC, MC, V. Metro: Colosseo. Bus: 60, 75, 87, 175, or 271.Tram: 3. Map p 136.*

★ **Colors** VATICAN Perfect for budget travelers in search of company, this friendly, colorful inn offers private and hostel-style rooms, as well as a kitchen and washing machine. *Via Boezio 31. ☎ 06-6874030. www.colorshotel.com. 8 units. Doubles 50€–75€. No credit cards. Metro: Ottaviano. Bus: 23 or 492. Map p 136.*

★ **Columbus** VATICAN This upscale inn, a stone's throw from St. Peter's, was once home to a long line of popes and cardinals. Many of the somber-toned rooms preserve their original 16th-century wood ceilings and stucco work. *Via della Conciliazione 33. ☎ 06-6865435. www.hotelcolumbus.net. 92 units. Doubles 160€–320€. AE, DC, MC, V. Bus: 30, 40, or 64. Map p 136.*

Della Lunetta CAMPO DE' FIORI Spartan accommodations in a prime location. *Piazza del Paradiso 68. ☎ 06-6875929. 40 units. Doubles 85€–120€. MC, V. Bus: 40, 62, 64, 70, 87, 492, or 571. Map p 135.*

Des Artistes TERMINI Attractive decor and a social, international clientele make this two-star a standout in the otherwise dreary sea of budget accommodations near the train station. *Via Villafranca 20. ☎ 06-4454365. www.hoteldesartistes.com. 32 units. Doubles 60€–190€. MC, V. Metro: Castro Pretorio. Bus: 75 and 492. Map p 139.*

Domus Tiberina TRASTEVERE In one of the most authentic parts of Trastevere, Domus Tiberina is a cozy B&B with a Mediterranean feel. *Via in Piscinula 37. ☎ 06-5803033. www.domustiberina.hotel-roma.net.*

A Des Artistes double with rose petals sprinkled on the bed.

The Excelsior Hotel at night.

10 units. Doubles 140€–180€. AE, MC, V. Bus: 23, 271, or 280. Map p 135.

★★★ **Eden** VIA VENETO Understatedly but unmistakably luxurious, the Eden is a soothing contrast to the over-the-top decor of most Veneto hotels. The rooftop Terrazza bar and restaurant are romantic beyond belief, with gorgeous views. *Via Ludovisi 49. ☎ 06-478121. www.hotel-eden.it. 121 units. Doubles 650€–750€. AE, DC, MC, V. Metro: Spagna. Bus: 52, 53, 63, 95, or 116. Map p 139.*

★★ **Excelsior** VIA VENETO Embrace the in-your-face glitz at this landmark palazzo, where spacious guest rooms are a giddy maelstrom of tassels, brocades, velvets, and gilt, and bathrooms are regally clad in colored marble. *Via Veneto 125. ☎ 06-47081. www.excelsior.hotelinroma.com. Doubles 425€–540€. AE, DC, MC, V. Metro: Barberini. Bus: 52,53, 63, 95, or 116. Map p 139.*

Forte SPANISH STEPS Decor is a bit frumpy, but rooms have Internet connections and satellite TV. The value for location, on one of Rome's loveliest streets, can't be beat. *Via Margutta 61. ☎ 06-3207625. www.hotelforte.com. 21 units. Doubles 140€–230€. AE, MC, V. Metro: Spagna. Map p 138.*

★ **Gladiatori** ANCIENT ROME You can almost reach out and touch the Colosseum from this refined and cozy boutique inn, whose roof bar offers views so intoxicating you won't even need a martini. *Via Labicana 125. ☎ 06-77591380.*

A sumptuous suite in the Hassler Hotel.

A studio room in the Hotel de Russie.

www.hotelgladiatori.it. 17 units. Doubles 260€–290€. AE, DC, MC, V. Metro: Colosseo. Map p 136.

★★★ **Hassler** SPANISH STEPS While other nearby five-stars have larger rooms and more facilities, the Hassler still lives up to its reputation for luxury with its impeccable service and views—oh, the views!—from the upper floors. Got even more money to burn? Book one of the positively swoon-inducing suites. *Piazza Trinità dei Monti 6. ☎ 06-699340. www.hotelhasslerroma.com. 100 units. Doubles 520€–670€. AE, DC, MC, V. Metro: Spagna. Map p 138.*

★★ **Hotel de Russie** PIAZZA DEL POPOLO Clean, neoclassical lines lend an airiness to this luxury newcomer popular with visiting movie stars. The hotel's U-shape encloses a fabulous terraced garden, with bars, restaurants, and fountains sweeping up toward the Pincio. *Via del Babuino 9. ☎ 06-328881. www.hotelderussie.it. 125 units. Doubles 600€–725€. AE, DC, MC, V. Metro: Flaminio. Map p 138.*

★ **La Lumière** SPANISH STEPS Spacious rooms at this boutique newcomer are lovingly decorated in a vaguely French country style, with soft blues and mauves and beautiful hardwood floors. *Via Belsiana 72. ☎ 06-69380806. www.lalumieredipiazzadispagna.com. 10 units. 150€–300€. AE, MC, V. Metro: Spagna. Map p 138.*

★ **Lancelot** ANCIENT ROME Rooms at this old-fashioned and unbelievably friendly three-star are large and mercifully well priced, attracting many return visitors and families on a budget. *Via Capo d'Africa 47. ☎ 06-70450615. www.lancelothotel.com. 60 units. 152€–248€. AE, MC, V. Metro: Colosseo. Bus: 60, 75, 87, 175, or 571. Map p 136.*

★★ Locarno PIAZZA DEL POPOLO Artistic types love this slightly shabby peacock of a hotel: The Art Deco furnishings are worn in places, but a feeling of old-world elegance remains. Ask for a deluxe room in the eastern annex, as rooms in the main building are dowdy and a bit melancholy. ***Via della Penna 22. ☎ 06-3610841. www.hotellocarno.com. 66 units. Doubles 190€–330€. AE, MC, V. Metro: Flaminio. Map p 138.***

Mach 2 AIRPORT Exactly what you'd expect 1.6km (1 mile) from the airport—suburban and plain, but with all-important sound-barrier windows, shuttle service to the terminal, and a flight-related name. The nifty Museo delle Navi (Roman Ships Museum) is nearby. ***Via Portuense 2465. ☎ 06-6507149. www.hotelmach2.it. 33 units. Doubles 113€–150€. AE, MC, V. Train to Fiumicino Città. Off map (p 136).***

Margutta PIAZZA DEL POPOLO Kudos to the saintly management who've kept the quiet and cheerful Margutta so affordable in this ultraexclusive area. ***Via Laurina 34. ☎ 06-3223674. 24 units. Doubles 115€–135€. AE, MC, V. Metro: Spagna. Map p 138.***

★ Navona PIAZZA NAVONA Close to all the best bars and restaurants, the Navona is a warm, welcoming, amazing bargain. ***Via dei Sediari 8. ☎ 06-6864203. www.hotelnavona.com. 35 units. Doubles 125€. AE, MC, V. Bus: 30, 40, 62, 64, 70, 87, 116, or 492. Map p 135.***

Panda SPANISH STEPS On a cafe-filled street in the heart of Rome's pricey shopping district, the Panda is a basic, pleasant choice, where a weeklong stay costs less than an Armani suit. ***Via della Croce 35. ☎ 06-6780179. www.hotelpanda.it. 20 units. Doubles 90€–110€. MC, V. Metro: Spagna. Map p 138.***

Pomezia CAMPO DE' FIORI While it offers few frills, the Pomezia provides more coziness and harmony of decor than other Campo de' Fiori two-stars. ***Via dei Chiavari 13. ☎ 06-6861371. 25 units. Doubles 90€–120€. AE, MC, V. Bus: 40, 62, 64, 70, 87, 492, or 571. Map p 135.***

A typical room in the Panda pensione.

The facade of the Raphael Hotel is blanketed in green ivy.

★ **Ponte Sisto** CAMPO DE' FIORI The largest and best-equipped inn in this prime zone between Campo de' Fiori and Trastevere, the Ponte Sisto has great marble bathrooms and a big garden courtyard. *Via dei Pettinari 64. ☎ 06-686310. www.hotelpontesisto.it. 106 units. Doubles 310€–400€. AE, DC, MC, V. Bus: 23, 40, 62, 64, 70, 87, 116, 271, or 280. Map p 135.*

★ **Radisson SAS** TERMINI Fans of minimalism and modernity will forgive this luxury hotel (formerly called "Es") its seedy location and slightly cold feeling. The sleek and fabulous roof bar (with pool) offers hypnotizing views over the tracks of Termini station. *Via Filippo Turati 171. ☎ 06-444841. www.rome.radissonsas.com. 235 units. Doubles 205€–285€. AE, DC, MC, V. Metro: Termini. Bus: 70. Map p 139.*

★ **Raphael** PIAZZA NAVONA The Raphael impresses all with its unforgettable facade of cascading ivy and a stunning rooftop restaurant, but disappoints some with its smallish standard rooms. *Largo Febo 2. ☎ 06-682831. www.raphaelhotel.com. 70 units. Doubles 210€–350€. AE, DC, MC, V. Bus: 40, 62, 64, 70, 87, 492, or 571. Map p 135.*

★★ **Santa Maria** TRASTEVERE An amazing find in hotel-deprived Trastevere, the Santa Maria feels like a 16th-century motel, with simple chalet-style rooms and a pretty courtyard with orange trees. *Vicolo del Piede 2. ☎ 06-5894626. www.htlsantamaria.com. 19 units. Doubles 155€–210€. AE, MC, V. Bus: 23, 271, or 280. Tram: 8. Map p 135.*

★ **Sant'Anna** VATICAN The overall theme at this comfy but dated three-star is mismatched opulence—it's as if rooms were thrown together with finds from a yard sale at the Vatican, down the street. *Borgo Pio 133/134. ☎ 06-68801602. www.hotelsantanna.com. 20 units. Doubles 175€–200€. AE, MC, V. Bus: 23, 30, 40, 62, or 492. Map p 136.*

★ **Smeraldo** CAMPO DE' FIORI Well-priced but cramped, this *centro storico* "emerald" has a few shining facets, including Internet access and air-conditioning in rooms, and a pretty roof garden. *Vicolo dei Chiodaroli 9. ☎ 06-6875929. www.smeraldoroma.com. 50 units. Doubles 110€–140€. AE, MC, V. Bus: 40, 62, 64, 70, 87, 492, or 571. Map p 135.*

★ **Sole al Biscione** CAMPO DE' FIORI Rooms are basic (and can be loud when school groups lodge here), but the multilevel courtyard garden, open to all guests, overflows with Roman charm. *Via del Biscione 76. ☎ 06-68806873. www.solealbiscione.it. 60 units. Doubles 95€–140€. No credit cards. Bus: 40, 62, 64, 70, 87, 492, or 571. Map p 135.*

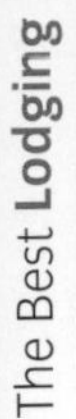

A suite at the Valadier hotel.

★★ **Valadier** SPANISH STEPS Like an aging Italian film star, the Valadier shows its years and still oozes sex appeal. Interiors recall a 1930s ocean liner, from the lacquered wood in its stateroom-sized doubles to its smoky piano lounge. *Via della Fontanella 15. ☎ 06-3611998. www.hotelvaladier.com. 48 units. Doubles 200€–370€. AE, DC, MC, V. Metro: Spagna. Map p 138.*

★★ **Villa San Pio** AVENTINE Staying at this elegant converted villa, with antique furnishings, rich fabrics, and the tranquillity of leafy Aventine Hill, is like visiting your long-lost, old-money Roman relatives. *Via S. Melania 19. ☎ 06-5745231. www.aventinohotels.com. 100 units (in the Aventino hotel group). Doubles 240€. AE, DC, MC, V. Metro: Circo Massimo. Bus: 95 or 175. Map p 136.* ●

10 The Best Trips Out of Town

Tivoli: Hadrian's Villa

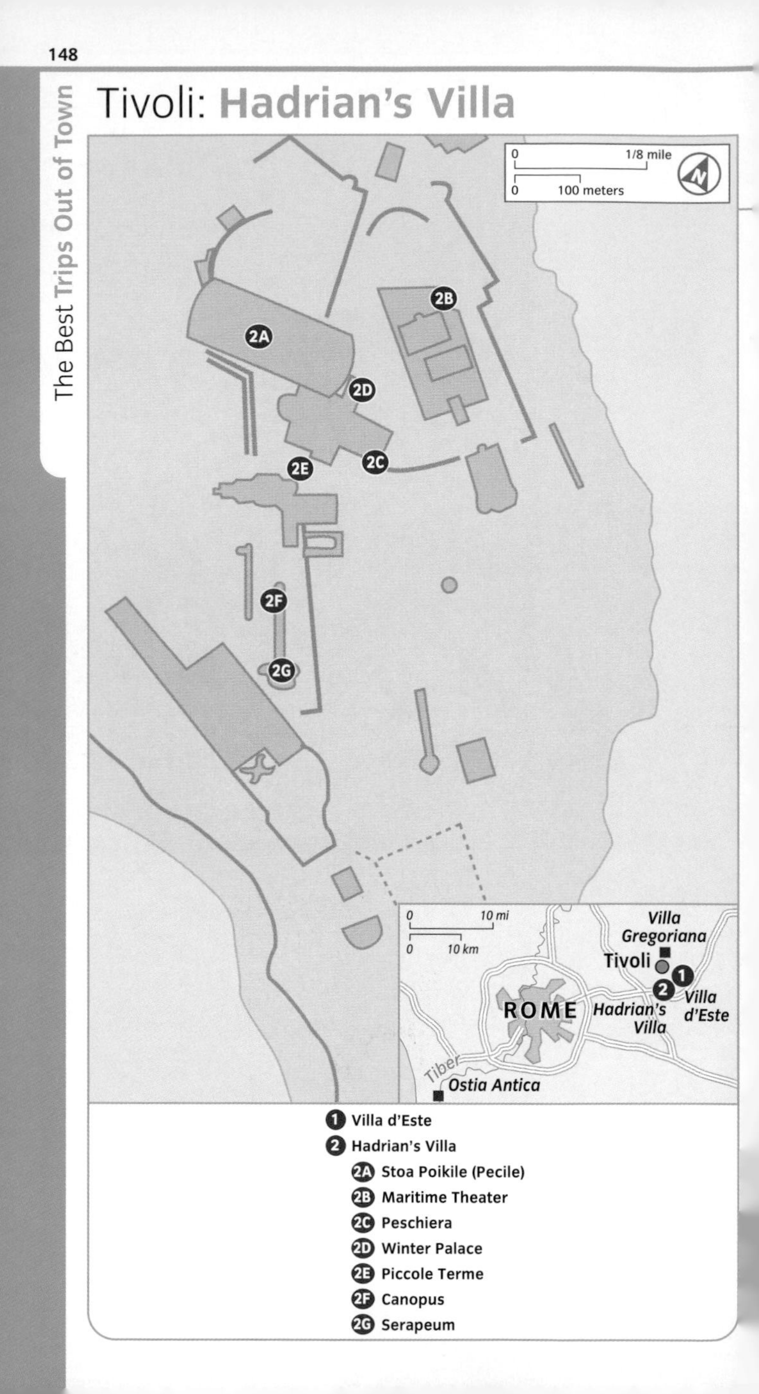

1 Villa d'Este
2 Hadrian's Villa
2A Stoa Poikile (Pecile)
2B Maritime Theater
2C Peschiera
2D Winter Palace
2E Piccole Terme
2F Canopus
2G Serapeum

The most classic Roman day trip, Tivoli lies about 32km (20 miles) west of the city and is home to the fountain-filled 16th-century Villa d'Este and the fantastically unique ancient ruins of Villa Adriana. Transportation to Tivoli can be slow; allow a full day.

❶ ★★★ **Villa d'Este.** It's all about the fountains at this pleasure palace, commissioned in 1550 by Renaissance noble and cardinal Ippolito d'Este. Throughout the lush, steeply sloping gardens, whimsical grottoes, rushing flumes, reflecting pools, musical fountains, and bizarre gurgling "trees" delight and charm. *45 min. Piazza Trento 1.* ☎ *0774-312070. 6.50€. Tues–Sun 9am–6:15pm May–Sept; 8:30am–4pm Oct–Apr. From Rome: Cotral bus from Metro Ponte Mammolo, about 45 min. From Villa Adriana, regional bus to Tivoli, about 15 min.*

❷ ★★★ **Hadrian's Villa (Villa Adriana).** Hadrian's sprawling estate (A.D.118–34) was as much a summer retreat from the stifling air in Rome as it was a place where the emperor could fulfill all his fantasies in architecture.

Near the entrance, the ★ **Stoa Poikile** pool was once surrounded by a shady colonnade. The delightfully inventive ★★★ **Maritime Theater** was where the emperor meditated and swam laps. The ★ **Peschiera** was a giant aquarium, handy for seafood dinners this far inland. The attached ★ **Winter Palace** has some of its heating system intact, as well as great views toward Rome. At the ★ **Piccole Terme (Small Baths),** look for marvelous stuccoes on the ceiling vaults. The exquisite ★★★ **Canopus,** a long pool with broken Assyrian arcades and statuary, terminates in the ★★ **Serapeum,** a dining room whose front "wall" was a thin sheet of water, fed by the aqueduct above, that cooled the air. *1½ hr. Villa Adriana (Tivoli).* ☎ *0774-382733. 6.50€. Daily 9am–6:30pm Apr–Sept; 9am–5pm Oct–Mar. From Rome: Cotral bus to Villa Adriana from Metro station Ponte Mammolo, about 45 min. From Villa d'Este (Tivoli town), regional bus to Villa Adriana, about 15 min.*

The statue-filled Canopus at Hadrian's Villa.

Ostia Antica

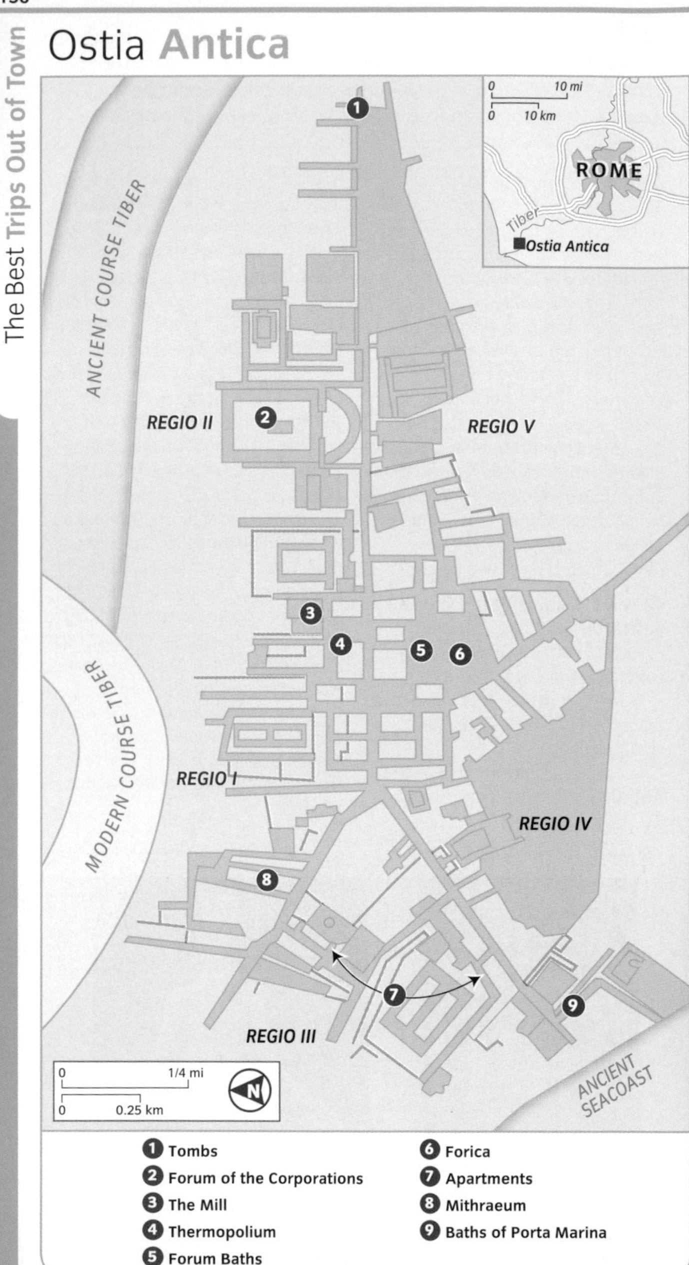

The port of ancient Rome lay where the Tiber flowed into the Mediterranean (*ostia* is "mouth" in Latin). The seacoast receded, and the river course changed, leaving ★★★ **Ostia Antica** landlocked and obsolete. Surrounded by trees and rarely crowded, the ruins are varied, extensive, and fun to explore, even better than Pompeii for understanding how the ancients used to live. The visit can easily be done in half a day, or combined with a trip to the beach at Ostia Lido (p 156) for a full day's excursion. Bring a picnic, or eat at the site's pleasant cafe.

1 **Tombs.** The road leading into the ancient town proper is lined with tombs; as was the custom throughout Rome, burials had to be outside the city walls.

2 ★★★ **Forum of the Corporations.** Farther into town, behind an ancient theater, is this wonderful former square where the shops of various importers have mosaics that indicate their cargo, from oil to elephants.

3 ★★ **The Mill.** Here, grinding stones and bread ovens are still in place.

4 ★★ **Thermopolium.** These hard-to-find ruins once served as a stylish snack bar, serving hot and cold food and drinks.

5 ★ **Forum Baths.** Notice especially the pipes that heated the marble-clad walls of these baths.

6 ★★ **Forica.** This tour-group magnet was the public latrine, with neat rows of toilets still open to the sewer below (now neutral-smelling).

7 ★ **Apartments.** All over the site, modest-to-extravagant apartment clusters are open for wandering—be sure to visit the posh ★ **Garden Apartments,** the ★ **Insula of the Charioteers,** and the ★ **House of the Dioscuri.**

A lovely mosaic from the Ostia Antica.

8 ★★ **Mithraeum.** This creepy chamber is found under the Baths of Mithras and was where 2nd-century-A.D. initiates of the god of Mithras performed rituals.

9 ★★ **Baths of Porta Marina.** Check out the hilarious ancient mosaics of bodybuilders here.
2–3 hr. Viale dei Romagnoli 117. ☎ 06-56358099. 4€. Apr–Oct Tues–Sun 8:30am–7pm; Nov–Mar 9am–5pm. Train to Ostia Antica from Stazione Porta San Paolo (Metro: Piramide), about 30 min.

Pompeii & Naples

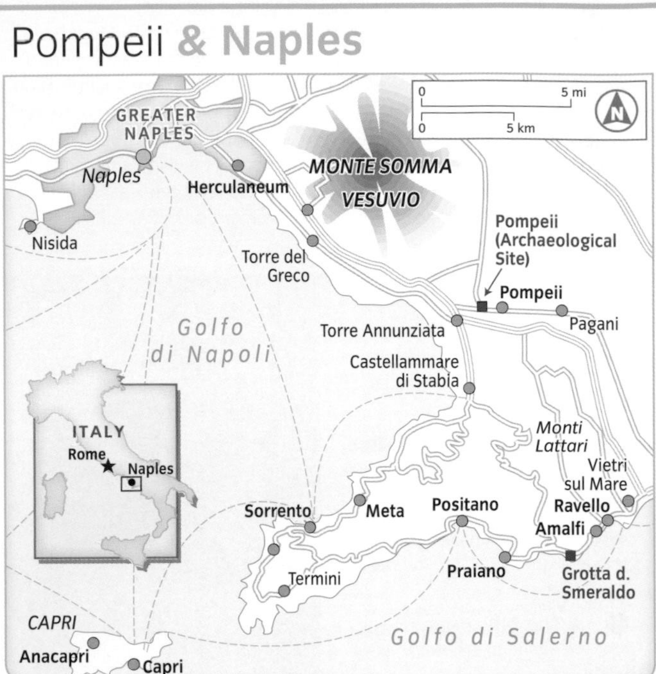

The ancient Roman town of Pompeii, buried by the devastating volcanic eruption of Mount Vesuvius in A.D. 79, is the most visited cultural site in Italy. At 3 hours away, Pompeii may not be the most convenient day trip from Rome, but it's worth the trip. For a real treat, stop in the city of Naples on the way back for a panoramic drive through Italy's most naturally stunning city.

Getting There

Take the train to **Napoli Centrale** station (about 2 hr.), then a **Sorrento-bound** *Circumvesuviana* (commuter train) to **Pompei Scavi** (about 30 min.). The *Circumvesuviana* also stops at Ercolano (the excavations of ancient Herculaneum).

★★★ **Scavi di Pompei.** Pompeii is a vast site—to see the best of it, you'll have to cover a lot of ground. Pick up a map at the entrance to get your bearings. While not everything is well preserved, what has survived will strike you as uncannily sophisticated and often luxurious. The **Forum** was the center of civic life in Pompeii, but not its most interesting attraction today (except for the plaster casts of bodies stored along the north side). To the east are the **Forum Baths,** with their elegant condensation management system and locker-room cubbyholes. **House of the Vettii** is popular for its racy frescoes and preserved kitchen implements. The fabulous **House of**

The plaster cast of a man killed by the eruption of Mt. Vesuvius at Pompeii in 79 A.D.

the Faun, House of Menander, and **House of the Tragic Poet** are where the wealthiest Pompeiians lived. At the eastern end of the site (a 20-min. walk from the entrance) is the **Amphitheater,** with the gladiators' barracks adjacent. On your way back, be sure to see the **Lupanare** (the town brothel, with X-rated frescoes above each door), the charming and fantastically preserved **Small Theater,** and the **Stabian Baths,** which has great vaults and more plaster casts of crawling bodies caught in desperate attempts to survive. (Most deaths during the eruption were actually caused by asphyxiation from the volcano's toxic fumes.) **Villa of the Mysteries,** famous for its beautiful and enigmatic frescoes, is a good 10-minute walk north of the main part of the site. *at least 3 hr. Entrance: Porta Marina. ☎ 081-8575347. 10€. Daily 8:30am–5pm Nov–Mar; 8:30am–7:30pm Apr–Oct.*

★★★ **Naples.** Sadly, most people think of petty scams and organized crime when they think of Napoli, but it's still safer than most big cities—and heart-stoppingly beautiful. Don't miss such knockout sights as **Piazza Plebiscito,** seaside **Chiaia** and **Via Partenope, Castel dell'Ovo,** the heights of **Vomero** and tony **Posillipo,** and **Palazzo Reale,** as well as such characteristic neighborhoods as **Spaccanapoli** and **Quartieri Spagnoli.**

Fat City

As the birthplace of pizza and Sophia Loren (in nearby Pozzuoli), *bella Napoli* is known for its bounty—even the main drag in Pompeii is called Via dell'Abbondanza ("street of abundance"). From Cape Misenum to Sorrento, the Bay of Naples is leaping with the best fish the Med has to offer. The fertile volcanic soil on the sunny slopes of Mt. Vesuvius is home to citrus groves that yield softball-size lemons. Thanks to a unique combination of sea air and local grass, Naples' region, Campania, is the only place in the world where real *mozzarella di bufala* can be produced. Make time for sipping fresh-squeezed lemonade, crunching into amazing fried calamari, or sinking your teeth into a fat slice of Neapolitan pizza with a huge hunk of melted mozzarella on top.

Castelli Romani

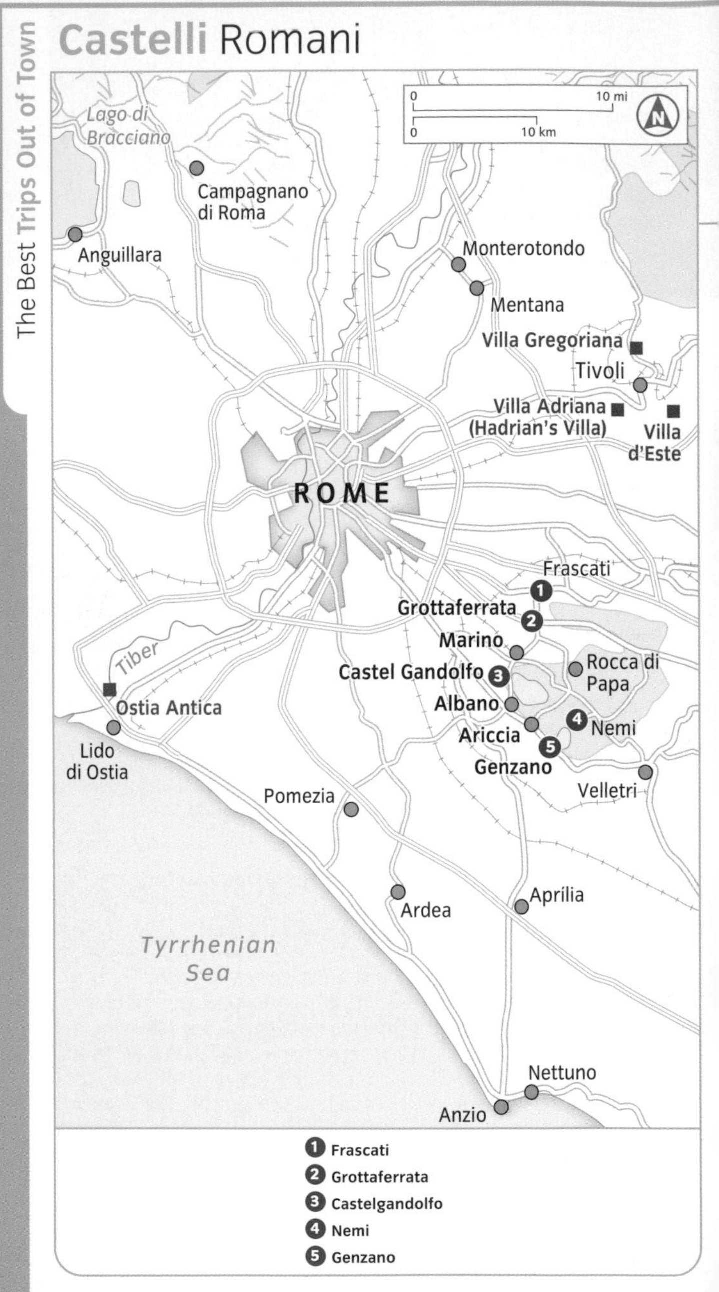

The best way to see these charming "Roman castles" (hill towns) just south of the city is to rent a car (p 162). On the way, stop and see the spectacular ruins of Roman aqueducts at the **Parco degli Acquedotti** (heading south on Via Appia Nuova, turn left on Viale Appio Claudio). Alternatively, the Castelli Romani are served by COTRAL buses from the Anagnina Metro station. There's also a direct train from Termini to Frascati.

❶ ★★ **Frascati.** The biggest but not the prettiest of the Castelli, Frascati is lively and has tons of restaurants and hole-in-the-wall osterie where townies (mostly old men) gather on rickety benches to sip the local *mescita* (rough-and-ready white wine, poured straight from great big wooden casks). Just below the town, adjacent to the train station, are the gardens and main house of the 17th-century **Villa Aldobrandini** (☎ 06-9420331), whose imposing, broken-pediment facade can be seen all the way from Rome's Janiculum Hill (p 59, bullet ⓫) on a clear day. The main building and gardens were designed by Giacomo della Porta and Carlo Maderno.

A statue at the Villa Aldobrandini in Frascati.

❷ ★★ **Grottaferrata.** Henry James wrote that this town "has nothing to charm the fond gazer but its situation"—high on a hill, with dramatic views over the Appian Way and Rome—"and its old fortified abbey," the wonderful 11th-century **Abbazia di San Nilo** (☎ 06-9459309), an example of medieval architecture rare for the Roman region.

❸ ★★ **Castelgandolfo.** Overlooking volcanic Lake Albano, clean and elegant Castelgandolfo has been the popes' summer retreat since the 1500s—the 17th-century palace here is technically part of the Vatican. The town piazza has a fountain by Bernini, who also designed the Church of San Tommaso di Villanova, with its acrobatic stuccoes by Antonio Raggi.

❹ ★★ **Nemi.** Set on the lip of an ancient volcanic crater, Nemi is by far the most picturesque of the Castelli, and famous for its strawberries. Gorgeous Lake Nemi—formed by the water that collects in the crater—was called "Diana's Mirror" by the ancients because the surrounding woods seemed to suit the goddess of the hunt.

❺ ★ **Genzano.** On the other side of the lake from Nemi, Genzano is at its best the week after Corpus Christi, when the streets are covered with flower petals for the *Infiorata* festival.

Beaches & Etruscan Sites Near Rome

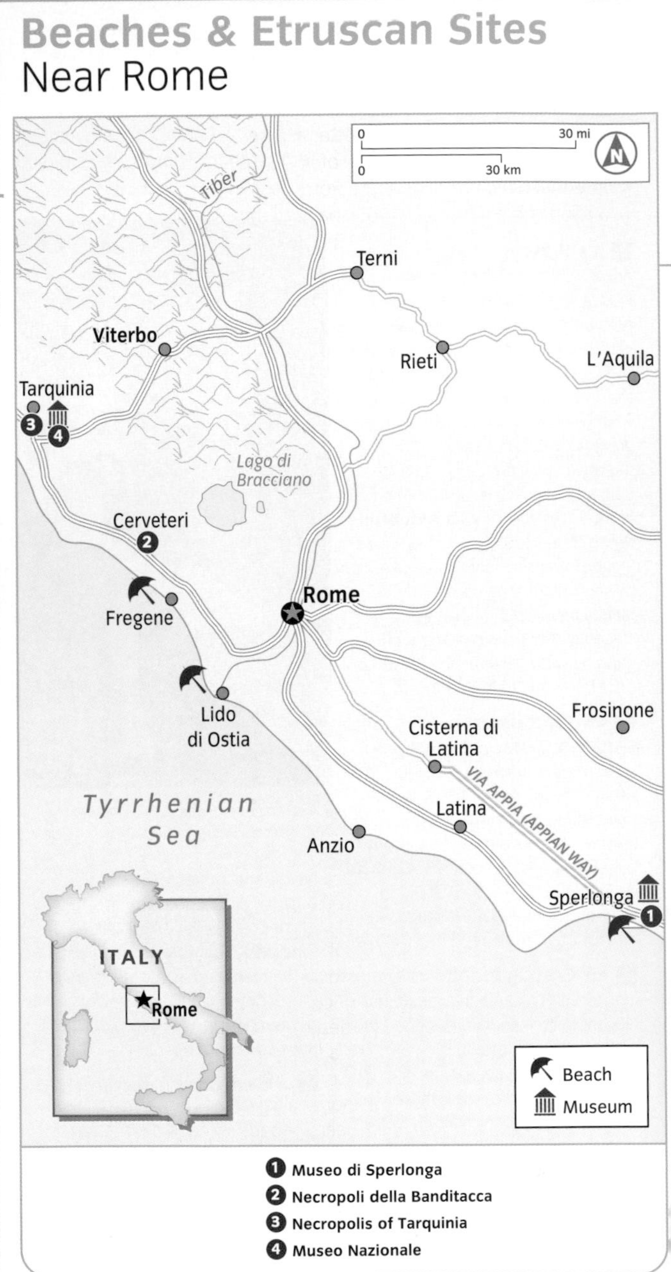

1 Museo di Sperlonga
2 Necropoli della Banditacca
3 Necropolis of Tarquinia
4 Museo Nazionale

The Roman *litorale* (seacoast) has never won any Mediterranean beauty contests, but there are several convenient and pleasant places to escape when summer in the city gets to be too much. When you tire of beachcombing, head northward along the coast-hugging Via Aurelia to the ancient sites of **Cerveteri** and **Tarquinia.** Here you'll find fascinating physical evidence of the Etruscans, the sophisticated culture that ruled Italy before the Romans. Much of the jewelry and other finds from these cavernous painted tombs can be seen at Rome's Villa Giulia museum (p 30, bullet ❷).

Fregene. The preferred seaside destination for upper-middle-class Romans, Fregene lies right underneath the path of jets on the final approach to Fiumicino airport. The topography isn't particularly gorgeous, but the see-and-be-seen crowd of super-bronzed bathers makes for quite a spectacle on its own. Go to beachfront **Il Mastino** (Via Silvi Marina 18; ☎ 06-434568) for an unforgettable lunch of spaghetti with clams. ***COTRAL bus from Lepanto Metro station, about 1 hr.***

Ostia. Even if you have only half a day to spare, you can still make it to Ostia, Rome's closest seashore. The water here is far from sparkling, but it's lively, with plenty of beach clubs (and dark sand that Romans say accelerates tanning). At the *spiaggia libera,* or "free beach," bus no. 7 from Cristoforo Colombo train station

The lovely beach at Sperlonga.

A Day at the Beach

The beaches here, like so many of the best places in this country, are bustling with a deeply rooted social culture. **Beach clubs** *(stabilimenti)*—pleasant, and nearly identical—consume much of the coast near Rome, and typically charge between 10€ to 12€ for access to their shores; the daily fee includes a **lounge bed** *(lettino)* and **shade umbrella** *(ombrellone)*, and use of changing rooms and shower facilities. Regardless of shape or age, about half of Italian women go topless at the beach, and half of the men wear Speedos. As for the water, while it's not exactly crystalline near Rome, it's plenty clean for swimming—and no matter where you go, you'll find take-out huts serving delicious cold mozzarella and tomato sandwiches or plates of steaming pasta with fresh Mediterranean seafood.

takes you to rugged dunes and wider stretches of sand, which make for a much more attractive setting, but there are few facilities. ***Train from Porta San Paolo (Piramide Metro station) to Ostia Centro, Stella Polare, or Cristoforo Colombo, about 35 min.***

★★ **Sperlonga.** Well worth the trek from Rome, charming Sperlonga has two main beach areas. The crescent-shaped bay south of the point is the more picturesque, with wide swathes of sand. On the headlands above, Sperlonga town looks like a Greek village, with whitewashed walls, narrow alleys, and spectacular vistas over the water. At the southern end of the bay is **Museo di Sperlonga** (☎ 0771-548028), with its marble sculptures of Polyphemus; and the attached, 2nd-century **Villa di Tiberio,** with its whimsical sea-grotto dining room. ***Train to Fondi (D or R train toward Napoli), then bus to Sperlonga.***

★★ **Cerveteri.** Called *Kysry* by the Etruscans and *Caere* by the Romans, this town near the seacoast was one of Italy's great Etruscan cities and may date back as far as the 9th century B.C. It is home to the immensely atmospheric **Necropoli della Banditaccia,** whose labyrinth-like paths between thick trees and huge *tumulus* tombs feel like something out of an *Indiana Jones* adventure sequence. The typically Italian lax site supervision means you can clamber all over everything, which is great fun. *🕘 1 hr. Via della Necropoli. ☎ 06-9940001. Tues–Sun 8:30am–sunset.*

★★ **Tarquinia.** The **necropolis** of Tarquinia may not be as lush or ancient-feeling as the one at Cerveteri, but the tombs here have vivid, beautifully preserved wall paintings. In the town, the **Museo Nazionale** (located in the noble Palazzo Vitelleschi) houses prized terracotta winged horses from the 4th century B.C., among the greatest Etruscan masterpieces ever found, as well as exhibits and sarcophagi excavated from the necropolis. Tarquinia itself is a very pretty medieval town, with several good restaurants. ***🕘 2½ hr. (necropolis and museum). ☎ 0766-856036. 6.50€ for both sites. Necropolis Tues–Sun 8:30am–1 hr before sunset; museum 8:30am–7:30pm. COTRAL bus from Lepanto Metro station to Civitavecchia, then change buses to Tarquinia, about 1½ hr.*** ●

Inside the Necropoli at Cerveteri.

The
Savvy Traveler

Before You Go

Government Tourist Offices

IN THE U.S.: 630 Fifth Ave., Suite 1565, New York, NY 10111 (☎ 212/245-4822); 500 N. Michigan Ave., Suite 2240, Chicago, IL 60611 (☎ 312/644-0996); and 12400 Wilshire Blvd., Suite 550, Los Angeles, CA 90025 (☎ 310/820-1898). **IN CANADA:** 175 Bloor St. E., South Tower, Suite 907, Toronto, ONT, M4W 3R8 (☎ 020/7408-1254). **IN THE U.K. & IRELAND:** 1 Princes St., London, W1B 2AY (☎ 020/7408-1254; www.italiantouristboard.co.uk). **IN AUSTRALIA:** Level 4, 46 Market St., Sydney, NSW 2000 (☎ 02/9262-1666).

The Best Times to Go

APRIL TO JUNE and **LATE SEPTEMBER TO OCTOBER** are the best months to travel in Italy. Starting in mid-June, the summer rush really picks up, and from **JULY TO MID-SEPTEMBER** the country teems with visitors. **AUGUST** is the worst month: It can get uncomfortably hot, muggy, and crowded, and the entire country goes on vacation at least from August 15 to the end of the month—many Italians take off the entire month. Many hotels, restaurants, and shops are closed (except at the spas, beaches, and islands, which are where 70% of the Italians head). From **LATE OCTOBER TO EASTER,** most attractions go on shorter winter hours or are closed for renovation. Many hotels and restaurants take a month or two off between **NOVEMBER AND FEBRUARY,** spa and beach destinations become padlocked ghost towns, and it can get much colder than you'd expect (it might even snow).

Festivals & Special Events

SPRING. The 42km (26 miles) of the **Maratona di Roma** are run the 3rd Sunday in March. During the **Settimana dei Beni Culturali** one week in April (www.beniculturali.it), admission is free to many museums and monuments. In late March and early April, azaleas cover the Spanish Steps in the **Mostra delle Azalee. Settimana Santa (Holy Week)** and **Pasqua (Easter)** in March or April are the biggest Catholic holidays of the year, with the pope partaking in dramatic ceremonies daily. Every April 21, Rome celebrates its birthday **(Natale di Roma)** with fireworks over the Campidoglio. Workers' unions organize a huge free rock concert at San Giovanni on **Primo Maggio** (May 1). The **Italian Open** brings the VIPs of the world tennis circuit to the Foro Italico (the Forum) for 10 days in May. Firemen pour buckets of rose petals over the heads of the congregation at the Pantheon on **Corpus Christi.**

SUMMER. Estate Romana (June–Aug) brings concerts to ruins, and open-air cinemas to piazzas. The miraculous snowfall of August 5, A.D. 352, is reenacted every year in Santa Maria Maggiore with a flurry of white flower petals during the **Festa della Madonna della Neve.** Get out of town, or wish you had, on **Ferragosto** (beginning Aug 15)—a 2-week holiday when *everyone* in Rome takes a vacation.

FALL. The pope says Mass at the Verano Cemetery on **Ognissanti (All Saints' Day),** November 1. For the **Giornati dei Defunti (Day of the Dead)** on November 2, Romans visit the graves of family members.

WINTER. To celebrate the **Immacolata Concezione** (Dec 8), firemen shimmy up a column in Piazza di Spagna to place a wreath on the arm of the Virgin Mary. Nativity scenes *(presepi)* spring up all over town in the weeks leading to **Natale (Christmas).** Italians ring in **Capodanno (New Year's)** by partying in the

ROME'S AVERAGE DAILY TEMPERATURE & MONTHLY RAINFALL

	JAN	FEB	MAR	APR	MAY	JUNE
Temp. (°F)	49	52	57	62	72	82
Temp. (°C)	9	11	14	17	22	28
Rainfall (in.)	2.3	1.5	2.9	3.0	2.8	2.9
	JULY	**AUG**	**SEPT**	**OCT**	**NOV**	**DEC**
Temp. (°F)	87	86	73	65	56	47
Temp. (°C)	31	30	23	20	13	8
Rainfall (in.)	1.5	1.9	2.8	2.6	3.0	2.1

streets, setting off fireworks, and casting unwanted furniture out windows. On January 5, a witch called **La Befana** "lands" at Piazza Navona, signifying the arrival of **Epiphany** (Jan 6) and the end of the holiday season.

The Weather

Rome's generally mild climate means that you can enjoy visiting the city year-round, and eat dinner outside April through October. Summer (especially late July and Aug) can be hot and humid, making for less-than-ideal touring weather. May and October are generally the best months for sightseeing, with sunny days, temperatures between 60°F and 80°F (15°C–26°C), and beautiful light. March is often rainy, and November feels the first bite of autumn. January and February are the coldest months, though winter temperatures rarely drop below 40°F (4°C).

Useful Websites

- **www.adr.com**: Information about Rome's airports
- **www.comune.roma.it/sovraintendenza/english/home/home.asp**: Within the official site of the city of Rome is an English-language portal to the city's monuments, museums, and cultural events
- **www.enjoyrome.com**: The website of the well-established independent tourist office is in English and has all kinds of practical information
- **www.museidiroma.com**: Information about Rome's museums (not exhaustive, and in Italian only)
- **www.romaturismo.com**: Official site of the Rome Tourist Board, with photos and brochures you can download for free
- **www.trenitalia.com**: Schedules, fares, and online booking for the national train system
- **www.vatican.va**: The Vatican's excellent official site; see also the comprehensive site for the Vatican Museums at http://mv.vatican.va
- **www.wantedinrome.com**: Rome's main expatriate publication has a good online classified section; otherwise, content is mediocre
- **www.weather.com**: Up-to-the-minute worldwide weather reports

Cellphones (Mobiles)

World phones are the only U.S. phones that can be used in Italy. Italy (like most of the world) is on the GSM (Global System for Mobiles) wireless network. GSM phones function with a removable plastic SIM card, encoded with your phone number and account information. In Italy, you can buy an inexpensive phone and SIM card for about 100€ and buy prepaid minutes in increments of 5€ to 20€.

You can also rent one in the U.S. before leaving home from **INTOUCH USA** (☎ **800/872-7626;**

www.intouchglobal.com), **ROADPOST** (☎ **888/290-1606** or 905/272-5665; www.roadpost.com), or **CELLHIRE** (www.cellhire.com, www.cellhire.co.uk, www.cellhire.com.au).

U.K. mobiles all work in Italy; call your service provider before departing your home country to ensure that the international call bar has been switched off and to check call charges, which can be extremely high. Also remember that you are charged for calls you *receive* on a U.K. mobile used abroad.

Car Rentals

All roads might lead to Rome, but you don't want to drive once you get here. Because the reception desks of most Roman hotels have at least one English-speaking person, call ahead to ask about the best route into Rome from your starting point. You're usually allowed to park in front of the hotel long enough to unload your luggage. You'll want to get rid of your rental car as soon as possible or park it in a garage.

You can opt to use the rental car to explore the countryside around Rome or to drive to another city. You'll save the most money if you reserve a car before leaving your home country. If you want to book a car in Rome, **HERTZ** is at Via de Muro Torto, near the parking lot of the Villa Borghese (☎ **06-3216831;** Metro: Barberini); and **AVIS** is at Stazione Termini (☎ **06-4814373;** Metro: Termini). **MAGGIORE,** an Italian company, has an office at Via di Tor Cervara 225 (☎ **06-229351;** bus: 447A). There are also branches of the major rental agencies at the airport.

From the U.K., I recommend **WWW.HOLIDAYAUTOS.CO.UK**. All prepaid vouchers include insurance—which can be astronomical in Italy. Book online with them for the minimum guaranteed £10 discount.

Getting **There**

By Plane

Chances are you'll arrive at Rome's **LEONARDO DA VINCI INTERNATIONAL AIRPORT** (☎ **06-65951** or 06-65953640), popularly known as **FIUMICINO,** 30km (19 miles) from the city center. (If you're flying by charter, you might land at Ciampino Airport, discussed below.)

After you leave Passport Control, you'll see two **INFORMATION DESKS** (one for Rome, one for Italy; ☎ **06-65954471**). At the Rome desk, you can pick up a general map and pamphlets Monday through Saturday from 8:15am to 7pm. The staff can help you find a hotel room if you haven't reserved ahead. A **CAMBIO** (money exchange) operates daily from 7:30am to 11pm, offering surprisingly good rates.

There's a **TRAIN STATION** in the airport. To get into the city, follow the signs marked TRENI for the 30-minute shuttle to Rome's main station, **STAZIONE TERMINI** (arriving on Track 22). The shuttle runs from 6:37am to 11:37pm for 9.50€ one-way. On the way, you'll pass a machine dispensing tickets, or you can buy them in person near the tracks if you don't have small bills on you. When you arrive at Termini, get out of the train quickly and grab a baggage cart. (It's a long schlep from the track to the exit or to the other train connections, and baggage carts can be scarce.)

A **TAXI** from da Vinci Airport to the city costs 45€ and up for the 1-hour trip, depending on traffic. The expense might be worth it if you have a lot of luggage or don't want to bother taking a train. Call ☎ **06-6645,** 06-3570, or 06-4994 for information.

If you arrive on a charter flight at **CIAMPINO AIRPORT** (☎ **06-794941**), you can take a COTRAL bus (☎ **800-150008** within Italy), which departs every 30 minutes or so for the Anagnina stop of Metropolitana Line A. Take Line A to Stazione Termini, where you can make your final connections. Trip time is about 45 minutes and costs 1€. A **TAXI** from this airport to Rome costs the same as the one from the da Vinci Airport (above), but the trip is shorter (about 40 min.).

By Car

From the north, the main access route is **AUTOSTRADA DEL SOLE (A1),** which cuts through Milan and Florence; or you can take the coastal route, **SSI AURELIA,** from Genoa. If you're driving north from Naples, you take the southern lap of **AUTOSTRADA DEL SOLE (A2).** All the autostradas join with the **GRANDE RACCORDO ANULARE,** a ring road encircling Rome and channeling traffic into the congested city. Long before you reach this road, you should study a map carefully to see what part of Rome you plan to enter, and mark your route accordingly. Route markings along the ring road tend to be confusing. **IMPORTANT:** Return your rental car immediately, or at least get yourself to a hotel, park your car, and leave it there until you leave Rome. Don't even try to drive in Rome—the traffic is just too nightmarish.

By Train, Bus, or Metro

Trains and buses (including trains from the airport) arrive in the center of old Rome at the silver **STAZIONE TERMINI,** Piazza dei Cinquecento (☎ **892021**); this is the train, bus, and Metro transportation hub for all of Rome and is surrounded by many hotels (especially cheaper ones).

If you're taking the **METROPOLITANA,** follow the illuminated red-and-white M signs. To catch a **BUS,** go straight through the station's outer hall to the sprawling bus lot of Piazza dei Cinquecento. You'll find **TAXIS** there as well.

The station is filled with services. At a branch of the Banca San Paolo IMI (at Tracks 1 and 24), you can exchange money. **INFORMAZIONI FERROVIARIE** (in the outer hall) dispenses information on rail travel to other parts of Italy. There's also a **TOURIST INFORMATION BOOTH** here, along with baggage services, newsstands, and snack bars.

Getting **Around**

By Car

Don't drive in the center of Rome. Period.

By Taxi

Licensed taxis are white or, less commonly, yellow. Be sure your cab has the red SPQR insignia on the driver's door. Cabs can be difficult to hail on the street, particularly during the day. Always insist on the metered fare, never an arranged price. The meter starts at 2.33€ from 7am to 10pm Monday to Saturday, and at 4.91€ from 10pm to 7am every day. On Sunday and holidays from 7am to 10pm, the meter starts at 3.36€. As a guideline, a daytime fare between Termini and the Vatican (one of the longer distances in the city center) should be about 13€. Add the tip by rounding up to the next whole euro—if the fare is 7.40€, leave the driver 8€.

By Metro

The **METROPOLITANA,** or **METRO,** for short, is the fastest means of transportation, operating daily from 5:30am to 11:30pm. A big red M indicates the entrance.

Tickets are 1€ and are available from *tabacchi* (tobacco shops, most of which display a sign with a white T on a brown background), many newsstands, and vending machines at all stations. Some stations have managers, but they won't make change. Booklets of tickets are available at *tabacchi* and in some terminals. You can also buy **PASSES** for 1 to 7 days (see "By Bus & Tram," below).

Building an underground transportation system for Rome hasn't been easy because every time workers start digging, they discover an old temple or other archaeological treasure, and heavy earth-moving has to cease for a while.

By Bus & Tram

Roman buses and trams are operated by an organization known as **ATAC** (Azienda Tramvie e Autobus del Comune di Roma), Via Volturno 65 (☎ **800-431784** for information).

For 1€ you can ride to most parts of Rome, although it can be slow going in all that traffic, and the buses are often very crowded. Your ticket is valid for 75 minutes, and you can get on many buses and trams (as well as the Metro) during that time by using the same ticket. Ask where to buy bus tickets, or buy them in *tabacchi* or at bus terminals. You must have your ticket before boarding because there are no ticket-issuing machines on the vehicles.

At Stazione Termini, you can buy a **1-DAY TICKET** *(biglietto giornaliero)*, which costs 4€, or a **WEEKLY TICKET** *(biglietto settimanale "carta")*, which costs 16€. These passes allow you to ride the ATAC network without buying individual tickets. A **TOURIST PASS** costs 11€ and is valid for 3 days. The tourist pass, the 1-day ticket, and the weekly tickets are valid on buses, trams, and the Metro—but never ride the trains when the Romans are going to or from work, or you'll be smashed flatter than fettuccine. On the first bus you board, you place your ticket in a small machine, which prints the day and hour you boarded, and then you withdraw it. You do the same on the last bus you take during the valid period of the ticket.

Buses and trams stop at areas marked FERMATA. At most of these, a yellow sign displays the numbers of the buses that stop there and lists all the stops along each bus's route in order, so you can easily search out your destination. In general, they're in service daily from 6am to midnight. After that and until dawn, you can ride on special night buses (they have an N in front of their bus number), which run only on main routes. It's best to take a taxi in the wee hours—if you can find one.

At the **BUS INFORMATION BOOTH** at Piazza dei Cinquecento, in front of the Stazione Termini, you can purchase a directory complete with maps summarizing the bus routes.

Although routes change often, a few reliable ones have remained valid for years, such as **NO. 75** from Stazione Termini to the Colosseum, **H** from Stazione Termini to Trastevere, and **NO. 40** from Stazione Termini to the Vatican. But if you're going somewhere and are dependent on the bus, be sure to carefully check where the bus stop is and exactly which bus goes there—don't assume that it'll be the same bus the next day.

On Foot

Seeing the city on foot (and getting a little lost while you're at it) is the best way to get oriented. Many main sights are very close together, and the *centro* is mostly flat (the seven hills are elsewhere). A walk from the Pantheon to the Spanish Steps, for instance, takes only 10 to 15 minutes.

Fast **Facts**

APARTMENT RENTALS For short- or long-term furnished rentals in Rome, check out the classifieds in the English-language magazine ***Wanted in Rome*** at its website (www.wantedinrome.com/clas) or at newsstands. The most comprehensive (and overwhelming) classified newspaper for long-term room or apartment rentals is the Italian-only ***Porta Portese, at its website*** (www.portaportese.it) or at newsstands.

ATMS/CASHPOINTS The easiest way to get euros is at an ATM (or Cashpoint), using your bank or credit card. Keep in mind that credit card companies charge interest from the day of your withdrawal, even if you pay your monthly bill on time. There are ATMs ***(bancomat)*** all over central Rome; you'll be charged at least a 3€ fee (in addition to whatever your home bank charges for international withdrawals). Cash tends to run out by Saturday night and isn't replenished until Monday afternoon, so think ahead. Also, find out your daily limit before you leave home.

BABYSITTING Most mid- to upper-range hotels can arrange babysitting services; otherwise, call the American Women's Association (☎ 06-4825268) for a list of reliable sitters. The Angels agency (☎ 06-6782877), run by Brit Rebecca Harden, arranges English-speaking nannies for wealthy Italian families and can help you, too.

BANKING HOURS Teller windows are open Monday to Friday from 8:45am to 1:30pm and from 2:45 to 4pm. Queues can be painfully slow.

B&BS The **Bed & Breakfast Italia** agency, Corso Vittorio Emanuele 284 (☎ 06-6878618; www.bbitalia.it), has a dizzying array of accommodations, ranging from private apartments in historic *palazzi* to more spartan sleeps with shared bathrooms. Rates range from 25€ to 80€ per person per night. **My Home Your Home,** Lungotevere dei Mellini 35 (☎ 06-97613280; www.myhomeyourhome.it), has fewer but more luxurious listings. Rates are 100€ to 200€ per person per night.

BIKE RENTALS Rome's busy, Vespa-infested streets are not especially bicycle-friendly, but the parks make for good riding, and Sundays are largely traffic-free and pleasant city-wide. Just outside the entrance to the Spagna Metro station, **Spagna Rent,** Vicolo del Bottino (☎ 339-4277773), rents bikes by the hour or the day, convenient for riding in the Villa Borghese nearby. **Tranchina,** Via Cavour 80 (☎ 06-4815669; www.scooterhire.it), between Termini and the Colosseum, rents bikes as well as mopeds. **Enjoy Rome,** Via Marghera 8A (☎ 06/445-1843; www.enjoyrome.com), offers a fun and educational guided bike tour (25€) several times per week, March through November.

BUSINESS & SHOP HOURS Most Roman shops open at 10am and close at 7pm from Monday to Saturday, closing for 1 or 2 hours at lunch. Designer boutiques, chain stores, and shops in heavily touristed areas do not close for lunch and are open Sunday. Smaller shops are often closed Monday morning and Saturday afternoon. Most restaurants are closed for *riposo* (rest) 1 day per week, usually Sunday or Monday.

CLIMATE See "Weather," p 161.

CONCERTS See "Tickets," below.

CONSULATES & EMBASSIES **United States Consulate and Embassy,** Via Veneto 119 (☎ 06-46741; www.usembassy.it). **Canadian Consulate,** Via Zara 30 (☎ 06/445-981; www.canada.it). **British Embassy,** Via XX Settembre 80 (☎ 06-42200001; www.britain.it). **Australian Embassy,** Via Antonio Bosio 5 (☎ 06-852721; www.italy.embassy.gov.au).

CREDIT CARDS Credit cards are a safe way to carry money. They also provide a convenient record of all your expenses, and they generally offer good exchange rates. You can also withdraw cash advances from your credit cards at banks or ATMs (Cashpoints), provided you know your PIN. If you've forgotten yours, or didn't even know you had one, call the number on the back of your credit card and ask the bank to send it to you. It usually takes 5 to 7 business days, though some banks will provide the number over the phone if you tell them your mother's maiden name or some other personal information. Keep in mind that when you use your credit card abroad, most banks assess a 2% fee above the 1% fee charged by Visa, MasterCard, or American Express for currency conversion on credit charges. But credit cards still may be the smart way to go when you factor in things like exorbitant ATM fees and higher traveler's check exchange rates (as well as service fees).

CUSTOMS Customs *(dogana)* at Italian airports tends to be lax; unless you're carrying a great deal of luggage or look suspicious, no one will bother to inspect you as you clear the arrivals area. By law, anyone arriving from outside the EU is allowed to bring up to 200 cigarettes, two bottles of wine, and one bottle of liquor into Italy, duty-free. There are no limits for anyone, foreign nationals included, arriving from another EU country. File through the "Blue Exit" lane at Customs.

DENTISTS See "Emergencies," below.

DINING Breakfast in Rome traditionally consists of a cappuccino and pastry at the local bar, not a full, sit-down meal, though most hotels offer some kind of continental breakfast. Cafes and snack bars are typically open 6:30am to 8pm, later in tourist areas; many are closed on Sunday. Restaurants are open for lunch 12:30 to 3pm, and for dinner 7:30 to 11:30pm (the last seating is usually at 10:30pm). Attire has gotten more casual at Roman restaurants in recent years. Jeans are acceptable almost everywhere—but shorts are frowned upon, except in really touristy areas.

Most informal Roman restaurants will accept reservations, but they're often not necessary, particularly if you arrive around 8pm (arrive earlier and you'll be dining alone). More formal restaurants do require reservations. You should contact your concierge at the time that you book a room, and ask him to book a table (you can tip him on arrival). Children are generally welcome everywhere.

DOCTORS See "Emergencies," below.

ELECTRICITY Like most of continental Europe, Italy uses the 220-volt system (two round prongs). American (110-volt) electronics with dual voltage (laptops and shavers) can be used with a simple adapter. Other appliances like hair dryers require a clunky voltage converter; using such appliances with simple adapters (not converters) will most likely fry the appliance and blow fuses. U.K. 240-volt appliances need a continental adaptor, widely available at home but impossible to find in Italy.

EMBASSIES See "Consulates and Embassies," above.

EMERGENCIES Italy has several emergency phone numbers: The *Polizia* are at ☎ 112; the *carabinieri* (they speak more English than the regular police), ☎ 113. Call ☎ 115 for the fire department. For an ambulance, call ☎ 118. Emergency care in Roman hospitals is efficient—and free for all foreign citizens. U.K. nationals should ensure they have a completed and validated E111 form to receive full health benefits in Italy. The system for these has just changed. For 2005, every visitor needs to apply for a new form, as the old ones expired on December 31, 2004. From January 1, 2006, visitors will need the European Health Insurance Card to receive free treatment. For advice, ask at your local post office or see www.dh.gov.uk/travellers. Should you find yourself in need of medical attention, ask to go to the nearest *pronto soccorso* (emergency room). Hospitals abound in Rome, though **Ospedale Fatebenefratelli** on Tiber Island, Piazza Fatebenefratelli 2 (☎ 06-68371), is one of the best. For dental emergencies, head for **Ospedale Dentistico George Eastman** in the Policlinico medical complex at Viale Regina Elena 287B (☎ 06-844831). **Ospedale Bambino Gesù,** Piazza Sant'Onofrio 4 (☎ 06-68591), on the Gianicolo, is central Italy's premier pediatric hospital.

EVENT LISTINGS The weekly *Roma C'e* (1€ at newsstands) has the most thorough listings for concerts, theater, dance, opera, movies, guided tours, and other happenings. There's a small English section in back. The monthly *Time Out Roma* is even more complete, though not always as up-to-date, and is in Italian only. The "Roma" sections of the daily newspapers *Corriere della Sera, La Repubblica,* and *Il Messaggero* list major events.

FAMILY TRAVEL Italian hotels and restaurants are generally very accommodating to children. See p 133, for the best family-friendly accommodations. Rome's many city parks (p 89) offer respite from the stress of sightseeing in a chaotic urban environment. See also "Babysitting," above.

GAY & LESBIAN TRAVELERS **Circolo Mario Mieli di Cultura Omosessuale** (☎ 06-5413985; www.mariomieli.org) is the best gay and lesbian resource in Rome. **Arcigay** (☎ 06-8555522; www.arcigay.it) and **ArciLesbica** (☎ 06-4180369) offer political and recreational forums and phone help lines.

HEALTH CLUBS Day memberships are offered at the **Roman Sports Center,** at the Villa Borghese underground parking structure (☎ 06-3201667); and at **Fitness First,** at Termini station/Via Giolitti 44 (☎ 06-47826300). Single yoga and Pilates classes are offered at **Moves,** Via dei Coronari 46 (☎ 06-6864989), near Piazza Navona.

HOLIDAYS Celebrated in Rome are New Year's Day (Jan 1); Epiphany (Jan 6); Easter and Easter Monday (Mar or Apr); Liberation Day (Apr 25); Labor Day (May 1); St. Peter's Day (June 29, Rome only); Ferragosto (Aug 15); All Saints' Day (Nov 1); Immaculate Conception (Dec 8); Christmas (Dec 25); and St. Stephen's Day (Dec 26). Shops and most restaurants are closed, and it can be very difficult to find accommodations in Rome over these holiday weekends.

INSURANCE Check your existing insurance policies and credit card coverage before buying travel insurance. You may already be covered for lost luggage, cancelled tickets, or medical expenses. If you aren't covered, expect to pay between 5% and 8% of your trip's cost for insurance. For trip-cancellation and lost-luggage insurance, try **Travel Guard International** (☎ 800/826-4919; www.travelguard.com) or **Travel Insured International** (☎ 800/243-3174; www.travelinsured.com). North Americans interested in getting medical insurance, including emergency evacuation coverage, can contact **Travel Assistance International** (☎ 800/821-2828; www.travelassistance.com).**For U.K. citizens,** insurance is always advisable, even if you have form E111 (see "Emergencies," above). Travelers or families who make more than one trip abroad per year may find an annual travel insurance policy works out cheaper. Check www.moneysupermarket.com, which compares prices across a wide range of providers for single- and multi-trip policies.

INTERNET Most Roman hotels have Internet access—dial-up or broadband connections in guest rooms, a hotelwide wireless network, or an Internet terminal in the lobby. **EasyEverything,** Via Barberini 2–16 (☎ 06-42903388), is open 24/7. Its rates are 2€ to 3€ per hour. For those with laptops, there are a few "hot spots" (wireless networks)—the cafe/tearoom **Gran Caffè La Caffettiera,** Piazza di Pietra 65 (☎ 06/679-8147), near the Pantheon, has great atmosphere.

LIMOS Try **Bob's Limousines & Tours** (☎ 06-5211192; www.romelimousines.com); or try **RomaLimo** (☎ 06-5414663; www.romalimo.com).

LOST PROPERTY Always file a police report if you wish to submit an insurance claim. Items left on buses and Metros, or at other city-run agencies, may turn up at the **Oggetti Smarriti (Lost Objects)** office in Trastevere at Via Bettoni 1 (☎ 06-5816040). For property left on trains, try the Oggetti Smarriti desk at Termini station (near platform 24).

MAIL & POSTAGE Stamps *(francobolli)* for the *Poste Italiane* can be purchased at post offices or at most tobacco shops *(tabacchi)* and hotel reception desks. Though the national mail has made vast improvements in recent years, many still swear by the Vatican mail. The *Poste Vaticane* has offices and mail drops only in Vatican City; postage costs the same as the Italian mail postage.

MONEY Italy's currency is the euro (at press time, equal to $1.30/£.68). The best way to get cash in Rome is at ATMs or Cashpoints (above). While credit cards are accepted at almost all shops, restaurants, and hotels, always have some cash on hand for incidentals and sightseeing admissions. For the most up-to-date currency conversion information, go to www.xe.com.

OPTICIANS Eyeglasses can be repaired and contact lenses can be purchased (no written prescription required) at any *ottica* (optician's), also the only place to buy contact lens solution.

PARKING You don't want to drive a car once you're in Rome. Finding street parking is a nightmare in the city center, and parking laws are beyond confusing. Either turn in your rental car once you arrive or, if you plan to take a number of day trips while you're there, consider parking at the **ParkSi** underground lot at Villa Borghese, Via del Galoppatoio 33 (☎ 06-3225934).

PASSES Rome does not have a comprehensive sightseeing pass; for archaeological sites, there's a 7-day, 20€ pass that includes admission to the Colosseum, Palatine, Baths of Caracalla, all three locations of the Museo Nazionale Romano, and

Crypta Balbi, as well as Villa dei Quintili and the Tomb of Cecilia Metella on the Appian Way. The pass can be purchased at any of the above sites; it pays off if you visit three or more sites.

PASSPORTS Always keep a photocopy of your passport with you when you're traveling. If your passport is lost or stolen, having a copy significantly facilitates the reissuing process at your consulate. While in Rome, keep your passport and other valuables in your room's safe or in the hotel safe *(cassaforte)*. See "Consulates and Embassies," above, for more information.

PHARMACIES *Farmacie* are recognizable by their neon green or red cross signs. They are the only places to buy over-the-counter medications like ibuprofen or cough syrup. Most pharmacies can fill prescriptions from home (some will even do so without a written prescription). A few pharmacies, like those at Piazza Cinquecento 49–53 and at Via Nazionale 228, are open late. Pharmacy hours are confusing, but all pharmacies, when closed, have signs in their windows indicating the addresses of open pharmacies in the area.

SAFETY Violent crime is virtually nonexistent, but petty theft and scams can be a problem. Pickpockets, some of them Gypsies, expertly work the tourist areas, crowded buses, and Termini station. Men should not carry wallets in back pockets, and women should carry handbags close to their bodies, securely fastened. Petty thieves do not prey on locals, so attitude and awareness will keep you from being targeted. Gypsies normally travel in groups of two or three, with babies slung across their chests. Other pickpockets dress like typical businesspeople and can be harder to spot. Always be suspicious of any individual who goes out of his or her way to "befriend" you in a densely touristed area. Otherwise, Rome is quite safe—walking alone at night is usually fine anywhere in the *centro storico*. For more information, consult the U.S. State Department's website at www.travel.state.gov; in the U.K., consult the Foreign Office's website, www.fco.gov.uk; and in Australia, consult the government travel advisory service at www.smartraveller.gov.au.

SCOOTER RENTALS The best way to "do as the Romans do" is to rent a scooter. Just show respect for pedestrians and other drivers in the chaotic city traffic. The fleet at **RomaRent,** Vicolo dei Bovari 7A (☎ 06-6896555; www.romarent.net), includes fun, bright orange Vespas. Rates are 42€ to 65€ per day. **Happy Rent** and **Tranchina** (see "Bike Rentals," above) also rent scooters by the hour or the day.

SENIOR TRAVELERS Non-EU seniors are entitled to precious few discounts while in Rome, although AARP (☎ 800/424-3410) members can save on airfare and car rentals arranged prior to departure. **Elderhostel** (☎ 877/426-8056) organizes well-priced "study trips" to many world destinations from the U.S., including Italy; the courses are geared toward active seniors, and accommodations may be spartan.

SMOKING On January 10, 2005, a revolutionary nationwide smoking ban went into effect in bars and restaurants. Whether the legislation will stick remains to be seen; smokers remain ubiquitous, and are tolerated almost everywhere.

SPECTATOR SPORTS One of the best experiences you can have in modern Rome is going to a Roma or Lazio football (soccer) game at the Stadio Olimpico (p 132). Tickets go on sale 6 days before games and cost 15€ to 90€. The season runs from late August or early September to May or June.

TAXES Non-EU visitors (with the exception of citizens from the U.K. and Ireland) who spend 155€ or more at stores with TAX-FREE stickers, are entitled to a VAT refund (up to 13% of the total purchase amount). The cashier will fill out a form, which you must present at the Customs office at the **last European point** of departure (for example, the Amsterdam airport, if you're flying to the U.S. with a connection in Amsterdam). Cash refunds are given in euros, which must then be changed. Credit card refunds can take from 6 months to never to be processed.

TAXIS It's usually (but not always) impossible to hail a taxi on the street. During busy hours, they're required by law to pick up fares only at taxi stands at the center of Rome, Piazza Venezia (east side), Piazza di Spagna (Spanish Steps), the Colosseum, Corso Rinascimento (Piazza Navona), Largo Argentina, the Pantheon, Piazza del Popolo, Piazza Risorgimento (near St. Peter's), and Piazza Belli (Trastevere). Taxis can also be requested by phone (☎ 06-3570, 06-88177, 06-6645, 06-4185, 06-4994)—the meter starts from the moment your cab is dispatched. Note that the taxi companies will ask you to call again later if they can't guarantee a cab within 13 minutes. Early-morning taxis to the airport can also be reserved in advance, at no extra charge, and are generally reliable. Fares within the city typically range from 5€ to 20€. Fare to or from the airport costs 40€ to 45€.

TELEPHONES Italy phased out its coin phones long ago. Phone booths *(la cabina)* take the *scheda telefonica* (plastic phone card) only, sold in denominations of 2.50€, 5€, and 7.75€ at *tabacchi.* Break off the perforated corner, and insert the card to get a dial tone. (Even if you have a prepaid long-distance calling card, you must insert a *scheda telefonica* to open the line.) Local calls (beginning with 06) usually cost 10¢ to 20¢; calls to Italian cell phones (beginning with 328, 338, 339, 340, 347, 348, and so forth) are wildly expensive—more than 1€ per minute.

TICKETS For concert and theater tickets, visit the venue box office or the **Orbis** agency, Piazza Esquilino 37 (☎ 06-4827403). For soccer tickets, go to the Roma Store, Lazio Point (p 131), or a **Lottomatica** (located inside many, but not all, *tabacchi*). Your hotel concierge may be able to help you; ask when you book your room (and offer a tip).

TIPPING Roman waiters—particularly those who cater to tourists—have grown accustomed to receiving gratuities of 15%, but Italians don't tip nearly that much, and waiters don't depend on them to feed their families. In general, rounding up a lunch or dinner bill is sufficient. (If, say, the check is 33€, leave 35€.) Check to see if the *servizio* is included; if it is, no additional gratuity is necessary. At the coffee bar, always add a few coins when you place your order (10¢ is perfectly acceptable, but 20¢ will get you faster service).

In hotels, a service charge of 15% to 19% is already added to the bill, but it's customary to give a small gratuity (50¢/day) to the chambermaid. You should tip a porter $1.50 for each bag carried to your room. A helpful concierge should also get a tip. Taxi drivers expect a tip of at least 10% of the fare.

TOILETS City-maintained public toilets are rare; those that do exist are often far from sanitary. Cafes, bars, and restaurants are required by law to let even non-customers use their restrooms, so don't be shy; just ask politely for the *bagno.*

TOURIST OFFICES The state-operated tourist bureau, or **APT,** Via Parigi 5 (☎ 06-36004399; www.romaturismo.com), provides maps, pamphlets, and other info. Much more helpful and friendly is the private tourist agency **Enjoy Rome,** at Via Marghera 8A (☎ 06-4451843; www.enjoyrome.com), which also gives out free maps and a city guide and arranges tours and accommodations.

TOURIST TRAPS Avoid restaurants with menus in eight languages, and—sad to say—any restaurant on a major tourist square such as Piazza Navona. Other tourist traps are the so-called "architecture/history/Latin students" who offer free tours in popular monuments (see "Tours," below). See also "Safety," above.

TOURS Rome has plenty of tour companies, but I recommend Enjoy Rome, Via Marghera 8A (☎ 06-4451843; www.enjoyrome.com), which offers a wide range of educational and entertaining group and private walking tours, bike tours, and bus tours. Guides are expats educated in art and history, or licensed Italian guides and archaeologists. Note: People offering "free tours" at places like the Forum and St. Peter's are often unqualified hacks.

TRAVELERS WITH DISABILITIES Many *centro storico* hotels and some lesser sites remain inaccessible to wheelchairs; call to inquire. The COIN agency, Via Enrico Giglioli 54A (☎ 06-23267504; www.coinsociale.it/tourism), provides up-to-date information about wheelchair accessibility at hotels, restaurants, monuments, and museums.

VAT See "Taxes," above.

Rome: **A Brief History**

6TH–5TH CENTURIES B.C. Following the expulsion of the seventh king of Rome, the Roman Republic begins. Roman law is codified in 450 B.C.

3RD CENTURY B.C. Rome defeats Carthage in the Punic Wars, opening the way for Mediterranean expansion.

2ND CENTURY B.C. Rome conquers Greece and adopts the Greek gods.

50S B.C. Caesar invades Britain and conquers Gaul (France).

44 B.C. Julius Caesar is assassinated on the Ides of March.

31 B.C. Octavian (Augustus) defeats Antony and Cleopatra at Actium, annexing Egypt.

A.D. 41 Caligula is assassinated; Claudius is emperor until he is poisoned in A.D. 54.

A.D. 64 The Great Fire destroys two-thirds of the city of Rome. Universally loathed emperor Nero is blamed for doing nothing to stop it.

A.D. 64 OR 65 St. Peter is crucified upside down at the Circus of Nero, on the future site of Vatican City.

A.D. 72–80 To satisfy the public's growing appetite for blood sport, the Colosseum is built.

A.D. 98–117 The reign of Trajan. The empire reaches its zenith; the power of Rome extends throughout Europe and on every shore of the Mediterranean.

3RD CENTURY A.D. During the "troubled century," Rome loses territory to barbarian invaders.

A.D. 313 Constantine legalizes Christianity.

A.D. 330 Byzantium (modern Istanbul) is renamed Constantinople and becomes the new capital of the Roman Empire.

5TH CENTURY A.D. A power vacuum leaves Rome defenseless. The city takes a beating from repeated barbarian invasions. Historians cite A.D. 476 as the end of the Western Empire.

7TH–9TH CENTURIES A.D. The popes govern a small and scattered population in Rome. The structures of antiquity begin to fall into ruin.

9TH–11TH CENTURIES A.D. A conflict-ridden "alliance" between the popes and the Holy Roman Empire brings centuries of bloody warfare.

11TH–13TH CENTURIES A.D. The popes—now essentially princes, descended from Italian nobility—use their influence to extend the reign of the Church throughout Italy.

1303–1377 Temporary removal of the papacy from Rome to Avignon.

1508 Michelangelo begins his frescoes in the Sistine Chapel.

1527 Charles V sacks Rome; the city is held hostage for 7 months.

1555 Roman Jews are ordered to live in the Ghetto.

1590S–1650S The baroque period flourishes: Caravaggio, Borromini, and Bernini lavish their talents on churches, piazzas, and fountains.

1798 Pope ousted by the invading French army.

1848 Rebels declare "the Roman Republic," which is quashed by French troops.

1870 Rome becomes the capital of a newly united Italy.

1922 Mussolini makes the "March on Rome" by train.

1929 Vatican City becomes a sovereign state with the signing of the Lateran Treaty.

1944 Rome is liberated from the Nazis.

1946 The *Repubblica Italiana* is created, ending the reign of the Savoia monarchs.

2001 The richest man in Italy, media tycoon Silvio Berlusconi, is elected prime minister for the second time. (He was prime minister very briefly in the 1990s.)

2001 AS Roma wins the *scudetto,* Italy's prized football (soccer) championship, for the third time.

2005 Pope John Paul II dies at the age of 84 after serving for 27 years. He is replaced by Pope Benedict XVI.

Roman **Architecture**

The architecture of Rome ranges from Roman temples and Byzantine basilicas to Renaissance churches, baroque palaces, and Fascist-era behemoths. Here is a brief overview.

Ancient Rome (6th C. B.C.–5th C. A.D.)

Everyone knows that arches and columns were the backbones of Roman buildings, but what about the rest of the buildings' structure? Some guidelines for making sense of the ruins:

Trevi Fountain, Rome.

- The lower the base of a building, the older its date; street level in Rome has risen about 9m (30 ft.) since ancient times. (Roman temples, such as the Pantheon, are a confusing exception to this rule, as temples were built on high podiums that are now flush with modern street level.)
- Round or irregular holes in ancient ruins indicate where metal has been removed (such as lead clamps that held a building together, or iron hooks that held decorations like sculpture or marble revetment).
- Rectangular holes are called "put-log holes," where beams were placed for scaffolding or to support a higher floor.
- Republican architecture was more modest than Imperial. Ruins with simple rectangular plans and plain tufa construction normally predate ruins with heavy marble or intricate vaulting.
- The use of concrete was perfected in the 1st century B.C.; any building utilizing concrete dates after that century.
- As lovely as they look to us today, brick walls never went naked in ancient Rome; they were always covered with marble paneling or stucco.

Early Christian & Romanesque (5th–9th C. A.D.)

The focus is on the interior. Churches are like geodes, with plain brick facades and dazzling jewel-tone mosaics inside.

Medieval (9th–14th C.)

The Middle Ages have largely disappeared from the architectural record in Rome. Santa Maria Sopra Minerva is the city's only Gothic church, its pointed arches and soaring vaults emphasizing heaven.

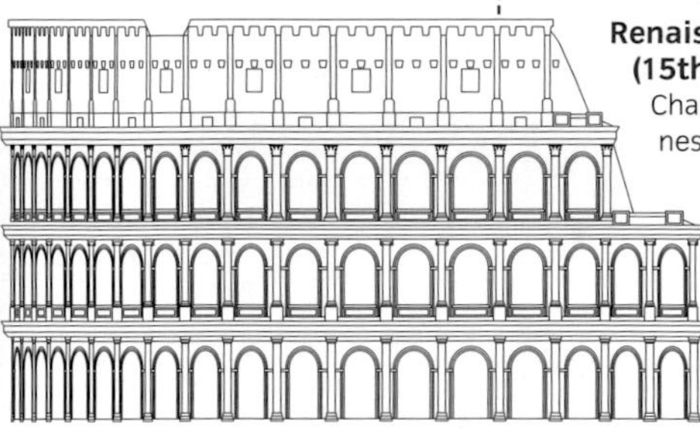

Colosseum, Rome.

Renaissance (15th–16th C.)

Characterized by stateliness, symmetry, and a rebirth of the classical orders, the best Roman architecture of this period is at Piazza del Campidoglio and Palazzo Farnese. Painting and sculpture are balanced, harmonious, and idealistic.

Baroque (17th–18th C.)

Think of the baroque as style with a serious caffeine habit—histrionic and playful, it defines the modern look of Rome. Architects like Bernini and Borromini employed such dynamic flourishes as jagged cornices and curvilinear tension (Sant'Agnese in Agone) to enliven monuments and public squares; sculptors (like Bernini) and painters (like Caravaggio) infused their subjects with naturalism and palpable, high-keyed emotion.

Rococo (18th C.)

Florid to the point of being frenzied—the baroque on methamphetamines.

Neoclassical (19th C.)

Safe and sedate, a return to the purest Greek and Roman forms.

Fascist/Rationalist (1920s–40s)

Buildings are bombastic, blocky caricatures of Roman Imperial monuments. Unweathered and insufficiently relieved by negative volume, they come off much harsher than their ancestors.

Useful Phrases & Menu Terms

Useful Phrases

ENGLISH	ITALIAN	PRONUNCIATION
Hello/Good morning	Buongiorno	bwohn-*djor*-noh
Hello/Good evening	Buona sera	*bwohn*-ah *say*-rah
Good night	Buona notte	*bwohn*-ah *noht*-tay
Goodbye	Arrivederci (formal)	ahr-ree-vah-*dehr*-chee
Hi/Bye	Ciao (or "salve"; informal)	chow
Yes	Sì	see
No	No	noh
Please	Per favore	*pehr* fah-*vohr*-eh
Thank you	Grazie	*graht*-tzee-yey
You're welcome/ Go ahead	Prego	*prey*-go
Do you speak English?	Parla inglese?	*pahr*-lah *een-gleh*-zeh?
I don't speak Italian	Non parlo italiano	nohn *parl*-loh ee-tah-*lyah*-noh
Excuse me (apologizing, interrupting)	Mi scusi	mee *skoo*-zee
Excuse me (getting through a crowd)	Permesso	pehr-*mehs*-soh
OK (agreeing)	Va bene	vah *beh*-neh
Where is . . ?	Dov'è . . ?	doh-*vey*
the bathroom	il bagno	eel *bahn*-nyoh
a restaurant	un ristorante	oon reest-ohr-*ahnt*-eh
the hospital	l'ospedale	oh-speh-*dah*-leh
a hotel	un albergo	oon ahl-*behr*-goh

How much does it cost?	Quanto costa?	*kwan*-toh *coh*-sta
What time is it?	Che ore sono?	kay *or*-ay *soh*-noh
The check, please	Il conto, per favore	eel kon-toh *pehr* fah-*vohr*-eh
When?	Quando?	*kwan*-doh
Yesterday	Ieri	ee-*yehr*-ree
Today	Oggi	*oh*-jee
Tomorrow	Domani	doh-*mah*-nee
Breakfast	Prima colazione	*pree*-mah coh-laht-tzee-*ohn*-ay
Lunch	Pranzo	*prahn*-zoh
Dinner	Cena	*chay*-nah
What time is it?	Che ore sono?	kay *or*-ay *soh*-noh
Monday	Lunedì	loo-nay-*dee*
Tuesday	Martedì	mart-ay-*dee*
Wednesday	Mercoledì	mehr-cohl-ay-*dee*
Thursday	Giovedì	joh-vay-*dee*
Friday	Venerdì	ven-nehr-*dee*
Saturday	Sabato	*sah*-bah-toh
Sunday	Domenica	doh-*mehn*-nee-kah

Numbers

1	uno	*oo*-noh
2	due	*doo*-ay
3	tre	tray
4	quattro	*kwah*-troh
5	cinque	*cheen*-kway
6	sei	say
7	sette	*set*-tay
8	otto	*oh*-toh
9	nove	*noh*-vay
10	dieci	dee-*ay*-chee
11	undici	*oon*-dee-chee
20	venti	*vehn*-tee
21	ventuno	vehn-*toon*-oh
22	venti due	*vehn*-tee *doo*-ay
30	trenta	*trayn*-tah
40	quaranta	kwah-*rahn*-tah
50	cinquanta	cheen-*kwan*-tah
60	sessanta	sehs-*sahn*-tah
70	settanta	seht-*tahn*-tah
80	ottanta	oht-*tahn*-tah
90	novanta	noh-*vahnt*-tah
100	cento	*chen*-toh
1,000	mille	*mee*-lay
5,000	cinque milla	*cheen*-kway *mee*-lah
10,000	dieci milla	dee-*ay*-chee *mee*-lah

Toll-Free Numbers & Websites

Airlines

AER LINGUS
☎ *800/474-7424 in the U.S.*
☎ *01/886-8844 in Ireland*
www.aerlingus.com

AIR CANADA
☎ *888/247-2262*
www.aircanada.ca

AIR FRANCE
☎ *800/237-2747 in the U.S.*
☎ *0820-820-820 in France*
www.airfrance.com

AIR MALTA
☎ *800/756-2582 in the U.S.*
☎ *356/2169-0890 in Malta*
www.airmalta.com

AIR NEW ZEALAND
☎ *800/262-1234 or -2468 in the U.S.*
☎ *800/663-5494 in Canada*
☎ *0800/737-000 in New Zealand*
www.airnewzealand.com

ALITALIA
☎ *800/223-5730 in the U.S.*
☎ *8488-65641 in Italy*
www.alitalia.it

AMERICAN AIRLINES
☎ *800/433-7300*
www.aa.com

AUSTRIAN AIRLINES
☎ *800/843-0002 in the U.S.*
☎ *43/(0)5-1789 in Austria*
www.aua.com

BMI
No U.S. number
☎ *0870/6070-222 in Britain*
www.flybmi.com

BRITISH AIRWAYS
☎ *800/247-9297*
☎ *0870/850-9-850 in Britain*
www.british-airways.com

CONTINENTAL AIRLINES
☎ *800/525-0280*
www.continental.com

DELTA AIR LINES
☎ *800/221-1212*
www.delta.com

EASYJET
No U.S. number
www.easyjet.com

IBERIA
☎ *800/772-4642 in the U.S.*
☎ *902/400-500 in Spain*
www.iberia.com

ICELANDAIR
☎ *800/223-5500 in the U.S.*
☎ *354/50-50-100 in Iceland*
www.icelandair.is

KLM
☎ *800/374-7747 in the U.S.*
☎ *020/4-747-747 in the Netherlands*
www.klm.nl

LUFTHANSA
☎ *800/645-3880 in the U.S.*
☎ *49/(0)-180-5-838426 in Germany*
www.lufthansa.com

NORTHWEST AIRLINES
☎ *800/225-2525*
www.nwa.com

OLYMPIC AIRWAYS
☎ *800/223-1226 in the U.S.*
☎ *80/111-444-444 in Greece*
www.olympic-airways.gr

QANTAS
☎ *800/227-4500 in the U.S.*
☎ *612/131313 in Australia*
www.qantas.com

SCANDINAVIAN AIRLINES
☎ *800/221-2350 in the U.S.*
☎ *0070/727-727 in Sweden*
☎ *70/10-20-00 in Denmark*
☎ *358/(0)20-386-000 in Finland*
☎ *815/200-400 in Norway*
www.scandinavian.net

SINGAPORE AIRLINES
☎ *800/742-3333 in the U.S.*
☎ *65/6223-8888 in Singapore*
www.singaporeair.com

SONG
☎ *800/359-7664*
www.flysong.com

SWISS INTERNATIONAL AIRLINES
☎ *877/359-7947 in the U.S.*
☎ *0848/85-2000 in Switzerland*
www.swiss.com

TAP AIR PORTUGAL
☎ *800/221-7370 in the U.S.*
☎ *351/21-841-66-00 in Portugal*
www.tap-airportugal.com

TAROM ROMANIAN
☎ *212/560-0840 in the U.S.*
☎ *4021/2041000 in Romania*
www.tarom.ro

THAI AIRWAYS INTERNATIONAL
☎ *800/426-5204 in the U.S.*
☎ *(66-2)-535-2081-2 in Thailand*
www.thaiair.com

TURKISH AIRLINES
☎ *800/874-8875 in the U.S.; 212/339-9650 in NY, NJ, CT*
☎ *90-212-663-63-00 in Turkey*
www.flyturkish.com

UNITED AIRLINES
☎ *800/241-6522*
www.united.com

US AIRWAYS
☎ *800/428-4322*
www.usairways.com

VIRGIN ATLANTIC AIRWAYS
☎ *800/862-8621 in continental U.S.*
☎ *0870/380-2007 in Britain*
www.virgin-atlantic.com

Car-Rental Agencies

ADVANTAGE
☎ *800/777-5500*
www.arac.com

ALAMO
☎ *800/327-9633*
www.alamo.com

AUTO EUROPE
☎ *800/223-5555*
www.autoeurope.com

AVIS
☎ *800/331-1212 in Continental U.S.*
☎ *800/TRY-AVIS in Canada*
www.avis.com

BUDGET
☎ *800/527-0700*
www.budget.com

DOLLAR
☎ *800/800-4000*
www.dollar.com

HERTZ
☎ *800/654-3131*
www.hertz.com

KEMWEL HOLIDAY AUTO (KHA)
☎ *800/678-0678*
www.kemwel.com

NATIONAL
☎ *800/227-7368*
www.nationalcar.com

THRIFTY
☎ *800/367-2277*
www.thrifty.com

Index

Photo **Credits**

p viii: © John Lawrence/Getty Images; p 5, top: © S. Bavister/Robert Harding Picture Library Ltd/Alamy; p 6, top: © Martin Moos/Lonely Planet Images; p 11, top: © Image Source/Alamy; p 12, bottom: © Sami Sarkis/Sarkis Images/Alamy; p 15, bottom: © Martin Moos/Lonely Planet Images; p 16, bottom: © Alvaro Leiva/AGE Fotostock; p 17, top: © Hotel Hassler; p 19, bottom: © Charles & Josette Lenars/Corbis; p 20, top: © Francesco Venturi/Corbis; p 24, bottom: © Bettmann/Corbis; p 26, top: © Peter M. Wilson/Alamy; p 26, bottom: © Charles & Josette Lenars/Corbis; p 30, bottom: © A.H.C./AGE Fotostock; p 31, top: © Doug Scott/AGE Fotostock/SuperStock; p 35, bottom: © DK Images/Index Stock Imagery; p 35, top: © Massimo Listri/Corbis; p 39, top: © Martin Moos/Lonely Planet Images; p 39, bottom: © Jonathan Smith/Lonely Planet Images; p 42, bottom: © Martin Moos/Lonely Planet Images; p 47, bottom: © R.P. Kingston/Index Stock Imagery; p 49, top: © Bill Ross/Corbis; p 50, bottom: © Javier Larrea/AGE Fotostock; p 51: © IML Image Group Ltd/Alamy; p 53, bottom: © Richard T. Nowitz/Corbis; p 54, bottom: © Walker/Index Stock Imagery; p 55, top: © Ian M. Butterfield/Alamy; p 57, top: © Ted Spiegel/Corbis; p 58, top: © CuboImages srl/Alamy; p 59, bottom: © Gari Wyn Williams/Alamy; p 62, top: © Max Rossi/Reuters/Corbis; p 63, top: © Bettmann/Corbis; p 63, bottom: © Ted Spiegel/Corbis; p 67, top: © Popperfoto/Alamy; p 69, bottom: © Hubert Stadler/Corbis; p 70, top: © Nicolas Sapieha/Corbis; p 71, bottom: © Franz-Marc Frei/Corbis; p 73, bottom: © Bill Ross/Corbis; p 75: © Dallas & John Heaton/SCPhotos/Alamy; p 82, top: © Vittoriano Rastelli/Corbis; p 82, bottom: © Kathy de Witt/Alamy; p 85, top: © Martin Moos/Lonely Planet Images; p. 86, top: © Owen Franklin/Corbis; p 88, bottom: © Al Sogno; p 92, bottom: © Archivo Iconografico: © S.A./Corbis; p 93, bottom: © John Heseltine/Corbis; p 95, bottom: © Araldo de Luca/Corbis; p 96, top: © Ruggero Vanni/Corbis; p 100, bottom: © Francesco Venturi/Corbis; p 101: © PCL/Alamy; p 109, bottom: © Checchino Restaurant; p 111, bottom: © Digital Vision Ltd./AGE Fotostock; p 112, bottom: © James Jackson/Getty Images; p 113, top: © Lisa Romerein/Getty Images; p 115: © Hotel Hassler; p 116, bottom: © Martin Moos/Lonely Planet Images; p 121, top: © David Noton/Getty Images; p 122, top: © Richard T. Nowitz/Corbis; p 122, bottom: © Martin Moos/Lonely Planet Images; p 124, top: © Martin Moos/Lonely Planet Images; p 125: © Bettmann/Corbis; p 126, top: © John & Lisa Merrill/Corbis; p 130, top: © Francesco Venturi/Corbis; p 131, top: © Franz-Marc Frei/Corbis; p 131, bottom: © Massimo Listri/Corbis; p 132, bottom: © Vincenzo Pinto/AFP/Getty Images; p 133: © Hotel Hassler; p 134, bottom: © Aldrovandi Palace Hotel; p 140, bottom: © Martin Moos/Lonely Planet Images; p 141, bottom: © Hotel des Artistes; p 142, bottom: © Hotel Hassler; p 143, top: © Hotel de Russie; p 144, bottom: © Martin Moos/Lonely Planet Images; p 146, top: © Valdier Hotel; p 147: © Araldo de Luca/Corbis; p 149, bottom: © Roger Wood/Corbis; p 151, middle: © Vanni Archive/Corbis; p 153, top: © Roger Ressmeyer/Corbis; p 155, middle: © AA World Travel Library/Alamy; p 157, middle: © Archivo Iconografico: © S.A./Corbis; p 158, bottom: © Frank Chmura/Alamy; p 159: © David Hanover/Corbis

 Cliff and Nancy Hollenbeck are authors, photographers, and filmmakers in the travel industry. They have authored more than a dozen books on travel, photography, and business subjects. Cliff has twice been named Travel Photographer of the Year by the Society of American Travel Writers. Cliff and Nancy have traveled throughout and photographed Italy for many years. Italy has also inspired Cliff to compose and produce two music CD albums of Italian arias.